CAST YOUR net

CAST YOUR net

*A Step-by-Step Guide
to Finding Your Soul Mate
on the Internet*

ERIC F. FAGAN

THE HARVARD COMMON PRESS
BOSTON, MASSACHUSETTS

The Harvard Common Press
535 Albany Street
Boston, Massachusetts 02118

Printed in the United States of America

Printed on acid-free paper

Library of Congress Cataloging-in-Publication Data

Fagan, Eric F.
    Cast your net : a step-by-step guide to finding your soul mate on the internet / Eric F. Fagan.
        p. cm
    Includes index.
    ISBN 1-55832-189-6 (pbk. : alk. paper)
        1. Dating (Social Customs)—Computer network resources. 2. Man-woman relationships—Computer network resources. 3. Mate selection—Computer network resources. 4. Personals—Computer network resources. 5. Internet.

HQ801.F253 2001
306.7'0285—dc21

                                        00-053927

Special bulk-order discounts are available on this and other Harvard Common Press books. Companies and organizations may purchase books for premiums or resale, or may arrange a custom edition, by contacting the Marketing Director at the address above.

10 9 8 7 6 5 4 3 2 1

I dedicate this book to the spectrum of those I love the most.

To Ma and Dad. Gone, granted, but you've never escaped my mind. You did a great job as parents; you were always there for us kids. You'd delight to see me now.

To Douglas, Stuart, Nancy, Craig, Kip, and Garrick—the greatest gang of kids a father could wish for. How proud I am of all of you.

To Ute for bringing my life to its peak. You are the sun shining on a never-ending road of love.

To Don and Sheila, stellar siblings. In my heart, we are still all kids.

And of course in a class of your own, Peanut…and Annie.

Contents

Acknowledgments

My heartfelt thanks to Mary Ellen Lind, who spent many hours editing my early efforts. May your Corvallis garden and your dreams flourish beyond your wildest expectations.

Also to Sheri Schaeffer, who generously gave of her time to set some of my thoughts on the right path. May you continue to grace the tennis courts and ski slopes for untold years. God grant Daisy many years with you in accompaniment.

My warm thoughts and thanks also to those of you who have provided much of the material I have quoted.

And to my daughter, Nancy, who preceded, and not surprisingly has surpassed me as a writer, for tips along the way.

Also to editor Sharon Broll, who shaped and molded my jumble into a finished product that tells the story as I had intended. And to Helen "Maggie" Carr, whose vast knowledge of the language helped tighten all the rivets. You brought the final work to a lustrous finish with your creative insight.

And finally to my love, Ute. You have filled the void in my life by proving that what I set out to do on the Internet could actually be accomplished. My thanks as well for your unflagging support and enthusiasm, and your unwavering love.

Introduction

The elevator to success is out of order. You'll have to use the stairs...
one step at a time.

—Joe Girard

Only I can change my life. No one can do it for me.

—Carol Burnett

In September 1998 I logged onto the Internet in search of my soul mate. It was a wild, often hilarious (now, but not then) quest that ended in absolute success. My looks are average; I'm not charismatic; my youth is a fading memory. I lay claim to no particular talents. At the time I had scant Internet experience; my knowledge of romancing women online was zilch. Further, my knowledge of browsers, search engines, and the like could have fit on the head of a pin. I knew more about speaking Sanskrit. Yet I had a pretty good idea of what I wanted in a female partner, and I was unwilling to settle for anything less.

I began my Internet adventure by stumbling upon one of the larger matchmaking services. Wow! Women galore! All shapes, sizes, ages, looks, inclinations, and locations. I whipped up a barebones (thirty to forty words) profile, and sent out forty-five email messages the first day. Within hours I began to receive a flood of extensive responses from my second-preference picks—but little or nothing from the type of women who truly interested me.

My social life was at ground zero, so even if I wasn't thrilled with the quality of the field I had the time necessary to handle the replies. This effort in turn generated another tide of response, and then...chaos. Some women wanted to make telephone contact; some wanted to meet. Others fired back questions I was expected to answer. I lost track of who was who and who wanted what. I finally stopped emailing new candidates, but I continued to flounder.

Blunder followed blunder. My email to Claire was accidentally addressed to Irene. My compliments on a picture sent by Susan in Phoenix inadvertently went to Carmen in San Jose. I had numerous face-to-face meetings with various women. In each case, for one reason or another, we didn't fit under the same umbrella. When the smoke cleared after the first three months, my search for a soul mate had advanced not an inch. I began to wonder if my teenage technique of cruising the streets after hours in a convertible might not be a more fruitful alternative.

After some somber rethinking (and being light one convertible), I changed my approach, revised my profile, organized myself, came up with a positive plan, and charged off anew. Over ten months, I attempted contact with more than four hundred women. Half ignored my overtures completely; the rest communicated with me to one degree or another. I met with twenty ladies in various states from Hawaii to Maine.

Then, at last, success. Ute, the treasure of my life, surfaced in Oahu.

The Online World

As we roar into the twenty-first century, 110 million Americans have hooked up to the Internet. Nearly 80 million unmarried adults are living alone in the United States. Link these together, and a mind-boggling singles market emerges. Just as e-buy and e-commerce for goods and services have rocketed far beyond the forecasters' dreams, so has Internet exploration for lasting social connections. The advantages of Internet matchmaking over the tried-and-not-so-true traditional methods of meeting a mate (singles bars, blind dates, newspaper personal ads, video dating services, and so forth) are diverse and compelling.

• *Numbers*. Among the major players in the field, Match.com boasts that 3,100,000 people had used their services as of April 1, 2000. A competitor, Matchmaker.com, claims a like figure. Americansingles.com weighs in with over 1,000,000 registered members. Many other sites have hundreds of thousands of members. On July 23, 2000, the *New York Times* commented:

"61% of American singles will look for a date on the Internet this year." Singles are becoming increasingly dissatisfied and frustrated with trying to find a mate in bars, churches, social clubs, supermarkets, bowling alleys, and at work. Going door-to-door brings negligible results. For more on how to begin your search, see Chapter Two.

• *Matching.* On the Internet you have the ability to look for the love of your life based on criteria that you specify in advance. For example, you can designate a search to bring up only men who are between five feet six and six feet two, slim/athletic, don't smoke, are of a particular religious persuasion, have no kids living with them, and live within 25 miles of you. Or a woman not over five feet two, between the ages of thirty and forty, who lives in Los Angeles. See Chapter Four.

• *Be all you want to be.* Searching on the Internet enables you to put your best foot forward, and with a chic slipper or macho boot. You can publicize your talents to your heart's content by creating a profile that touches on all the exotic elements of the real You. See Chapter Three.

• *Browsing.* You have the ability to inspect any number of potential soul-mate candidates to your heart's desire without their ever knowing you peeked. (To save a few trees, throughout the book I'll refer to a soul-mate candidate as an SMC.) Once you find someone of interest, you can explore that SMC in depth. See Chapter Six.

• *Convenience.* You can search and communicate any time of the day or night.

• *Screening.* Email contact is an excellent way to dig deeper into an SMC's likes and dislikes before meeting. You can track down characteristics that are red flags for you personally. An exchange of pictures can give you an idea of what to expect in a face-to-face meeting. See Chapters Six and Seven.

• *Interacting.* Some people have the ability to say the right thing at the right time: The timely quote, the one-liner, or the astute observation. Not me. My clever remarks generally come to mind, if at all, hours or days after the need arises. On the Internet, as I will show you, such quickness with language isn't necessary. You have endless time to create opening lines, days to come up with appropriate responses. See Chapter Five.

• *Minimizing risk.* Anyone who has ever read or seen the movie *Looking for Mr. Goodbar* realizes the risk inherent in meeting strangers in a bar. Or anywhere else for that matter, without having some sort of an idea what you are getting into. On the Net you are able to preserve your anonymity. With care, your correspondent will not know your phone number, address, full name (or even part of it, if you wish), or true email address. See Chapters Four and Seven.

• *Minimal cost.* Services that provide you with the capability to search their membership typically cost no more than $10–15 a month. Some offer a free trial period of a week or so. Some of the better ones are free. See Chapter Two.

Granted, there are some disadvantages to casting your net online.

• *Identities are concealed.* The woman who is capturing your heart with her romantic overtures could actually be a fourteen-year-old boy. Maybe even a chimp that has learned to type. You can overcome this problem to a large degree by swapping pictures. Still, there is no guarantee until, and unless, you actually meet. Photos may date back to a day when the SMC was slimmer, had more hair, did not (or did) wear a beard, was in better shape, and so on. See Chapter Six.

• *You can't get a chemistry reading.* Only a face-to-face meeting will give you the chance to check for sparks. An SMC who crafts the written word beautifully may be tongue-tied in person. Or be obnoxious to you and/or others. Or have dragon breath. Or any of a dozen things that may preclude furthering a relationship. See Chapter Eight.

• *Distance.* Someone who might appear at first blush to be an ideal SMC may live 500 miles away, or 3,000. Maybe even in a different country. Do you go for it? Or do you just keep on looking? See Chapter Nine.

• *Time online.* Finding the Right Person can be time-consuming. Things may not go as quickly or in the precise direction you want. Frustration and discouragement may come to roost on your shoulders. There are ways to handle this. See Chapter Ten.

• *Making the same mistakes.* Using a new medium to scratch up a loved one doesn't mean that you will automatically avoid all the same old potholes on Love Road. See Chapter One.

And then there are the perceived disadvantages. Let me debunk them right now.

• *Embarrassment.* In an interview I read on *Match.com*, a woman said that when someone suggested using the Internet to look for a mate she was offended. "I wanted to find a man to share my life with, but I didn't need to resort to computer dating!" she claimed. Even after finding her soul mate via the Internet, she wrote, "admitting to the whole world that you met your husband-to-be *on the Internet* would be pretty embarrassing, don't you think?"[1]

"I met my love late one night in a neighborhood bar" is an improvement? How about, "I found the love of my life in the deli section of the supermarket"? Or, "After eight pathetic and painful experiences, a blind date finally worked out for me"?

Internet trysts have acquired cachet. Recently, articles in *Time*[2] magazine and *Newsweek*[3] touted the advantages of Internet dating for busy professionals.

• *Lurking psychos.* The Internet has no monopoly on creeps. They can pop up in singles bars, on blind dates, at night school, and at church socials. But there is an extraordinary difference between face-to-face and Internet connections. When you lose interest in an Internet relationship, you can end it by clicking your Delete button, in the comfort of your home. Try getting rid of an amorous or talkative suitor(ess) as easily.

Certainly horror stories circulate. A Web site, *www.wildxangel.com,* lists numerous faux pas as told by the victims. But in every instance, you will find that the complaining individual ignored common sense. For instance, there are several stories about gullibles of both sexes who have lent their credit cards to first-time Internet dates, and then were surprised when substantial charges showed up. With appropriate guidance, people can avoid such fiascos.

Privacy is a must. The email you send and receive is filtered through the matchmaking site's own mail system; only the site itself knows your real email address. Members cannot connect directly without the consent of both persons.

• *Fear of the unknown.* There is very little written about Internet matchmaking to tell you where to go and what to do when you get there. This book will guide you in both respects, every step of the way.

1. "How I Met My Match," *Mix 'n' Match,* January 20, 2000, www.match.com.
2. "You've Got Male"; *Time,* February 15, 1999, p. 83. "Are You with Anyone?", *Time,*
   Special Edition, February 5, 2001, p. 32.
3. "Valley of the Doll-less," *Newsweek,* August 16 1999, p. 59.

What This Book Will Do for You

This book will show you how to find your soul mate, the person with whom you want to enjoy the rest of your life, through the Internet. It will give you the confidence to enjoy working at this demanding but rewarding task. It will detail the steps to locate, contact, and reel in that elusive mate, by combining common sense and determination. That person may be anywhere in the world; no matter—your computer is the modern-day flying carpet. Anything is possible through the Internet.

In these pages you will encounter the hopes, wishes, mistakes, thoughts, challenges, techniques, and accomplishments of scores of individuals who have experienced the wonders (and disappointments) of searching for their soul mate on the Internet. Many of those I quote were soul mate candidates with whom I had contact. Others were good enough to respond to questionnaires I emailed to people to research their thoughts and attitudes. In many cases, profiles came from my direct search. To protect privacy, I have changed names and altered slightly the content of messages and profiles, while keeping the lessons to be learned intact. Many SMCs are from smaller towns not readily locatable without a local guide. To ease the lesson in geography, I have rerouted some of these to the nearest recognizable metropolitan area.

We will be talking about finding someone *for keeps*—your soul mate for the rest of your life. So you will be weeding out those individuals who (a) have lifestyles and goals that are incompatible with yours, or (b) are not looking *for keeps*. You will learn to identify the positives that you really want in a relationship, and to eliminate past negatives. You will then learn to craft a profile to put yourself forward in the right place in the best light. You will become adept at questioning a range of SMCs, and then analyzing their responses and reactions to you.

Together, we'll develop your skills in handling the problems that are inherent with kids, pets, and out-of-town rendezvous. You'll find help in avoiding the most common mistakes, and staying on your feet when a variety of items that can go wrong, do.

It will be work, usually pleasant, sometimes frustrating, and often not easy. But the saying, "The harder I work, the luckier I get" applies to exploring SMCs as much as to any endeavor.

Follow the steps, work through the exercises, and fill out the charts. Use the best judgment you can in each circumstance, and learn from your mistakes. There is more help available to you, as you will see at the end of the book. Keep in mind that your own safety is paramount (and if you think this doesn't apply to men, check out the video *Fatal Attraction*). *Above all, take your time!* Indulge yourself. Heighten your pleasure as your eagerness to meet with an SMC grows. Put a Post-It on your monitor, NO RUSH!

The process I describe will work if you are careful and thoughtful at each step. You have a golden opportunity to first explore many of the facets of your SMC's character and inclinations. Then you can find out what the SMC looks like and whether the chemistry works. Your SMCs are looking just as hard for you as you are for them. Don't short yourself. Or them.

What This Book Will NOT Do for You

1. This is the wrong book if you just want dates or short-term relationships.

2. These pages will not teach you how to romance the person of your dreams whom you find on the Internet.

3. There are no sex tips here.

A profusion of other books, supermarket magazines, and videos serve such purposes. If you aren't ready for THE relationship, pass on this book. Not everyone comes to the well for that reason. But if you truly want to find the person with whom you are willing and eager to spend the rest of your life, you're in the right place at the right time.

What You Will Need

You can take advantage of this book, even if you score your computer aptitude abilities in the single digits (including 0). Let me first list what it would be nice for you to have, and then I will make some other suggestions.

Ideally you should have

- a computer

- an Internet connection

- the ability to browse Internet sites

- a basic knowledge of email.

If you lack a computer, perhaps a family member or a friend will oblige. If not, many public libraries now offer the use of computers coupled with Internet access. You will also find Internet coffee shops strewn about cosmopolitan areas that will charge you a small fee to connect up.

If you know little or nothing about email or the Internet and its terminology, turn to a friend or family member. There are also inexpensive books such as *The Complete Idiot's Guide to the Internet* that can get you started. High schools and junior colleges overflow with courses on Internet navigation. The same is true for adult education classes. We'll cover some of the basics below.

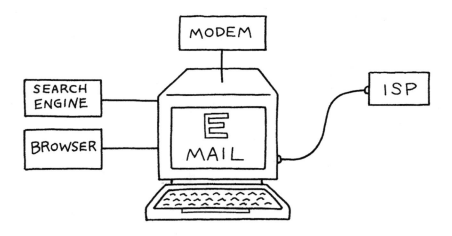

Computers 101—the Nuts and Bolts of the Internet for Non-Mechanics

For those of you who have not yet had the time or the inclination to bring yourselves fully up to speed technically, let's go over a few terms. Feel free to skip this section if you're computer literate.

Using the Internet is similar to owning a car that needs gas and oil and has a two-way CB radio installed. The *ISP* is your gas, and a *modem* is your oil. The *browser* is your car, which you "steer" by typing in addresses. If you aren't sure where to go, you need a road map—*a Search Engine. Email* is your CB radio equivalent. Just as CB radios work very well even if you don't own a car, email can work even if you don't have a computer of your own. Now let's make sense out of all this by looking a little more closely at the five terms listed in italics.

• *ISP (Internet Service Provider)—your "gas."* Your computer connects to the Internet via your telephone (or cable) line. Different companies (ISPs) provide this hookup service through their own computers. When you click on the Internet button, your computer dials into the ISP's computer, and voilà! You are on the Internet. To find ISPs in your area, look in the Yellow Pages under "Internet." Telephone companies such as AT&T, Sprint, and MCI also offer Internet services. The cost for some time now has been about $20 a month for unlimited use. In other words, no matter how much time you spend on the Internet using the telephone line, the $20 covers it. One caution. Run the phone number your ISP provides past your local phone company. Make sure it is a toll-free call. If it isn't, you might want to call a local college, university, or library to see what other ISP service is available in your immediate area.

The ISP you pick will give you explicit instructions on how to hook up to their computer. If necessary, a live person will guide you through the steps over the phone. Each ISP also throws in a free browser and email services.

AOL, Prodigy, AT&T, and CompuServe are commercial online services, all variations of ISPs. They provide entertainment features in addition to Internet services. Not all give you unlimited use of the Internet, however. Be sure to ask about this.

• *Modem—your "oil."* This is a checkbook-sized gadget usually located inside your computer that enables your computer to send and receive data over a telephone line. Plug one end of a regular telephone cord into the slot in your CPU (computer). The other end goes into any telephone wall jack. Unless you have two telephone lines, you get your pick: telephone or Internet. You can't do both at once with only one line; you can make a telephone call or be hooked up to the Internet. (DSL and cable technology are exceptions to this rule. With these connections you can be on the Internet and the telephone at the same time, though they are more costly than regular ISP service.) You can leave in place the telephone cord connecting your computer with the phone jack. That's not a problem. If your computer is more than two years old, you may not have a modem inside. You can buy one at an electronics store or repair shop. Generally they will put it in for free. Or you can buy an external model that has a cord to plug into the back of your computer. Another cord goes right to the phone jack.

• *Browser—your "car."* This is a computer program that enables you to search through the Internet to find all the matchmaking sites listed in Chapter Two. On every browser there is a rectangular box near the top of the screen that will initially have something like *"http://www.microsoft.com"* filled in. This is called an "address"; in this case it is Microsoft's address. To go someplace else on the Internet, you replace the *"http://www.microsoft.com"* with the address of the Web site you want to visit.

• *Search engine—your "road map."* This is a site that allows you to find other sites when you don't have their addresses. One such search engine is *www.dogpile.com* (there is a slew of such search engines). At Dogpile, you find a box near the top with "Dogpile Search" right above it and "Fetch" to the right side of it. Type anything you want in the box, such as "matchmaking," click on Fetch, and the Dogpile computer goes to work. It makes a lightning check of the whole Internet. After a few seconds, a screen comes up with a list of entries that pertain to matchmaking. Sort through them, and click on the underlined wording to get to the address of any site that interests you. Of course, just as when you pull a net of fish up out of the ocean, there will be a lot for which you have no use.

• *Email—your two-way "CB radio."* Every home has a mailbox. The mailperson delivers your mail by putting it inside the box. If you want to send a letter, you put it in the mailbox, and the mailperson whisks it away for delivery. Similarly, you will need an Internet "mailbox" to receive and send email messages. This is yet another free computer program.

You need a basic email program, such as Outlook Express, to connect up to the mailbox. It is in this program that you make up, send, receive, and, manage messages. Virtually all computers that still run have such a program. Ask a friend, relative, or the teenager next door for help if you can't find it or figure it out.

If you have your own computer and are connected to your own ISP, you will have a personal mailbox from which you can send and receive email, compliments of the ISP. If you are using someone else's computer, including that of your local library, you can set up an Internet mailbox free at any site, such as *www.yahoo.com, www.hotmail.com, www.surimaribo.com, www.netaddress.com* or dozens of others. If you are familiar with using a search engine, simply type in "free mailboxes" (include the quotation marks) and take your pick. Try Dogpile for practice in finding these mailboxes. Once you have a free mailbox on such a site, you can send and receive email at any time through any computer.

Matchmaking sites make the handling of email a breeze. As you bring up a member's profile to review, there is generally a button you can click on to send email to that member. Clicking on the button will bring up an email form that is preaddressed to the member. You simply type in your message and type something in the Subject section (though this isn't always necessary). Click on Send, and your message takes flight.

MORE HELP FOR THE
NEW-TO-THE-INTERNET CROWD

Sprinkled throughout the book are Side Trips. These are points that clear up computer terms or procedures in language anyone can understand. Those of you who are old pros at this sort of stuff will probably want to skip these. Some of it may seem astonishingly basic. It is, if you know more than I did when I started.

In Summary

Your soul mate is out there! Convince yourself of that. You may be short, fat, thin, well-proportioned, balding, well-groomed, mustachioed, lacking education, gorgeous, outgoing, inept at social graces, handicapped, or any combination of the above. Perhaps in addition, you are shy, can't do math, and are no good at small talk. You may hate crowds, horses, vegetables and fruit, and love poodles and Rush Limbaugh. You may be heterosexual or gay or have inclinations in both directions. Maybe you bathe infrequently. No matter; there are thousands of individuals who will qualify as your soul mate! Let me repeat: There are thousand of persons who will qualify as your soul mate! People out there are digging through the cybernetic haystack for someone who looks, talks, thinks, and walks just like you—and you will feel the same way about them! For the first time in history, you have an opportunity to run across any number of them—through the Internet. In the luxury of your own living room.

That's it. That's all you need to know to get rolling. Now let's get started on your plan.

1 Laying the Foundation

The hardest thing in life to learn is which bridge to cross and which to burn.

—LAURENCE PETER

Don't expect mangoes when you plant papayas.

—MIMFA A. GIBSON

One of my favorite activities is backpacking. Caveman bathroom facilities and insects are part of the fun. When a loving partner early on announced, "I'll go backpacking as long as you can guarantee indoor plumbing and no bugs," I should have taken this red flag to heart. Instead, our relationship ultimately foundered on several similar issues on which we disagreed.

Many of us looking for a soul mate are coming off a divorce or a relationship that ended on an unhappy note. Even widow(er)s who have lost a loving spouse can probably think of something to improve, strengthen, or build upon. Seldom do we get a second chance to do things right in life; love is the exception, especially if you take stock of past mistakes and resolve to fashion a remedy. At the same time, you have a wonderful opportunity to look back to see what was solid and enjoyable.

So before you start scouting out a replacement for your last partner, let's take a few moments to analyze what was good and what bends could be straightened. Every relationship has its delights. Find the positives, and determine to enjoy them with your next partner. Decide as well what was missing in your relationship that caused it to droop or spit sparks. And pinpoint each feature that you can very well do without. Let's begin by making a list of the characteristics, good and bad, of your past relationships. First we'll talk about the basics—your partner.

Charting Your Partner

Everyone needs to feel loved, wanted, and respected. Beyond these basics, individuals who mesh well with their partners are much more apt to survive the long haul. Human nature has worked this way ever since the first saber-toothed tiger poked an unwelcome snout into the cave. Mutual comfort in a relationship equates to longevity.

Most of us give little or no thought to what attracts us to a potential partner. So let's do that right now. First let's take a look over our shoulder; then we'll review. Fill in the characteristics of your last partner(s) of significance in the History chart below. Ignore the "You" column for the moment. Make checks, write in yes or no, and add comments. Feel free to stir in whatever other characteristics occur to you. Do whatever it takes to give you a realistic picture of each past relationship. As an aid, try to find pictures of each partner. The passage of time tends to distort memory. Don't gloss over shortcomings; be brutally honest.

As a double check on your objectivity, after you fill it out, ask a close friend who knew both you and your ex-partner(s) to go over your completed chart. Pay close attention to where your opinions differ.

HISTORY

Characteristic	Partner 1	Partner 2	Partner 3	YOU
APPEARANCE				
Height				
Weight range				
Race				
Ethnic background				
Hair color				
Hair length				
Hairstyle				
Age range				
Trim/average/heavy				
Other?				

Characteristic	Partner 1	Partner 2	Partner 3	YOU
STYLE				
Glasses				
Style of jewelry				
Style of dress				
Good dresser				
Dresses appropriately				
Other?				
HEALTH AND FITNESS				
Alcohol use				
Drug use				
Nutrition-conscious				
Smoker				
Athletic				
Active				
Overall health				
Other?				
EDUCATION				
Schooling				
Computer literacy				
Improves self				
Inquisitive/curious				
Other?				
PERSONAL INTERACTION				
Dependable				
Flexible				
Patient				

Characteristic	Partner 1	Partner 2	Partner 3	YOU
PERSONAL INTERACTION (continued)				
Fussy eater				
Annoying habits				
Clean				
Nagger				
Companionable				
Carried baggage				
Honest				
Arrogant				
Punctual				
Needy				
Argumentative				
Generous				
Enjoys private time				
Extrovert/introvert				
Fun at a party				
Well-mannered				
Considerate				
Easygoing				
Fun to be with				
Other?				
ENTERTAINMENT				
Likes to read				
Enjoys music				
Enjoys dancing				
Likes to travel				
Active in sports				
TV watcher				
Likes to cook				

Characteristic	Partner 1	Partner 2	Partner 3	YOU
ENTERTAINMENT (continued)				
Likes theater				
Likes ballet				
Likes to eat out				
Likes movies				
Enjoys community activities				
Internet user				
Other?				
LOVE STUFF				
Romantic				
Sexually abusive				
Sexually enjoyable				
Vocalizes affection				
Uncritical				
Warm and affectionate				
Loving				
Supportive				
Easy to anger				
Hostile to you				
Hostile to others				
Jealous				
Verbally abusive				
Faithful				
Attentive				
Considerate				
Flirts with others				
Physically abusive				

Characteristic	Partner 1	Partner 2	Partner 3	YOU
LOVE STUFF (continued)				
Willing to commit				
Other?				
VIEWPOINT				
Adventuresome				
Upbeat				
Energetic				
Open/reserved				
Extrovert/introvert				
Sense of humor				
Religious				
Encouraging				
Political				
Supportive				
Other?				
FINANCIAL				
Employed				
Ambitious				
Likes his/her job				
Good job prospects				
Workaholic				
Financially secure				
Good investment, business sense				
Other?				

Characteristic	Partner 1	Partner 2	Partner 3	YOU
MISCELLANEOUS				
Likes animals				
Has/wants children				
Morning or night person				
Political				
Other?				

Now take a look at what you have. Pluck out the warming aspects that you want to see carried over to a new relationship. These don't have to be earthshaking items. You might appreciate a partner being on time, or one who calls to tell you of a potential delay. Perhaps you appreciate something as simple as one who makes you a cup of coffee when you are tired. Or maybe even when you *aren't* tired.

Next, consider what was missing that you would like to have seen. Perhaps your list includes someone who would take the time to learn new things: a foreign language, the intricacies of bridge, or the thrill of equitation (the art of inducing horses to jump over high obstacles they would just as soon go around). Or one who enjoys taking in an arty flick.

Finally, decide what you will eliminate next time around the course. If you have multiple ex-partners to compare, you are likely to see similar patterns. Have partners been verbally abusive? Were they critical of you? Did all of your partners have the same negative characteristic(s)? If so, there's a reason. Psychologists tell us that people are attracted over and over to the same sort of partner because of familiarity with the type. If this predilection leads to a healthy relationship, fine. If not, this is your opportunity to set yourself on a happier track. Let's look at three examples.

Diane, thirty-six, in Salt Lake City:

"It took me the longest time to figure out why I ended up with one jerk after another. Then it finally dawned on me that I was picking guys I thought had a lot of self-confidence. Instead, they were really just arrogant. I kept ending up with men who had to possess and control me, and who were insanely jealous. When I finally realized that self-confidence and arrogance didn't have to go hand in hand, I came up with a great guy."

Phil, forty-seven, in Atlanta:

"I've never had any trouble attracting women in their twenties, but they never lasted long. A constant diet of nightlife and partying got old. And the stuff they called music! In a few months, I would start looking around again. A friend finally wised me up when she said I reminded her of Sam in *Cheers*. In one *Cheers* episode, Sam was killing himself trying to keep up with a younger woman. My friend fixed me up with a forty-two-year old with plenty of energy, but more my style. I finally had someone in my own generation, talking my language."

Corinne, thirty-one, in Tulsa:

"My ex-boyfriend was a master of deception. He had five different stories every time I caught him in some fabrication. Thus when I started looking on the Internet, I was particularly on the alert for inconsistencies. Anything that doesn't fit with something a guy tells me earlier, I'm outta there."

Charting Yourself

Next let's work on the same chart for you. Fill in the fourth column of the History chart with *your* characteristics in past relationship(s). And keep in mind that your traits may change from partner to partner, particularly if you have learned from mistakes. Take your time and be honest with yourself. Add anything about you that is important but doesn't show up on the chart. Highlight your good points; in a later chapter, you will be emphasizing these in your profile.

Put down your faults as well—you are the only one who is going to see them! It is the rare breakup where fault is one-sided. If you think you might be having a problem being honest with yourself, ask a friend for a candid opinion. Or copy the blank chart and invite a friend to fill in your characteristics. Alternatively, you might consider talking over your strong and weak qualities with a counselor who specializes in relationships.

Perhaps you can discuss the list with a support group to which you belong. My soul mate Ute was once part of such a women's group. One evening a member trotted out a long list of characteristics she hankered for in a male partner. Naturally, the group felt that no such perfect human being existed. The discussion of the Ideal Male was helpful to all the participants, however, and Ute learned much about herself that evening as a by-product. She told

me that many of the essentials she wanted in a man held no interest for others, and vice versa. She realized how much she delighted in the outdoors and needed a partner who would enjoy it with her. For another member of the support group, however, the perfect mate was a man who preferred spending time aboard cruise ships rather than traipsing uncertain trails in the woods.

Look at the characteristics you listed for yourself. Just because some attribute did not fit with an earlier partner does not mean that you must change. When a square hole doesn't accommodate a round peg, neither the peg nor the hole is at fault. When cats and dogs refuse to socialize, is either species the culprit? Many relationships come to grief merely because the characteristics of the partners are at odds.

For example, my sister, Sheila, had a quick irreverent wit. Her husband, Mickey, was slow to grasp the humor of her comments. Funny to her was sarcastic to him. Arguments frequently ensued. Tempers and often household items would fly. Sheila was an early riser who usually greeted the dawn playing classical guitar. Mickey preferred to start the morning at ten, and without music, thank you. This was another source of friction and identifiable flying objects. Ultimately the two divorced because numerous such small pieces of their puzzle didn't fit together.

If there is something you don't like about yourself, you have two choices: fix it, or accept and live with it. You may be overweight, smoke, or indulge in long TV or Internet sessions to the exclusion of exercise, for instance. Decide whether you are willing to do anything about these frailties, and then either make your move, or put it out of your mind. If you choose the latter, look for a soul mate who will take these attributes in stride and consider them as part of your persona, rather than as shortcomings.

The worst mistake you can make is to advertise for a partner, alleging you are something you are not, even if you intend to remedy the embroidery in the future. If you are thirty pounds overweight, don't claim that you are "average," because you are not. Be honest: specify that you are in the "a few pounds overweight" class. Or wait until you lose the thirty pounds before starting to look around. Otherwise, you may be trolling for SMCs who are looking for attributes *you don't have.* There are plenty of women who are willing to take on a hefty man, and vice versa. On any given day, a tour of your local supermarket will turn up such couples. One is twice the weight of the other, but there they are shopping away happily. Why waste time trying to attract SMCs who are looking for something you are not?

The Building Blocks of Your New Relationship—Your Potential Soul Mate

Let's begin to create the framework of a new relationship. We'll make lists of pertinent characteristics on which you are going to focus. In Chapter Three, these lists will help you to create an eye-catching, SMC-attracting profile. In Chapter Six, we'll use these lists to find your champion among the contenders.

Make three lists:

1. *A list.* Those attributes of a partner that you cannot do without, your "must-haves."

2. *B list.* The elements that you would prefer in a partner but are willing to do without as long as all the must-haves are in place. These fall under the category of "nice, but not necessary" items.

3. *C list.* Those characteristics that you absolutely will not tolerate, your "no-no's." Any one of these will eliminate an SMC.

The following were my personal lists. Your own may vary greatly.

MY A LIST (MUST-HAVES)

My A list defined a woman who was

> slim and fit
>
> intelligent
>
> physically appealing
>
> with a good sense of humor

who was also a

> bicyclist
>
> hiker
>
> backpacker (or at least willing to try)
>
> reasonably good housekeeper

and who

> enjoyed reading
>
> liked children
>
> had a fondness for dogs
>
> had some education beyond high school
>
> accepted the past as history
>
> used little or no alcohol

and was

> warm and affectionate

> clean

> sexually playful

> upbeat most of the time

> willing to try new ventures

> not self-conscious about her body

> aware of good nutrition

> generally not concerned about what others thought of her, and

> slept with her bedroom window open at night.

Lest you wonder about the importance of this last item, remember that one definition of marriage is "Sleeping in a room that is too warm next to a person who is sleeping in a room that is too cold." If you've been there, you'll understand.

MY B LIST (NICE, BUT NOT NECESSARY)

The frosting on the cake was to find a woman who was

> witty

> with only a passing interest in religion

as well as a

> jogger

> ballroom dancer

> tennis player

who was also

> a good cook

> frugal

and who

> liked to travel

> had class

> didn't live too close to her own kids

> liked computers

> watched very little TV, and

> enjoyed dressing casually.

MY C LIST (NO-NO'S)

A woman who used any form of drug, even just so-called recreationally, or anyone who was a

> smoker

> complainer

> night person

> non-dog lover

or who

> was intensely religious

> played Scrabble

> liked to gamble

> liked sailing, downhill skiing, beach activities, horses, or doing things in the desert

or had

> tattoos, or

> children living at home, especially beyond school age.

TIPS FOR CREATING YOUR OWN LIST

In short, you will compile lists of characteristics you must have (A), those you would prefer to see (B), and those you want to avoid (C), in your ultimate partner. This way you know both what you are looking for and what you must avoid. In Chapter Six we'll go into more detail about how to use these lists.

Don't compromise. Your search may take a little longer, but the effort will be worth it in the end. Diane, a forty-seven-year-old psychologist, discussed this with me once. She wrote:

> "The most constant theme I see in wayward relationships is the willingness of the woman to give up on her dreams. We are all too often confronted with our fear of being alone that we make all kinds of sacrifices to maintain a relationship."

This capitulation is not limited to women: men have the same weakness. And at practically all ages, beginning in their late twenties.

Don't give up your dream of finding the ideal partner. This is so important that I will repeat it again. You do not have to give up your dream of finding the ideal partner. Don't! And resist the urge to have a relationship—any relationship—rather than be alone. Weigh your choices. You can wait a bit longer to find exactly the soul mate who fits you, or you can accept less for the sake of having company. If you opt for the latter, you run the very real risk that sometime in the future you'll be traveling this road again, still looking for your soul mate.

If you need company, there are all sorts of people who would love to have you. You can volunteer for everything from caring for the aged to working with abused women and children. Little League umpires are always in short supply. Every road race needs someone to hand out cups of water as the mob rushes by. Nursing home residents are overjoyed to have someone with whom to play cards, share a joke, or listen to music. An automobile ride is near-Nirvana to most. Schools and libraries are always in need of volunteers to tutor or to help kids with their homework.

In Summary

If you don't like what's been happening in your past relationships, decide what worked and what flopped. Make note of ex-partner characteristics that caused problems in the past. Consider these "red flags" to avoid at all costs; don't risk renewed grief because you have carried one or more over into your new relationship. In addition, begin thinking of what you *must have* in a soul mate. At the same time, consider what you might want to improve about yourself; then either make the change or forget about it.

In her book *Desirable Men: How to Find Them,* Dr. Nancy Fagan developed a method of carefully assessing past relationships to avoid making the same mistakes.[1] The method is applicable to laying the foundation for success in finding your soul mate on the Internet. In discussing potentially destructive relationships she says,

> Time flies. Don't waste your time with the wrong type of man. Keep in mind that patterns are like the grooves on a record. Old records (relationship patterns) tend to have scratches that cause the needle to stick, creating an ugly repetitive noise rather than enjoyable music. The only [way to create] beautiful music is to pick up the needle and put it on a new groove.

And yes, besides being very competent in her field, Nancy is my daughter, and I'm extremely proud of her.

Make up the three lists of characteristics I've mentioned in this chapter. These will help you to put together your profile in Chapter Three, and to sift the SMC wheat from the chaff in Chapter Six.

Now let's get down to the business of finding where the action is.

---

1. Rocklin, Calif. Prima Publishing, 1997, p. 23.

Looking for Love: Online Starting Points

If you don't know where you're going, you will probably end up somewhere else.

—Laurence Peter

The people who get on in this world are the people who get up and look for the circumstances they want, and, if they can't find them, make them.

—George Bernard Shaw

My mother and sister were fearless travelers. As a teacher, my sister, Sheila, had summers off. She, my mother, and a great, lovable slurpy ox of a dog of indeterminate heritage, Foxie, would take to the roads in a VW van. They would roam the highways and byways of our country for the season, sleeping in the van—all three of them.

On their initial venture, however, a hurdle sprang forth immediately. Sheila had invested heavily in maps to guide them some 100,000 miles or so

around the country, beginning in Lowell, Massachusetts. Their starting point was Rte. 110, just at the outskirts of Lowell. Loaded and ready to leave, engine running, with maps pasted all over the dash of the van, and Foxie panting in anticipation, my sister suddenly disembarked and went back into the house. "Dad," she pleaded, "How do I get to Rte. 110?"

Getting to the Playing Field

You also will want to get on the right road to turn up a soul mate. The best path to follow is the one that will take you to the major matchmaking sites. First, however, let's look at the various arenas out there, with a couple of worthwhile side trips.

CHAT ROOMS

Pro

There are plenty. People occasionally meet their soul mates in chat rooms.

Con

Trolling through chat rooms is one of the least productive ways to spend your time—it's like trying to find your heartthrob on CB radio. The chance that you'll find your soul mate is slim because you are limited to working with those individuals who are present in the chat room at the time you show up. In fact, your odds would be better just hanging around your local singles bar. I found that the vast majority of people are chatting not to find love, but merely for the sake of making contact. A chat room is a wonderful medium to dispel loneliness. Profiles are available, but they are generally sparse; few have pictures.

Chat rooms can be found on many, many sites. Yahoo, for example, has dozens. Go to the *http://chat.yahoo.com* site, click on "Complete room list," and you get your pick. Scroll way down to "Romance" where you will find a group of selections beginning with twenties, thirties, and up through sixties-plus-plus. There are also "rooms" for gays, lesbians, single parents, and the Pickup Bar.

Once in a chat room, you are connected with anywhere from five to thirty or more people, all of whom are sending messages, inane or mundane for the most part, back and forth. All of the messages appear on your screen as they are typed in by the chat room participants. Each message is accompanied by the author's "handle" or code name. "Candy Kid" or "Turncoat" are examples. In a smaller frame of the screen on the right is a list of the handles of all the people who are presently tuned into the chat room. Many will be participating by sending messages; others ("lurkers") will just be watching the action. A note comes up on your screen alerting you when someone new comes into the chat room, and when someone leaves.

You can jump in and send a message to anyone at any time. Type your offering in the box directly below all the messages and click Send. Your awe-inspiring words will appear on the screen for you and everyone else to see, with your name or handle attached.

In the sixties-plus group, the first handle I saw on the screen was *I-wanna-tease-ur (#@&%%)*. Others were also couched in singularly unsubtle terms. Half the screen was constantly taken up with announcements of people coming into and leaving the room. *Tower_of_Power* kept demanding to know why everyone was ignoring him. His inquiries were liberally sprinkled with earthy Anglo-Saxon phrases.

A neat feature enables you to chat privately with any individual you choose from the names of the online participants on the screen. Click on one of the names on the list and you get several options, including a peek at a quite basic profile of the chatter. I asked seventeen women, "Are you actively looking for a partner, or do you just enjoy chatting?" One said "Neither." Fifteen were just online for the chat. A seventeen-year-old girl was looking for a partner and had been in chat rooms for two years. Her response to my inquiry as to her success was "Not good."

Although I could bring up a chatter's profile, the information was rudimentary at best: name, state, marital status, age, and occupation. The majority of the profiles were missing most of this information, particularly the person's age. There was no intimation of height, weight, or other such essentials.

Of the ten romance-oriented chat rooms I visited, two conversational themes emerged: obscenity and inanity. The Health and Wellness room brought the same results.

In short, use chat rooms to pass idle time if crudities do not bother you. They are not a fruitful source of soul mates. In most cases, you are starting with bare-bones information. Gender is sometimes the only clue, and that may be suspect as well. Spending your time in chat rooms is the equivalent of trying to spot the American flag Neil Aldrich left on the moon. Enjoy yourself, but don't waste your time looking for your love.

BULLETIN BOARDS

Pro

All the members will have something in common, and there are as many bulletin boards as there are nighttime stars. Bulletin boards tend to be local if the site is specifically oriented toward matchmaking.

Con

Except for age, you start with a bare cupboard. You must ask for even the essentials: height, weight, marital status, and so forth. There are relatively few members to work with.

My first stop at Internet romancing was at a local bulletin board for outdoors-minded singles. The first problem was the dearth of any significant information about the members. I presumed that all were living somewhat in the vicinity of San Diego. Beyond that, I had only age and gender to go on. It didn't go on very well. An overwhelming majority of the two hundred members were male. Of the some fifty females, only one seemed in my ball game. She met my advances with "Thanks, but no thanks."

Although not impossible, finding a mate through a bulletin board will be hard slogging at best.

PERSONAL ADS

Pro

Free, and lots of places to post them. You can zero in on locations that specialize in specific geographical areas if you are so inclined.

Con

This tactic is on a par with placing ads in the personal section of the newspaper.

Of the more than fifty personal ad sites I visited, most had too few members or were local (but not to me). Large sites like Hotmail's *2000classifieds.com*, *AOL.com*, and *Yahoo.com* were the exceptions. All three have large member bases. Of the rest, however, many only redirected me automatically to another site, *One-and-only.com* being the location I was sent to most frequently. There was one pleasant exception: *www.introserve.com*, which is worth checking out. It is free, with some neat matching features. The drawback: It has only 60,000 members.

If you want to rummage around in this area, run "free personal ads" in your friendly search engine. Include the quotation marks this time. I tried a site, *About.com,* which is a personal ads directory, and came up with 96,337 locations where I could post personal ads; I skipped some of them.

NEWSGROUPS

Pro
There are zillions of them, covering every conceivable topic. You can locate groups of people with interests that are identical to yours.

Con
Great for topics like hiking and Barbie doll collecting. Trying to find a partner at "romance" sites brings up mostly pornographic links.

If you are not quite ready to dive directly into the ocean of SMCs looking for partners, joining a newsgroup with a focus on an activity that you enjoy can be more like taking an easy dip in the wading pool.

Ute, fifty-eight, Oahu:

"When I first decided to look for a new relationship, I had no confidence in my skills at communicating. I'd been single for almost ten years. I froze up at the mere thought of talking with a single man my age. I hadn't the faintest idea of what to talk about beyond "What type of work do you do?

"I joined a hiking newsgroup and found a message from a fifty-year-old man looking for a hiking partner, male or female. This was great for me. I wasn't trying to find a romance at this point. I wanted to meet single men with whom I had a common interest so that I wouldn't be tongue-tied. This was a good way for me to build up my confidence without any pressure."

You can find newsgroups in two ways. First you can download into your computer a list of newgroups from your ISP. First you will have to set up your newsgroup receiving program. If a friend can't help, try the Technical Support staff at your ISP. They should be able to give you all the help you need to get on your sled and down the hill.

The second way is to enter the word "newsgroups" (the quotes aren't necessary) in the box of your search engine and click OK, or Go, or whatever button is next to the box. Pick and choose from what comes up. You can narrow your search by adding a word, such as "golf," to find newsgroups discussing just that sport. Type "golf newsgroups" in your search engine and include the quotes.

MATCHMAKING SITES

Pro

Many sites have extensive membership throughout the country; some with contacts throughout the world. You can refine your search by specifying quite a variety of factors in some cases. Also you can shield your email address and true identity.

Con

You pay one way or another. Some sites charge a monthly fee. Others ask you to pony up as emails are sent. Before signing up for any site, you need to understand how you will be charged, so you can avoid later surprises.

Certain matchmaking sites have fine-tuned the art of searching for a mate. Others are playing catch-up, but competition is forcing the major sites to improve constantly. Several provide first-class services. When you get down to business, setting up shop with one of these is the way to go.

Finding the Right Matchmaking Site for You

I started looking for matchmaking sites by putting the word "love" into a search engine. Big mistake. I turned up more pornographic sites than anything else. Evidently the concept of love has changed over the years. I finally came across the two directories of info-for-singles and matchmaking sites (all discussed in depth below) that put me on the right track.

The best site for *you* depends on several variables. Before you hoist your flag at any site, consider the following factors.

• *Money.* Free trials give you a chance to test-drive a site. As a practical matter, don't plan on meeting up with a sweetheart within the frame of the trial period; six months is more realistic. Granted, lightning strikes, but seldom. Don't elect the pay-for-each-event option; look for a monthly fee and compare it with the fees at other sites. Also ask if there is a price break for longer term memberships. Let's say you ante up for a six-month membership, and the thunderbolt zaps you in the second month. What is the site's cancellation policy? Do you get any of your money back?

• *Time investment.* Ask yourself how much time you can devote to the Cupid process. Sites like *2ofakind.com* (discussed later in the chapter), for instance, will do most of the heavy lifting for you. You fill out a simple profile and go about your chores; 2ofakind's friendly computer will scout its field and come up with two picks a week for you.

If instead you want to beat the bushes yourself, consider whether a site lends itself easily to the type of geographical search you wish to prance off upon. Some sites allow you to search regions of the country, the West Coast, for example. Other site searches are all or nothing: the whole country or one state at a time, which means that you might be making half a dozen separate searches each time you log on. One site may allow city searches (including a bit of the surrounding area) such as Los Angeles, Orange, San Diego, and so forth, only. You may prefer a site that allows a pass at Southern California in one swoop.

Some sites require a minimal amount of profile info from you, with wordiness being optional. Others move you from screen to screen during the sign-up process only if you have filled out all the boxes on the previous screen. You can invest a remarkable amount of time filling out the array of essay questions required at some sites.

• *Flexibility.* All but one of the major sites now allows you to post pictures with your profile. Some permit just one photo; others allow up to five. Find out whether you can search by profiles that include pictures, skipping over the others. Some sites allow you to run searches for specific words in a profile, such as "card playing" or "skiing."

• *Additional sections and assistance.* Most of the major sites have Advice and Fun sections ranging from articles on dating to scheduled upcoming singles events sponsored by the site. You will find that the extent and quality of the material vary significantly.

ADDRESSES

All of the sites in this chapter start with "http://" so I have left that part off. Some of the addresses then have "www"; some do not. So only type in what is spelled out here. For example, to get to the People Match site you would type in "www.peoplematch.com/" after the "http://" part. On the other hand, to get to Casual Kiss you would type in only "casualkiss.com/" after "http://." Best to skip capital letters in the address, and put a backslash ("/") at the end of the address. Don't type in the quote marks that I just used in this paragraph.

After you insert the correct address, you have to nudge the computer into taking you there. Either press the Enter key or click on a Go button usually found to the right of the address box, and off you sail.

"Site" is shorthand for Web site, by the way. This refers to the collection of information you find at any given Internet address. At the Greyhound site, for instance, you can find information about fares, schedules, and so forth, for the national Greyhound bus system.

Of the some seventy-five matchmaking sites I visited, the following eight have the largest registered memberships as of January 1, 2001. Keep in mind that the sites count everyone who has breezed through and alighted on the site as a member. Many such members are long gone. Also the sites themselves provided the figures for total membership, as well as monthly increases, so we must take into consideration the natural enthusiasm of management.

WWW.2OFAKIND.COM

Registered members	120,000
New members each month	8,000
Free stuff	• Profiles of two potential matches
	• No cost to leave your profile on-site
Membership cost	$24 for 12 weeks

Of all the matchmaking sites, this one has a unique approach, though it will not be for everyone. You begin by filling out an "Introductory Letter" that serves as your profile. This section is extensive but easy to click through. You then define the type of match you wish, including gay or lesbian choices. For the most part, you merely highlight items in drop-down boxes. When you describe your own Traits and Interests, for instance, you can generally show three items per section. For instance, under Hobbies I could choose three out of eighteen possibles, ranging from animals to writing. Oddly enough, although there were eleven choices for Athletic Activities, running and jogging were not included.

This site posts excellent reviews by Yahoo and Playboy, but I felt somewhat handcuffed. All your matchmaking selections are made by the computer and then emailed to you. Set the age range you're looking in, and that's what you get. No browsing the younger set. In response to my query about this, 2ofakind president Sal Prano explained that the significance of "no browsing" is to ensure that only people who meet each other's qualifications can match; the genuine searcher wastes no time. That is an interesting, but nowhere universal viewpoint.

When it comes to outlining your potential match, you work with drop-down boxes in forty-four categories to indicate what you want in a partner. In some of the categories, such as Race, Religion, Weight, Smoking, and Parenting, you can indicate 1, 2, 3, or X according to the relative importance of each to you. A 1, for example, means "very important," whereas an X signifies that you couldn't care less.

Next you assign a grade from 1 (NOT Important) to 100 (VERY Important) to twenty-four characteristics encompassing the items you just filled in about yourself (Goals, Hobbies, Musical Tastes, Athletic Activities, and so forth). Mr. Prano explained the reasoning behind this feature to me: "The ability to rate not only *what you like* but *how much you like it* and *how important it is in relation to everything else* is the most significant distinction of our service."

I could identify with a scale of 1 to 10, but 1 to 100?

After you finish filling out the "Introductory Letter," the computer will scratch around for profiles of two potential matches and send them to you by email in the next couple of days. It will also send along a handle that the computer evidently feels is best for your persona. So the rest of your afternoon is free (at least from 2ofakind).

There are no photos, so you are shooting in the dark. 2ofakind focuses on compatibility, so you must arrange to exchange pictures on your own.

I logged in on a Tuesday and was notified that my matches would arrive on Friday. They did—profiles of Sandra in Gaviota, California, and Joan in San Diego, where I live, but I could only read their profiles. To contact either would cost me $24. The $24 would also include a twelve-week membership. Once I was enrolled and had paid my dues, 2ofakind was willing to send me its computer's two Best Bets for Eric each week for a total of twenty-four potential playmates. So I'd be paying a buck a shot for the computer's best efforts.

The site's advertising claims that you get only the first two matches for free. For some reason, the computer kept disgorging braces of new matches for me every couple of weeks or so for several months.

Even if you decide to keep your $24 in the bank, your profile stays in the computer and is subject to being matched and sent along as one of the two weekly morsels to another member. If a paying member contacts you, you will be able to return email messages to that individual. This is the fisherman's equivalent of being able to drop your hook in the water, without bait, without being able to troll, and without being able to look over the side of the boat to see when the fish is about to bite. Otherwise, if you get out your checkbook, 2ofakind's computer will continue to roll out weekly pairs of matches for you. You can contact any of these that strike your fancy. If you are unhappy after a "few weeks," Mr. Prano invites you to ask for a refund.

The drawback to the site is the limitation on selections. In a given week, there might be half a dozen interesting SMCs; the next week might be barren. You will never know, because the computer will feed selections to you only two at a time. Mr. Prano explains that this feature is intended to ensure quality control. Instead of receiving a succession of matches at one time with increasingly lower percentages of matching, each week you have a new opportunity to receive a higher-scoring match including the pool of new members. This is your call. My preference was to do my own sorting and scoring.

One member complained that the site connected him up with his ex-wife of twenty years. He further lamented that she refused to go out with him. Mr. Prano commented:

> "This couple obviously had a lot in common. That is what brought them together in the first place. The many complexities and other factors of making a relationship work over time are beyond the scope of any matchmaking service. All you can ask of any match system is that it give you as good a head start in regards to compatibility."

Mr. Prano makes a good point. The higher your compatibility, the better your odds of making a relationship work permanently. But with your ex?

WWW.FRIENDFINDER.COM

Registered members	4,000,000
New members each month	65,000
Free stuff	• Browse ten profiles a day
	• Email one member a day
Membership cost	$11 to $15 a month for three months
	$7 to $10 a month for one year

Like other sites, you can get right off the mark by filling in your age, gender preference, and state. Click on "Search." The age range does not always work. I asked for my usual range, but was served ages 19 and up.

To join, hit on "Click to join for FREE!" and off you go. The registration form is one page, and completing it takes only five minutes or so. You will also spend some time composing a couple of essays about yourself and the flavor of mate you prefer. At the end of registration, and seemingly part of it, are the Favorite Lists to Join. Be cautious; checking off lists is not necessary as these are merely advertisers. Start X-ing these boxes and you will receive promotional email for all eternity.

Before you begin fishing around for SMCs, you must have a password. When you register with FriendFinder, you give an email address. After you finish registering, FriendFinder's computer will come up with a password and email it to you. So after registering you must wait a couple of minutes and then go into your email to pick up the message from FriendFinder telling you the password that has been assigned to you. I got 59825. Knowing my capacity for remembering that for more than a few minutes, I went into "Update Profile" under the FriendFinder Account section, scrolled down to "Update Password," and changed 59825 to my usual.

FriendFinder has a large database to comb; the company claims to have four million registered members. When you cruise through this assemblage, you do so by state or by country. A nice feature tells you exactly how many SMCs of the gender you wish are available. For instance, there were over 13,000 women in California and only 308 in Wyoming. There are women from scores of countries listed as well, beginning with 3 women in Albania, to 135 in Venezuela.

In browsing, I found that most of the members I looked at had not been active on the site within the previous three to twelve months. If you use the Search method after upgrading ("paying" described later), I presume you may get more current results. I didn't do it, so I am only guessing.

FriendFinder provides a "free" membership, but with some handicaps. After creating your own profile (a requirement), you can only "browse" rather than "search." One big difference between searching and browsing is that in the latter the only variables that you can specify are state or country, gender, and age range. Also, you get closed down for the day after you've looked at ten profiles. You can fire off only one email daily. A screen comes up telling you that you need to upgrade to do further browsing. Pony up or come back the next day.

Upgrade prices are reasonable: $11–$15 (Silver or Gold membership) a month on a three-month basis, or $7–$10 a month if you spring for a year up front. The sheer number of available candidates makes this site worth taking a three-month shot. At the time I went into the site, there was a special offer. If you purchased the Gold membership ($15 a month for three months) FriendFinder was willing to throw in another 3 months for free. So for $45, you could get six months of service, a bargain at $7.50 a month. There are no refunds (except for certain limited reasons), so don't complain if you find your soul mate in only one month.

As an option when you join, you can make up a short email message to be returned to a sender automatically every time you receive an email. It might say, "I get so many emails that I can't always be prompt in replying. If I think you are compatible, I will get back to you" (suggested by the site) or perhaps, "I'm on vacation until the eighth, but I will get back to you." You can change the message at any time.

There is an interesting pester feature. If you check a certain box, whenever an SMC does not respond to your email within a couple of days, the computer will automatically send out a "did you get my message?" email for you. Sort of a love spam. I have reservations as to the advisability of using this feature. If you don't get a response, *that* may be the message the SMC intends.

A much more attractive feature is the ability to record a voice message. A member can click and hear your voice. A clever variation enables you to record a specific message that can then be sent directly to the SMC of your choice. You must download a small program to do this, but the instructions are fairly idiot-proof.

The site has hundreds of articles available on every conceivable subject concerning romance and related topics. There's a significant catch: all of them are composed by members. The incentive for contributing an article is a free upgraded listing. As a result, the vast majority of the articles are ineptly written, have various spelling and grammar errors, are merely complaints, or are some combination of the above. There are occasional valid tips, but there is a lot of information to slog through to get to them. It's sort of like trying to catch minnows bare-handed.

WWW.AMERICANSINGLES.COM

Registered members	1,700,000
New members each month	70,000
Freebies	• Search by gender and age only
	• Contact three members
	• Leave your profile on-site with up to five photos for viewing by other members
	• Add a one-minute audio to your profile
Membership cost	Various plans: $8.33 a month for a year to $19.95 for a single month

This user-friendly site starts off with a cool feature: a search by telephone area code. This allows you to sample the neighborhood stock without even having to register. Select and gender and age range, and fill in the area code(s) that interest you. Up will come all the profiles, featuring all shapes and sizes. No matter—this is just to give you a taste of the offerings.

To get some free appetizers, go to "Sign-Up Free" and register. In filling out the registration form, women have seventeen choices to describe their body build; men have sixteen. Males may select anything from "soft" to "ripped"; women can start with "slender" and go from "Rubenesque" to "zaftig." You can describe your religious persuasion as "atheist," but if you are agnostic, your only other choice is "Tell you later." I did not fill in the blank that asked me what my field of study was (forty-plus years ago?), and was precluded from going further until I did. Overall, registration was quick and easy. To gain access to the site on future occasions, you must remember a seven-digit number as your user ID.

Once you are registered, you are asked a series of questions about your interests. You mark your preferences by checking boxes next to activities or typing in your thoughts. The site will display your answers when your profile comes up in an SMC's search for you. Some of the boxes ask you to conceptualize major points in two hundred words or less: "What is your perception of an ideal relationship?" "What have you learned from past relationships?" If you don't fill in a certain minimum number of words, you can't go on. Thus you have to answer the questions even if you'd rather skip them.

You can upload (or mail) as many as five photos. Send them one at a time if you are uploading them, or the session will time out. To those of you who are novitiates, this means that your connection to the Internet will be terminated and you will have to start again.

Along with registration comes the capability to contact three other members; beyond that you have to start paying. You can *receive* emails without cost, but passivity isn't for the dedicated searcher. You can also leave your profile up on the site for other members to discover *you*, but you can't move the ball down the field any further yourself without trotting out your credit card.

The search mechanisms work well, though with some limitations. Start with "Search" and you can begin immediately to get a flavor of the offerings, but based only on gender and age range. When I asked for a search of women 55-65 in the United States, the computer dished up more than 500 profiles for viewing. The site has a worldwide scope, but you can only select one country at a time.

Once registered, you can insert your profile and broaden your search parameters. Unfortunately, height and weight are not in the parameters. In the first search I conducted, more than half the women were outside my height and weight range. Paid membership cures this. Once you lay your money down, you are given the ability to use more parameters in your search, an auspicious enhancement. So if you like what the site has to offer, click on "Guest Tour" on the Home Page for all the details of a paid membership: membership perks, cost, getting started, and the like.

There are additional side features. "Romance Central" offers a host of basic tips; "MatchNetTravel" features exotic and basic *trips*. The advice section is slim; submit your quandary, but don't hold your breath waiting to see your predicament resolved onscreen. TheBEAT is an interesting and informative newsletter with dating tips, hot topics, and the like. You can even check out your astrological compatibility with another member if your inclinations run in that direction.

The search capabilities are quite varied. You can enter a radius of up to 200 miles, entire states or portions of states, up to ten area code exchanges, or the whole mix. Check a box, and only profiles with photos will show up.

Do take advantage (most did not) of the cool "Voice Message" feature. You dial an 800 number and leave a message up to 30 seconds long. Play the message back to hear how you sound and make changes. The quality *is* excellent. When someone wants to check you out, they will get your message by clicking on the sound icon. Neat.

Vice President Bill Kelly explained AmericanSingles' objectives:

"I think a key difference between our site and others is that ours is oriented to serious long-term relationships. We actively patrol for 'sleazy' profiles. Even the length of the registration eliminates people looking for something to do Saturday night. Also, there are no links to our service from 'adult' sites."

AmericanSingles.com is part of the MatchNet.com family of matchmaking sites. Check out *MatchNet.com* and you will find JDate.com (165,000 Jewish singles), DeutscheSingles.de (50,000 single Germans), BeMatched.com (British singles), MatchNetFrance.com (850,000 Gallic singles), and Match-NetAustralia.com. All are constructed along the same format. Work your way through one, and you've got the hang of them all.

MATCHMAKER.COM

Registered members	4,000,000
New members each month	30,000–40,000
Freebies	Two-week free trial
Membership cost	Various plans: $12 a month for a year to $19.95 for a single month

This is one of the larger sites, with a variety of offerings. It extends services to those of all sexual persuasions. Matchmaker boasts that of its registered users, more than 300,000 are "active," exchanging 1.5 million emails a week.

There is a two-week free trial. You can select from seventy-four regional areas, or sixteen "Special Interest" areas ranging from Nudists to Teen Talk to Yenta. There are six "International" categories, as well as an "Ebony" selection. The site lacks a comprehensive search feature. You can search only by "Community." California alone would take twelve different searches; the United States would mean seventy-four separate trips to the well. "Search all areas" would be a welcome upgrade.

You can check the membership without registering. Once you set your ranges, the possibles will start coming up, slide-show style. Every 7 to 30 seconds, a new profile arrives (you get to set the flip rate). There is some basic info, and four buttons to click to get more info or make contact. Click one of the buttons, and you are introduced instead to the registration page for your two-week trial. Sorry, no extended peeks until you join the database.

Matchmaker requires patience. The sign-up process is tedious and time-consuming. Plan on spending a couple of hours if you are going to do it in depth. First, there are some seventy multiple-choice questions you must answer. When I signed up the choices were not always on target. For instance, you can only designate height and weight *ranges*. I weigh 140, and the only choice available to me was "under 150." I'm five feet eight, and I had two selections: five feet six to five feet eight or five feet eight to five feet ten. I selected the lower category.

A lot of the questions may simply not pertain to you. For example, I found the following fairly irrelevant for me:

"What is the style of your hair?" (bald on top was not an option)

"What color are your eyes?"

"Do you have a private place to take a partner?"

"How accessible is this system to you?"

"What is your favorite color?"

"Have you had or would you consider having a homosexual experience?"

You can't ignore any of the questions; all must be answered. Many of the answer selections are attempts at humor that do not get past inanity. When you finish the multiple-choice section, you then get to give your responses to the twenty-one *essay questions*! While you are laboring over them, expect your Internet connection to time out a lot. In fact, the site gives you fair warning:

> If you are going to take a long time to fill this section out, you may want to complete a few of the questions and then hit the Next button at the bottom until you reach the end and come back via the Edit/Essay link to complete the rest—otherwise your ISP may time you out due to them not seeing any activity on your internet connection.

Given that there seemed no likelihood of completing the questions in a *short* time, you had best heed the service's advice.

Many of the essay requirements seemed inconsequential, for instance,

"What were your favorite toys as a child?"

"When you were a child, what did you hope you would grow up to be?"

"If you could pick one superhuman power (such as comic-book characters have) what would you choose?"

"What do you have hiding under your bed?"

"What cologne/perfume gets your attention the quickest?"

Time to be careful: when you select your handle, or user name, Match-maker adds a three-digit number to the end of it. That, plus the password you select, will get you into the site in the future. If you forget either one, you are out of luck; Matchmaker does not keep these in their database. You would have to register all over again and answer all ninety-one questions. Matchmaker is considering making changes to resolve this problem.

Once you have completed this essay marathon, the computer cranks around a bit and comes up with a list of SMCs. Next to each name is a number, which reflects the percentage of their responses that match with yours. Click on any name, and that SMC's full profile will come up. You can then review his or her answers to all twenty-one essay questions. Again, even if you speed-read, expect a lot of timing out.

You cannot search by age; you must weed out candidates yourself. The site limited me to pulling up fifty names at a time. Of the first fifty, only seven were in the age group that interested me—over fifty. Twenty-seven were in their forties, ten were in their thirties, and seven were in their twenties.

Joy, 38, had been browsed 4,931 times. She had received only 267 emails. What happened? I found her to be an extremely attractive woman. If she had been in my age range, I would have zipped off an email immediately. But 95 percent of the lookers passed her by for one reason or another. If nothing else, this underscores a key message I am trying to get across to you: there is a stunning variety of likes and dislikes.

WWW.CLASSIFIEDS2000.COM

Registered members	208,000 active
New members each month	Undisclosed
Freebies	• Post personal data free for twelve-week increments
	• Add voice message to your profile
Membership cost	None

This is a site run by Excite.com. You can get there through Excite but going directly to Classifieds2000 is easier. Go down to the "Personals and Friends" section. Click on Relationships directly underneath, and you will arrive at a well-designed matchmaking section that compares favorably with top sites discussed in this chapter. Best of all, it is free!

Like many such sites, you do your own picking and choosing; the computer will not run matches for you. It will only bring up profiles in the ranges you specify. You must tote your own luggage here. Create your own entry, and start looking through those listed.

Although you can search without even joining, it is to your advantage to join because Excite offers some email options you will want. The sign-up process is quick and painless. First select a handle that is referred to as a "Member Name." I tried Fearless One, but it was already taken. The computer gave me some options, among which were FearlessOne1 and EricF36 (don't I wish!). Or I could try again.

You'll then be asked to answer twenty-seven questions, mostly by selecting responses from drop-down boxes that you can run through pretty quickly. Next you select the time period for which you want the ad to run, up to a maximum of twelve weeks. Presumably, you can renew. The note under "Headline"—"This is the first thing people will see about you"—is somewhat misleading. All that someone is going to read about you are the first few words of your headline. So brevity counts at this site. Use short words ("I love to ski," for example). The last box gives you roughly five hundred words to tell about yourself and your future Prince(ss). Apart from completing the description box, you can finish the whole business in about two minutes.

Checking the Private Profile box enables you to hide your picture. But when you send your profile to someone you pick out of the mob, your picture goes along automatically. You can email or upload a picture to the site; sorry, nothing by U.S. Postal Service. Online assistance is available for neophytes.

As of January 1, 2001, there were 208,416 ads to search. To join the melee, first select a category—Female seeking Male, Female seeking Female, and so forth. This brings you to the "Search Characteristics" area. In short order, you identify the type of person you are looking for by age, height, type of relationship, and seven other qualifications. A drawback is that you can designate height only in six-inch increments (five feet to five feet six, for instance). If you are a man looking for a woman from 5 feet to five feet seven, you will have to conduct a double search.

You can search a single city or combine multiple areas. Highlight four lines, and you cover the whole state of California. Keep clicking to your heart's content; pick the whole West Coast if you desire. Highlight the designation "All Areas" and the whole world becomes your playground. This is the most comprehensive and flexible search system of all the sites I visited. You can also bring up profiles that include voice messages (see later in this section), pictures, or both.

The database produces a list of ages, types of relationship sought, and locations. You also get the first few words of each headline. In addition, icons indicate which profiles come with pictures and voice mail. Clicking on the truncated headline brings up the rest of the headline, the full profile, and a picture if there is one.

If you like what you see, you have several options. Clicking on "Add to Hot List" does exactly that. You can then continue searching through other profiles. Later you can go to your Hot List, which will hold the icons of those members you have added. Click on the candidate's Hot List icon, and the same information as listed (headline, age, location) will be there. Click again, and you are in the candidate's profile. The complete info you saw in your initial search will reappear.

If immediate action is more to your liking, you can send email. Check a box, and your profile will go right along with it. No use causing your SMC to hold his or her breath any longer than is necessary. You can send your email with an anonymous return address (provided by Classifieds2000), or you can show your true address.

I ran a search using my standard parameters, and came up with forty-six candidates, twenty-four of whom showed pictures. I could have limited my selection to only those profiles with pictures. In the category I selected, some two dozen women had opted for the Premium Personal feature. For a one-time charge of $9.95, their profiles went to the top of the list, and their line items were of a different color. I have to question the value of this stratagem. If I were getting down to business (and I wasn't at this point), I would have gone through the entire list, regardless of placement or hues. Neither the color of their headlines nor the order of the list would have influenced me one way or the other.

Evidently there is no limit on the size of picture you can submit with your profile. Photos ranged from full-screen to ones that were 2½-by-4 inches. The quality varied greatly from professional to squinty.

I then reversed roles and searched as a woman looking for a man. I kept the criteria the same except changed the height range to five feet six to six feet. Up came 128 Eligibles, 50 of them with pictures. Only three of them had popped for Premium Personals. Those three had the advantage, if such, of being at the head of the pack.

A unique, though impractical attraction is the slide show presentation of SMCs. This feature is for the computer couch potato, a looks-only search. To initiate this innovation, go back to the page showing "Personals and Relationships." Click on the Slide Show category directly beneath. A second screen will come up. Intuitivity ends here. On the left at mid-page is a box with Slide Show, Personals, and Just Friends. Click on Personals. When the third screen comes up, follow the simple directions. This is a neat wrinkle, but you can designate only your gender and that of your SMC. Select a geographical search area and off you go. Pictures of SMCs in that area will pop up on the screen one at a time. You can specify how often, from five to thirty seconds. Best to pick thirty seconds to allow for downloading and scrolling. Click on the ">" symbol, and you can move immediately to the next SMC at any time.

If you see someone interesting, click on the picture. The slide show stops, and the SMC's profile comes up. The drawback of the show is that you get every SMC in your selected area. All ages, weights, heights, and druthers. You get the whole boxful of sweets, not just the batch you want. Remember from earlier that when I set the criteria and searched "Any Area," I ended up with forty-six candidates? When I specified the same area in the slide show, the computer lined up 9,876 beauties for my viewing. The first was a self-styled

> **"25-year-old beautiful Irish lass working on the continent as a stripper seeking marriage to a strong, extremely dominant man who understands SM and what it's all about. I am extremely sub and need a man who will control all aspects of my life."**

I decided not to invest the more than eighty-two-plus hours it would have taken just to look at all the lovelies, never mind try to sort out those who might fall outside my parameters. Even fourteen hours at the five-second-a-peep rate was far beyond my endurance. If I were a woman, I would have had 32,488 guys to drool over. That's a lot of beefcake-staring time.

Another unique feature, though of dubious value, is the "Blind Date" section. Fill out a tedious form, and you could possibly end up on a television show. With a blind date in tow, of course. Serious searchers will turn back at this point.

Providing a voice message is a great way to get a leg up on your competitors. In addition, most of those making use of the "Voice Message" feature generated messages that were only slight variations from:

> **"Uh, thanks for looking at my profile....My name is ———. If, uh, you like what you see in my profile, send me an email and I'll get back to you [followed by another five seconds of silence]."**

It's hard to state the obvious more clearly, but it's not really *what* you say; it's *how* you say it. One young lady read what turned out to be the first part of her profile. Even though it was obvious that she was reading from a script, she had a charming twinkle in her voice.

Use a little imagination! If you talk about a favorite subject, you are apt to do so with enthusiasm. Write down what you want to say and practice a few times. By doing so, you will get ahead of most of the few who use the Voice Message feature. For instance, I might have used something like this:

> "Hi. I'm sitting here at my computer looking out into the backyard at my favorite nonperson, my dog Peanut. I'm talking to you, and she thinks I'm talking to her, so the tail is going 100 miles an hour. In the distance I can see a mountain I'm going to hike up as soon as you come along. So if you would enjoy the company of a guy with a neat 60-pound moth-eaten dog, get in touch. Ciao."

Georgina, thirty-six, came up with an upbeat message:

> "Hi there. It would be so much more enjoyable to swim in the ocean, hike trails, or run with a partner. Can I entice you to join me? We'll stop for a bagel and ice cream afterward. You know how to get in touch with me. We'll have fun exploring."

Steve, twenty-seven, was mundane, but enthusiastic:

> "Man, this is like having to give a speech. There are lots of things I like to do, but making a speech isn't one of them. So you'll just have to get back to me. I'm a lot more fun one-on-one. See you later."

Regardless of the efficacy of some of Excite's gimmicks, this is a gem of a site, and a top contender for your efforts. So check it out, particularly because it's free. If I were still in the market, I wouldn't bother spending $9.95 to go to the top of this list. I would be hoping that someone would find me despite the lack of a pastel headline phrase.

Let's stray off the path again for a moment. When would you hide a profile? Why would you want to do that?

When I was foraging around pretty heavily on my favorite site, I had seen all the back issues and would inspect the new offerings every couple of days. Thus I felt I was pretty much on top of the crop. Mind you, I wasn't leaving it up to someone to stumble across *me*. But I found that by keeping my profile visible, I tended to attract women whom I had already decided were playing in different arenas. Every time one of these candidates contacted me, it took time to go into the site, pull up the profile, and respond nicely. I found I wasted less time corresponding with incompatible candidates if I hid my profile from the casual huntress. I would send my emails to new SMCs in batches. Then for the next couple of days, I would turn on my profile to reap results. Later I would go dark again.

LOVE.AOL.COM

Registered members	590,000 with photos
New members each month	Undisclosed
Freebies	Personal ad with plenty of space to describe yourself and your SMC
Membership cost	Free

Clicking on "Create a Personal" brings you ultimately to a series of boxes to check off and fill in. User-friendly stuff. You have only twenty-five letters for your headline, which AOL terms a "Love Banner." You move easily from screen to screen putting checks in boxes. If you don't like any of the offerings, select "No Preference" or "Prefer Not to Say." In half a dozen boxes, you get to insert at reasonable length explanations about yourself and what you'd like in an SMC. Skip any of the boxes you wish; come back at a later time to change or add responses. The "Like to Do" and "Anything Else" boxes together give you roughly five hundred words to spell out your enticements. Finally, you can mail or email a photo.

If you don't have a photo in your computer, AOL will make one for you inexpensively and quickly. Mail a picture to AOL with a SASE and $3. In a hurry? Send an extra buck for three-day service. If you need the photo cropped—maybe you need an old flame or family member removed—toss in another dollar. AOL does the rest, and sends your picture back to you on a floppy disk. The photo can be up to 1 MB, which can make for a big picture. Directions onsite tell you how to email to AOL the photo you now have on the disk. If you are technologically challenged, go to a computer friend or family member. The advantage of having a digitized picture like this on your computer is that once you get the hang of emailing it, you can shoot off the same picture to other matchmaking sites.

To poke around in the leaves at *love.aol.com,* you can Browse or Search. To Browse, pick out the state of interest to you, and then the city. Up comes everyone in the selected city of the gender you elect—all shapes, sizes, and ages. If instead you elect to use the Search feature, you can look by state *or* city, but the dragnet is extensive. The preliminary questions are brief and to the point. Are you man or woman? Looking for man or woman? Variety (white, Asian, and so forth)? Add an age range and location, and the computer is ready to go. You can check by state or city only. To cover the country you would have to step to the plate fifty times; up to another forty-five if you select other countries.

You can check a box to view only profiles with photos. There is also a box where you can enter keywords. And that's it. The computer asks your preference as to body size and height when you fill out your own profile, but it cannot search by either such commodity.

Undaunted, I tried the "Quicksearch" feature. Quicksearch urges you to enter a keyword or two in a box off to the side. I entered "running and jogging." In a few seconds, I had 10,000 profiles for my viewing. These were profiles of all shapes, sizes, ages, and locations. Also both sexes. When I specified "Samba" instead, AOL dished up 185 choices for review, again completely undiscriminating. There seems to be no practical use for this feature; it won't help you narrow your search.

Equally as quixotic was the Browse feature. This leads to a map of states and a selection of countries that funnels you down to a city selection. You then evidently get everything that particular city has to offer. But at least of only one gender. The first selection that came up was a forty-one-year-old woman, who at 5 feet even was looking for a twenty-eight- to thirty-five-year-old man over six feet tall. The second was a tall nineteen-year-old who claimed to be "a friggin Amazon in heels." At five feet ten I had no reason to disbelieve. Like casting an ocean net indiscriminantly, when you browse *love.aol.com* everything comes up—SMCs of all ages, sizes, and propensities. The inability to rummage other than by one city (or occasionally by one county) at a time is a sharp limitation. To go through California alone would take over forty different browses.

When you find a profile of interest, you can contact the SMC at the email address shown on the profile. Everyone hands out their true email addresses, you included; no secrets here. An additional mode of contact is the "Buddy List." If you download some AOL software at the prompt (easily done), you can then chat online with your SMC—if your SMC is online. If your SMC doesn't have the software, he or she can also download it, and you are both off to the races. This puts you back in the chat room mode in essence, so why do it at this point? Later, this could be a useful feature for staying in touch with someone at the top of the short list. But you'll want to make sure that your SMC has measured up in all of your crucial categories before you start devoting time to passing along the news of the day.

KEYWORDS

Let's say you type the word "dancing" in the Keyword box. When you hit the Enter key, the computer fishes through all the profiles. It will scoop up all those profiles in which the word "dancing" appears, and show you a list of the results. If you put in two words, say "square dancing," the chances are that the computer will disgorge any profiles with either or both words. If you put quotation marks around the two words, the system may just search for the complete phrase. No guarantee, however.

After the computer goes through the files, it shows a split screen. In the right screen at the top is the total number of SMCs that the search has produced for you. Below that are the Love Banners (brief headlines) of up to fifty of the first group of SMCs. Click on one of the banners and an SMC's complete profile (and picture, if there is one) will come up in the left screen. I went for my usual age range in California. Up came 1,453 potentials. I went back and checked off "photos only." This narrowed the field to 768 picks. Adding "bicycling" and "bicycle" as keywords brought me to a more manageable 22 contenders. When I added "backpacking" to "bicycling" the computer kicked in another 7.

I removed the two keywords and tried adding heights: five feet three, five feet four, and five feet five. After a lengthy hourglass grind, during which time I went out and made myself a snack, the database informed me that there were no profiles to match my keywords. I got the same response when I tried the keyword phrase "a few extra pounds."

Overall, AOL's site is easy to use. Over a six-month period, AOL vastly improved its sign-up method. The price is right—it's free. You needn't be an AOL user to take advantage of the matchmaking service.

Because of the restrictions on searching, this site will appeal more to those with unlimited time and patience. The best I can suggest is that you put your profile up and hope for the best. But I would do my businesslike looking elsewhere.

WWW.YAHOO.COM

Registered members	Estimated 100,000 (undisclosed)
New members each month	Undisclosed
Freebies	Ad is good for thirty days
Membership cost	Free

The "Personals" section of Yahoo has a couple of nice touches, although its search capability lacks in several respects. Sign-up is quick and easy. Create a headline (termed an "Ad Title" by Yahoo), pick from half a dozen drop-down selections, click a few boxes, add some comments about yourself, and you step right into the ring. If you have trouble coming up with something to say about yourself, there is a basic ad-writing help section.

You can browse or search. The Search specs are limited to Ethnicity, Religion, Smoking, and Age. If you go to the "Advanced Search" feature, only two more elements are added: Drinking and Body Type. Even the latter leads to guesswork. Your choices include Slim/Waifish, Slender/Average, and Athletic/Fit. You are not allowed to select more than one body-type category per search. You can specify your particular interests as keywords, however, which is a welcome feature. You also have the option to require *all* of the keywords to be present in a profile, or *any* of them.

Your search area is confined to a particular city, state, or zip code. You can make only one choice, although if you select "No preference" you get to rove the entire country and beyond.

After you specify your search parameters, the service will tell you how many matches there are, and display them fifteen at a time. You see the age of the SMC, the date the profile was posted, and roughly the first fifty words of his or her profile. Click on More and you get the whole works.

I first went through the bantamweight division: Slim/Waif. The only match in my age range was Elsie225 in Eden Prairie, Minnesota. I went back and changed to the Slender/Average class. All five SMCs who showed up were five feet three. None indicated how slender or how average the candidate was. Only one match in Arizona deemed herself Athletic/Fit. A minor irritant was the failure of my age range selection to remain when I went back to change the body type. All the other selections stayed, but I had to reinsert the age each time I varied my search criteria. None of the profiles come with pictures. You must handle that on your own.

Yahoo offers some basic advice about email correspondence and the first face-to-face meeting. Some of the advice must be taken with a grain of salt. One capsule under "Meeting" says, "Let the other person bring up the idea of talking on the phone." If both individuals are reading this advice, the wait could be lengthy.

All in all, the price for this service is right, but you tend to get what you pay for. The ability to go to porno sites directly from Yahoo detracts and casts a needless shadow on Yahoo's matchmaking efforts.

WWW.MATCH.COM

Registered members	3,100,000
New members each month	130,000
Freebies	Seven-day free trial
Membership cost	Various plans: $8.33 a month for a year to $16.95 for a single month

Signing up is simple. If you want to start looking right away, the registration takes only a few minutes. You need only answer half a dozen questions, specify the age range you're looking for, and you're off. You are required to answer only a few multiple-choice questions with specifics that matter: your drinking and smoking preferences, for example. If you are in a hurry to get to the herd, you can skip the essay parts about you and what you want in a partner. Fill them in later.

Your search can range from a one-mile radius to the entire world. The service saves your criteria for future use. Thus once you have done your particular search, you can go back at a later time (a few days down the line, for example), and run a search using the same criteria. Next time through, you can specify that the search bring up only members who have joined since you last logged in. This brings about a minor drawback. You will also get any previous members who have made changes to their profiles since you last logged in, so there is a certain small amount of duplication. In Chapter Four we'll discuss how to set practical guidelines for searching through a matchmaking site.

The serious searcher will want to fill out Match.com's whole questionnaire. We'll cover this questionnaire in detail in Chapter Four. You then select your handle and password. If later you can't remember either or both of them, Match.com will email the information to you. If you also forget your own email address, you may be ready for the nursing home instead of Match.com.

In a sixteen-month period, the number of singles who had tried Match.com jumped by more than 2,000,000. This has to be a positive message. No question that many of these people took only the free trial, but the numbers are still impressive.

The cost is quite reasonable. For each month beyond your free trial period you will pay $16.95. Agreeing to a longer period, up to twelve months, gets you a rate as low as $8.33 a month. Further, your rate stays the same for all time beyond the period you sign up for. Initially I shelled out for a month, but later I switched to the six-month rate, $10.83 a month. When I went past the six months, my rate remained at $10.83.

In addition to a large membership and a practical approach, Match.com offers a handful of useful perks. If you so wish, anytime a new member comes on who seems to meet your criteria, Match.com will notify you by email.

There is a chat room, which is as dubious a genuine search method as any other chat room. There is also an interesting calendar provided to fore-warn members of upcoming events, and an online magazine with a host of informative topics such as "Should a Man Lie about His Age?" and "Vacationing Solo." At the Advice column, you can email your questions and concerns and read about those of others. In the "Profile Makeover" section, you will find tips on how to create an effective profile (some of which I disagree with), and examples of revised member profiles. Finally there is a "Tips and Strategy" section where you will find articles such as "How to Say No," "Birth Control Update," and "Should You Relocate for Love?" Match.com has also succumbed to the horoscope crowd. In all these sections, there are worthwhile archives of past articles.

PASSWORDS AND USER NAME LOG

One of my computer monitors is splashed with letters, numbers, and Web site addresses, à la black marker. These represent user names and handles I use to gain entrance to various sites. I also threw in some coded credit card numbers for the occasions when I am unable to resist the urge to make online purchases. The result is a near-indecipherable mess that falls far short of being a work of art.

To avoid such optical pollution, get a small notebook such as a steno pad to keep a record of these types of information. Put down the name of the site you have joined, as well as the entry data: handle and password. If you have more than one email address (I have three), indicate which address you gave to the site.

MATCHMAKING SITES IN A NUTSHELL

Match.com and AmericanSingles.com are the top contenders for the Matchmaking Site crown. Match.com's more extensive free trial period appeals, as does the quality of its extra features. AmericanSingles is playing catch-up in both departments. On the other hand, AmericanSingles has quick-and-easy voice messaging, which Match.com has not yet implemented. Both offer a large singles population to select from, at reasonable membership prices, which is the bottom line after all. You can't go wrong with either site. Classifieds2000 is a close third, with an appealing free-all-the-way membership.

Singles Directories

Although I have listed the major sites, you may want to strike out on your own. A singles directory will keep you busy beyond belief. There are two comprehensive ones. The first, Singlesites, also points to a sheaf of other directories.

SINGLESITES.COM

At *Singlesites.com* you will find links to more than five hundred sites that range from *kinkycontacts.com* to those tailored to a wide variety of religious persuasions. You will also see links to some thirty other singles directories. There are dozens of sites featuring "Beautiful ——— women"—fill in the blank for the nationality of your choice. Half of the women in Russia and most in Asia seem to be beautiful and looking for marriage. *Compulove.com*, for example, promises you "Beautiful unspoiled Filipinas."

You will even find a nudist site with a two-week free trial to ogle the National Geographic–type pictures (two million members without clothing) to your heart's content (*www.Nudist.matchmaker.com*). Sites galore offer advice on every conceivable subject remotely connected to dating and matchmaking.

WWW.CUPIDNET.COM

This site provides an even broader list of singles sites broken down into categories: matchmaking sites, national sites, international sites, religious sites, and so forth. There is some duplication in the categories, but no matter; the listing of over one thousand international sites alone has something for everyone. There are sites for Catholics, Christians, blacks, gays and lesbians, Mormons, Jews, teens, alternative lifestyles, astrological matchmaking, Muslims, and Jewish gays and lesbians, just for starters.

MARRYWHOMEVER.COM—AN ALTERNATIVE?

Actor/comedian Tom Arnold decided to go right to the well for a bride. He put up his own Web site, *www.marrytom.com,* and invited inquiry from "an adult single woman of childbearing age, good with children, willing to relocate, has goals, and self-confident enough to wear a bathing suit on vacation." Only one picture per applicant, please, to be uploaded online.

To join the parade, an interested woman had to fill out a form online. Besides blanks for name, address, phone number, and age (all mandatory), there was room for about seven hundred words to explain "Why Tom Arnold Should Marry You." A disclaimer was included explaining that Tom might not even date you, never mind marry you, and that you understood and agreed to that. In addition, there were eight questions regarding one's current Internet Service Provider, including "Would you like to find out about faster Internet Service?"

Within one week his site had enjoyed one million hits. Tom claims to have received and read 10,000 responses, which may have effectively kept him from enjoying any dates. At least part of Tom's success in this venture must be attributed to his discussion of his undertaking on national TV— David Letterman, *USA Today,* and the *Today* show. Tom's plan was to tour the country dating hand-selected females. If you have that kind of publicity, and lots of traveling money, go for it.

In Summary

Weigh the pros and cons of poking around on the Internet. If what you have been doing up until now has effectively produced potential partners for you, keep up the good work; maybe there's no need to shoot the rapids online. But if you are looking for new options, join the growing millions of singles now exploring matchmaking sites. First try those services that offer a free introductory period. Look at the additional features each site provides.

What kind of a time investment are you looking at? Plan on at least a six-month effort, so take the cost into consideration as well. Are you better off choosing a free service or paying for one that gives you more efficient and comprehensive search capabilities? Last, do you get a good feeling about the site—that the site is actively trying to help you on your love safari?

Now it's time to get down to the real art of designing your cyber self.

3 Creating Your Cyber Self

Advertising is the greatest art form of the twentieth century.

—MARSHALL MCLUHAN

The right name is an advertisement in itself.

—CLAUDE HOPKINS

I lack the temperament to be a fisherman. First, I don't have the patience. Second, I find it most unpleasant to retrieve a hook that a fish has consumed with gusto. In my preadolescent years, however, my parents would pack our family off to a rented cabin at Gillespie Pond in New Hampshire for a summer vacation. Our accommodations inevitably included a dock from which my younger brother, Don, and I would attempt to fish.

The crystal-clear water (it used to be that way!) was always about ten feet deep at dock end. We had no rod, just a length of nylon line wound on an H-shaped wooden spool, a sinker, and a hook at the end. The huge local worm population afforded costless culinary enticements to the subsurface residents. By dropping the baited hook straight down, we could observe directly the progress of our efforts, including the precise moment the fish took the bait. A yank on the line usually yielded the expected results. We would then haul in, unhook, and toss back the catch. On occasion our efforts produced the unexpected. One evening, we dragged in the same turtle three times in a row.

By now you should have a feel for the extent of the Internet matchmaking pond. Maybe one particular site has caught your eye. Now it's time to construct the lure that will draw prize specimens, rather than turtles. Let's begin putting the real You into cyber form. You will be fishing in a different sense, but the principle is the same. A profile, along with a well-prepared handle and headline, is your bait.

Handles

When you join, or at some sites if you just begin searching without joining, you will be asked to choose a name by which you will identify yourself to other members. Obviously, you don't want to broadcast your own full name. Anonymity eases the process of throwing back the fish you attract but don't want. These handles are variously referred to as "IDs" "User IDs," "Love IDs," and so forth.

A new potential SMC (soul-mate candidate, remember) may come in to canvass your site. Whenever you are not actively looking, your handle and headline represent your only presence in the marketplace. This is all you'll have to draw that SMC into looking at your profile. It isn't until someone makes contact with you that you realize you have a bite. At Gillespie Pond, we had only worms; we'll devise a much more attractive lure for SMCs.

Someone looking through potential matches does not waste a lot of time; there are too many profiles to scan. Your handle is a minor, but important attention getter. It opens the door to your personality a crack. Be careful you don't imply the wrong image. Anything with "69" in it, HotMama, StudCat, or the like, will fetch a horde of one-track minds.

Give some thought to your best qualities, and to the kind of person you want to attract. The following are actual uninspired handles that tell little or nothing about the SMC:

Carl04	nef14
Taffy07	dibl
friend123456	Minn5 [in Texas, yet!]
enjoy3302	flea1121
Golden04	Ruth007

Most sites will generate a few handles for you if you draw a blank, all of which are guaranteed to bring yawns. When Carl04 logged into his site and applied for a handle for the first time, he was told that "Carl" had already been taken, and would he go for something like "Carl04"? Most likely he was given a choice of two or three other such thrillers. Similarly, "Flea" found that she was not the first to come up with such an offbeat handle. So the computer tacked on a random number and suggested "Flea1121."

Compare the boring handles with these more imaginative and/or informative ones:

WOW_JUDY	Firefly
Metaphysician	LiveWire85
Lion4ram	Mzcharm
blackadder03	Fun4Bev
nopollyanna	Petitepackage
zestylady	BrendaStarr18
PhoenixRisen	DivineYoga
Trans4m	Skiguy2000
Runner4U	kayaker609
modernmaven	Sail4Me
AerobicsNut	Travel_myPassion

Give some thought to your handle. Try something that will make you stand out from the crowd. Dare to be different. If you have a personality trait that appeals, use it: HappyGoLucky, BusyBee, AlwaysUpbeat, FunOne [my soul mate Ute's selection]. Or invent something: TankTiger, ClickAndGo, Fandalasia, MindBoggler. It doesn't have to make sense, or even be a real word; just don't be dull. And keep in mind that any name with the slightest sexual connotation will attract the worst types.

If at a later time you come up with a different handle that appeals more to you, don't hesitate to change it. Every site has a section where you can alter all aspects of your profile, including handles and headlines. If another handle captures your fancy, switch.

My own first effort at a handle, my Internet nickname so to speak, was a tame EricF. I then noticed that the competition variously dubbed themselves, SilverFox, SturdyGuy, SuchaCatch, and so forth. So I went back to my college days when I was tabbed "Fearless Fagan" by my baseball coach, and came up with FearlessF. And it fit, because I have been a risktaker all my life (most often to my detriment).

Headlines

Most sites let you compose a phrase or sentence as your opening remark. This text is displayed at the top of your profile, and usually is also shown separately along with your handle. Your headline can set the tone for your profile. On some sites, users begin their search by looking only at headlines and handles. When they see something that appeals to them, they can click on the headline to go to the full profile. So if an SMC is shuffling around in the headline section only, you want to increase the odds that yours will catch his or her eye.

Headlines fall into five categories: clever, informative, ho-hum, aren't-we-all?, and god-awful. Following are some examples I found in my search.

Clever:

- Coauthor wanted for final chapter in adventure story!

- Thinking woman's man seeks thinking man's woman.

- Romancing the stone??? Here's a unique emerald...

- Tennis, anyone?

- VIP position available—job description: friend, companion, soul mate—with possibilities for advancement to a term relationship.

- If I were a car I'd be a Chevy—nothing fancy but always there for you.

- Knight in shining armor/court jester mix/free to the right home.

Informative:

- Slim, blue-eyed brunette who would love to hike the Maine woods with a special guy.

- California/Oregon beach lover and classic car buff.

- Love to travel, go to movies, theater, play tennis.

- Long-time vegetarian, now vegan, having fun with yoga and Zen, and you!

- Analytical man with big heart, loves music, wants kids.

- Come dance with me!…really dance…like swing and cha cha and waltz and tango. Let's embrace and glide across the dance floor!

- Captain looking for lady to cruise away and enjoy life in the warmth of the seas!

Ho-hum:

- Thirty-three-year-old male, located in Honolulu, Hawaii.

- On Toward Spring!

- Are you the right one?

- Could we be perfect partners/friends/lovers for the rest of our lives?

- Moderately handsome, usually articulate, semi-fit…

- Nicest guy on Long Island.

- Wannaknowme.

"Aren't we all?":

- Ready to meet that special someone.

- Unique mold—one of a kind!

- I am looking for that someone special who is happy within and can make a difference in my life.

- Woman seeking man.

- Normal nice guy looking for normal nice gal.

- Would you like to meet someone new and interesting? Try me!

- Looking for that special person.

- Looking for sincere relationship no games, jokes, or playing around.

God-awfuls:

- Looking for you, a friend first. Tired of scab-pickin' dirty liven' dudes making my gender look bad!

- Young at heart—no old farts.

- I can't believe I'm out here again—can someone relate to this?

- Why the Hell am I doing this?!

- Not a "bad boy" but good at all the bad boys' most desirable traits.

- Do you want a more interesting description?—say at least "want new match-description" in email to R——— at ———@online.no.

- Come fly with me (is that corny or what?).

My own first headline was so bad that I've forgotten it. After a bit of thinking, "For the ride of your life for the rest of your life…" emerged. That worked for me. Certainly you can do a tad better with a bit of effort.

So this gives you a glimpse of the competition. As you dig around on various sites, make notes of interesting headlines. Take some time with your own. Run it past a friend or two of the gender you want to attract. Your sparkling wit may be too subtle. Your creation may invoke a "huh?" rather than a "wow!" Put your thinking cap on and come up with something either clever or informative. Come alive!

By now you've put together your three A, B, and C lists (see Chapter One). You're thinking about a unique handle, and a headline that will magnetize eyeballs. So let's get to the heart of your campaign to lasso a soul mate: your profile.

Creating a Knockout Profile

At sixty-three, I had sampled many slices of life. My likes and dislikes abounded. And I realized there was a lot I wanted to tell about myself. After a month of fumbling, I finally got my profile into a semblance of working order. I couldn't get across all I wished to say in the 350 words to which the site limited me, so I created an 800-word addendum. Overkill? Nothing mys-

terious left? Those who can pack their entire history and outlook on life into 1,150 words must have spent their formative years in a cave.

Displaying the merchandise fully and detailing my wish list meant that I could eliminate an unsuitable candidate more quickly, and she could eliminate me. It worked marvelously. If you skimp on telling about yourself and your likes, you risk leaving out the one phrase or word that may catch your soul mate's eye.

Dr. Peter Moran, a noted economist, said of advertising:

"The more facts you tell, the more you sell. An advertisement's chance for success invariably increases as the number of pertinent merchandise facts included in the ad increases."

In just under ten seconds, enough time to read the first few lines of your personal profile, someone will form a first and possibly lasting impression of you. The experience is on a par with meeting a blind date for the first time. Your profile is equivalent not only to your initial greeting, but also to what you are wearing, your posture, your ability to make eye contact, and the firmness of your handshake, even your aftershave or perfume. Although there is no one profile style that suits everyone, a charming, humorous, poignant, creative, or otherwise unique approach may improve your results. You do yourself a disservice by settling for the bland and the concise. You'll want to take the same pains with your profile that you would with a first date. You wouldn't show up late, wear a stained jacket, or chew with your mouth open on a first date. Be just as attentive to your profile.

Consider yourself in contention for the best soul mate possible. If you don't make a favorable impression immediately, the SMC will simply move to the next profile and most likely never come back! But if you design a clear and accurate verbal picture of yourself and the major characteristics of the SMC you desire, you will be a winner in the matching game.

Your handle and headline will first excite curiosity that will lead an SMC to read your profile. But remember: you don't want to merely attract SMCs; you want to attract the ones who are right for you! If an SMC sees from your profile that you have a compatible outlook on life and similar interests, he or she will keep on reading. An accurate, well-fashioned, interesting profile will inspire an SMC to send emails to learn more about you.

LOOKING OVER THE COMPETITION

Before we get to the dos and don'ts, set a bit of time aside to study the competition. Male or female, the approach is the same. Let's say you are a thirty-year-old woman looking for a man in the range of thirty to thirty-five. Reverse roles and run a search of women thirty to thirty-five looking for men; this is your competition. Look through at least twenty profiles. See how your competitors bait their respective hooks. Take notes. If a phrase or a sentence strikes your fancy, don't hesitate to modify and adopt it into your own profile.

For instance, I found a profile comment, "No baggage, just a small suit-case under the bed." So I inserted it into my own profile to say, "I recently read, 'No baggage, just a small suitcase under the bed.' I have neither baggage nor suitcase, not even a small purse."

Others may seem to have more to brag about, or appear more fortunate than you in different areas. Don't lose any sleep over it. You are a unique individual. What you have to offer is precisely the best match for your soul mate. When I reviewed my competition, I saw many tall and distinguished-looking men with full heads of silvery hair (on top, I could comb my hair with a toothpick). Some appeared to come straight from a male-model catalogue. Others owned boats, fast cars, or both (I own a '73 VW and a bicycle), and sounded as if they were burdened with excess money. Still others appeared to be in excellent physical condition and had exciting professional jobs. But I still liked best the package I had to offer, and I hoped that my soul mate would as well—correctly, as it turned out! So other than getting an idea of what they are saying, ignore your competition. Your soul mate is looking for *you*, not for one of the close contenders.

Remember, too, that your purpose is *not* to come up with pen pals or just dates. Rather, you will be looking for red, yellow, and green flags as you play the soul mate search game. Red for "stop reading and go on to the next profile"; yellow for "Hmmm. Let's look into this item a bit more"; and green for "That's interesting. Let's talk [or keep talking]." For more on this see Chapter Six.

Once you have an idea of what your competitors are claiming, you'll have somewhat of a feel for a profile. Let's start building yours. And remember: don't try to do this work while you're logged onto a matchmaking site and are in the process of signing up. Instead, draft your text first on paper, or in your favorite word processor. Once you have it polished, go back into the matchmaking site you've elected and copy in your text.

We'll first list the dos and don't dos and then discuss them further.

Do

1. be honest!

2. tell lots about yourself.

3. talk about the activities you currently engage in.

4. list the activities you would be willing to try.

5. expand on one or two special interests or activities.

6. describe what you are looking for in a relationship.

7. include poems or witty quotes if that is your style.

8. include your picture with your profile.

9. use proper spelling, grammar, and punctuation.

10. refine your presentation.

11. get feedback.

Don't

1. be negative.

2. waste words stating the obvious.

3. brag about how good you look.

4. use sexual innuendo.

5. shout (use all capital letters).

6. use words that are unfamiliar to you.

7. use acronyms unless they are universally understood.

8. use unnecessary abbreviations.

9. disparage previous relationships.

Now let's look at each suggestion in more detail.

DO BE HONEST

You want to find SMCs who are interested in you, rather than in the person you wish you were. In other words, you're looking for someone who will love you as you are, right? Maybe someone who enjoys a video and popcorn at home on Saturday night? Or playing poker and having a few beers?

Ruthetta, twenty-seven, in San Diego:

> "I'm looking for a cowboy type whose idea of fun is first going to shoot some pool with a few beers, and then singing karaoke."

Marcel, fifty-five, in Baltimore:

> "My greatest enjoyment in life is sailing my forty-two-footer in the bay. I'm looking for a woman who is not afraid to roll up her sleeves and pitch in onboard. Don't be squeamish about taking care of fish we pull aboard. Beer drinker preferred."

Jeanne, forty-four, in Rutland:

> "So, I am not as wrinkle-free as I used to be, but maybe I am more interesting. Other things you will win: I have a great twelve-year-old daughter who is the nicest person in the history of the universe. I have a great eight-week-old puppy who is smarter than I am."

Perhaps you want an SMC who is turned on by the love handles that twenty, thirty, or forty extra pounds provide:

Joanne, thirty-three, in Richmond:

> "Hi Guy! Since you're reading this, and not passing it over, I'm going to assume that you already know that I'm not a Cher look-alike. If fat women turn you off, then you might as well just go on to the next ad. Now that we've got that out of the way, I've never married."

Or who agrees with you about opera, cats, jogging, and Howard Stern:

Ken, twenty-nine, in Atlanta:

> "Not sports or opera/theater-oriented."

So be truthful. Omission can be a form of dishonesty; don't avoid factors that you know might cause problems if left unsaid:

Trudy, forty-nine, in Tacoma:

> "Love to travel, garden, outdoors, nature. Grew up in the country; am planning to go back. You aren't looking at a city girl here."

Don't be concerned about putting down items that you feel might scare people off. Handle them right up front. If you are a late-night person, why waste time with an insane (to you) person who is going to want you up at 5:30 A.M. to jog? By telling it like it is, you will find a soul mate who steps to your drumbeat.

Maria, twenty-eight, in Wichita:

> "I smoke a lot, so you have to be used to that."

Spell out your must-have items; leave no doubts.

Jim, fifty-seven, in Grand Rapids:

> "You have to be intelligent and have a good sense of humor. You have to love life and be in a positive mode."

Meretta, forty-seven, in Chicago:

> "Humor is a must. I grew up in a family with a rich sense of humor that was evident daily. I enjoy verbal wit and play."

Also be frank in stating strong feelings in the other direction:

Eric, sixty-three, in San Diego:

> "I have no objection to a partner who drinks lightly socially, but I draw the line at drugs. I have no tolerance for any kind, not even marijuana. If you are into any, even just so-called recreationally, save us both some time and don't respond."

Paul, fifty-one, in Colorado Springs:

> "Two sports that do not hold my interest are downhill skiing (cross-country is fine), and horseback riding. I rode a horse once in my youth. It was an unusual experience for both the horse and for me."

DO TELL LOTS ABOUT YOURSELF

A matchmaking service generally allows 300–350 words for your profile. An SMC will read your petition to the end, but only if you write in an interesting manner. Don't ramble. Be unique. Don't mimic what others profess to be their heart's desires. You want your profile to stand out as unusual so that each SMC will say, "Man! I have to meet this one."

Begin by writing freely about yourself. At this point, don't count words. Write freely as much as you need to tell what you do, and why you do it. Specify the qualities that you are looking for in a partner. Keep writing. Tell how you want to interact with your partner, what you will share. Tell your

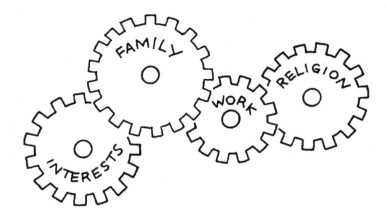

SMC why life with you will be more fun than with anyone else. If you have "eclectic tastes," don't just leave it at that; list some examples. Here are a few excerpts:

Fred, fifty-five, in Washington, D.C.:

> "I enjoy dancing (square and ballroom), astronomy (I built my own telescope and am working on a second), good movies, fishing, good food, travel (motor home, motorcycle for two), photography, reading, hiking in the Redwoods, almost all kinds of music (can't stand Punk Rock and Rap), fishing, shopping, reading, cooking, TV shows (*Washington Review*, and so forth), warm weather, did I mention fishing? learning new things, and learning tennis (one of my latest projects), and LOVE!"

Fred expands on some of his interests by giving us side notes in parentheses. Do you get the impression he likes to fish?

Twenty-five-year-old Lisa in Portland gives an insight into what life with her would be like:

> "I stay physically fit by running (I run three to five miles almost every day) and hiking (I made it to the top of Mt. Rainier last summer!). I am passionate about live theater and have made many trips to NYC especially to enjoy the shows. I also love to cook healthy foods, garden, and go hiking or picnicking with my neighbor's kids on weekends."

Gina, thirty-seven, in New York City, explains what her life revolves around:

"Theater, ballet, contemporary art, movies, and good fiction rate high. I'm a lap swimmer, pseudo polar bear who swims outdoors in the winter (in a heated pool, of course; I may be crazy, but not ridiculous). I've skied cross-country only once, but loved it. I can ice skate in one direction, and spent one hour on snowshoes. I loved the bunny slope at Aspen. Sailing might be fun if the destination is interesting. I love to travel to see urban and rural places on foot or by car. I've lived and traveled abroad."

And from thirty-five-year-old Gary in Los Angeles:

"My favorite activities are camping and backpacking. I have tried rock climbing and deep-sea fishing and love both! I like books (Plato to Elmore Leonard to Douglas Adams) and movies (*West Side Story* to *Gone with the Wind*) that make me think. I love dogs (two labs own me) and watching soccer games (I play at it also, but not too effectively, though I have fun)."

Fred, Lisa, Gina, and Gary have shown a range of tastes. Certainly there is more to each, but at least we have a flavor of the whole person. Now contrast those with the following *complete* profiles.

Cindy, fifty-four, in Oahu:

"I'm a divorced mother of three grown children. I am strong and independent and enjoy stimulating conversation among good company. I like the simple things in life such as a good book and a walk on the beach. Looking to find the same in a companion who has a solid foundation in old-fashioned values, and who approaches life with an open mind."

Cindy's sparse profile could use more fleshing out, more details. "Strong and independent" can be interpreted in a variety of ways. Strong in the sense of lifting weights or strong in the sense of being able to face down adversity? Independent financially, or in terms of stepping to her own tune? Cindy would do well to expand on this profile, and also on what she is looking for in a relationship. What are the "old-fashioned values" that will catch her interest? Often the best thing about the "good old days" is that they are gone.

Rosie, forty-nine, in Ft. Lauderdale:

> "Here I am living in Paradise, luxuriating in my pool, enjoying a Cabernet waiting for someone to join me. Do you love nature and its bounties? Have you ever had the opportunity to gaze at the delicious sight of the sun settling through palm trees and into tropic waters? Would you love to be a witness to the dewdrops shimmering in the moonlight? Join me in this magnificent setting and thrill at the sight of the sailfish dancing on the bay, and let our hearts ride with the pelicans gliding above them. If you would like to share these gifts of nature with me, what are you waiting for?"

There's no denying Rosie's emotional appeal in this profile, but what can we gather about her other than that she is interested in sailing and Cabernet? What does she do once she's out of the pool? Rosie could have easily expanded on her love of nature. Perhaps she enjoys rock hunting on the beach, canoeing through the backwaters, or following butterflies in season. We have no clues to other facets of her life, one or more of which may be just the ticket to attract her soul mate.

Go beyond adjectives. If you are "adventurous," explain in what way. If you claim to be "fit," clarify that it is a result of spending half an hour at the gym four days a week after work, for example.

Tom, thirty-seven, in London:

> "As I do, you enjoy the feeling of good health that radiates after exercise of whatever sort."

Ursula, thirty-three, in Fresno:

> "I love the peaceful quiet of a mountain stream, canoeing on a lake at dusk, or hiking in the Sequoias, or in the meadows of Yosemite."

Both of these SMCs go beyond mere listing of likes. Tom describes *why* he exercises. Ursula shares with us the tranquility she finds in the settings she portrays.

I like to run because it makes me feel good and keeps me in shape, but I wasn't necessarily looking for a woman who would run with me. Being willing to get up in the morning and come out to my races would have been good enough. And even better would be to find one who would run her own race at the same time. Of greater importance to me, I did want a woman who would bicycle and backpack right alongside me. My profile reflected this:

> "You are trim and fit, enjoy nature, backpacking once in a while, bicycling two or three times a week, and possibly jogging."

Write as if you are talking directly to your soul mate. Assume that the person reading your profile right now is your soul mate. Envision sitting comfortably over a cup of coffee with that SMC. Use the personal pronoun "you" as if you are speaking face-to-face, looking into the eyes of your reader. The following two paragraphs have the same content, but watch how the message comes across more intimately in example B:

A. "The woman I want must be willing to have kids. She will enjoy white-water rafting once a year, horses, dogs, and dancing to country music. She doesn't depend on TV for her entertainment, but instead likes to read and play bridge. I like plain eating and red meat once or twice a week."

B. "You are looking forward to having kids. You also enjoy whitewater rafting once a year and have a liking for horses and dogs. You will enjoy kicking up your heels with me to country music. Rather than TV, you get your entertainment from reading. What an added attraction if you also play a good hand of bridge. You have simple eating tastes and don't mind if I have red meat once or twice a week. I'll even do the cooking."

Notice that the first excerpt is impersonal wishful thinking—"I want..." "I like..." kind of stuff. The second one may elicit the response, "AHA! Yes! That's me!"

Describe your job. If the tale is unique, explain how you got there. For example, did you work your way up through the ranks, or were you fortunate enough to inherit Daddy's business? Have you been with the same organization for a long time?

Bill, sixty-two, in Seattle:

> "I was with the same company for thirty-eight years. I started in training as a busboy in one of their restaurants, and ended up as a vice president in charge of operations."

If you like your job, describe what you like about it:

Sara, twenty-six, in Anchorage:

"I'm college-educated with a great job as an operating room nurse in a local hospital. My job allows me plenty of time to enjoy life."

Joanna, thirty-four, in San Jose:

"I'm a Web site designer. I love my job. I can get lost in the intricacies of trying new things and putting it all together, and never even notice the day fly by."

It is unlikely that any of these SMCs will waste time grousing about the job at the end of the day.

If you don't care for your job, spare us the details. Contrast how two men who work in the same area of California feel about their calling:

Bob, thirty-two:

"I spend most of my time being a software engineer in the Silicon Valley get-rich-quick rat race. Beats standing on a street corner with a cup in my hand...I think."

Juan, forty-four:

"I'm a San Franciscan, work in Mountain View, and I see a lot of 101 South during the week. Actually, I like my job, even with the commute. I just put my mind in neutral. As a software engineer, I'm..."

If you've just embarked on a new career, convey the excitement that this change brings to your life. If you are going to school full-time as an adult, describe how you are supporting yourself.

Rhonda, thirty-nine, in Riverside:

"I am doing college the hard way. School evenings and weekends, driving 110 miles round-trip each time. I should have listened to my mother when I was younger, but I'll have my B.A. next year. I work as a sales clerk to support myself and my fourteen-year-old son, but the end of the tunnel is definitely in sight."

Be open about your parenting role. Humorist James Wilmot said, "Before I got married, I had six theories about bringing up children. Now I have six children and no theories."

If applicable, tell how many kids you have, how old they are, and what gender. Obviously a two-year-old girl will have a different effect on your leisure time than will a fourteen-year-old boy. Speak proudly of your children. Don't complain. Everyone knows the best child is wearing at times.

Michael, thirty, in Lincoln:

> "My five-year-old is a handful, but I love every minute of him (almost)."

Marlie, forty-six, in Helena:

> "I have three wonderful teenagers if you can believe it."

Dave, fifty, in Provo:

> "I have three children: fifteen- and sixteen-year-old girls and a twenty-three-year-old son. I love every child in the world but of course especially my own."

Being direct about your family responsibilities is essential, even if your having children puts off an SMC. You are looking for a soul mate who will accept your family situation.

Monica, forty-two, in La Jolla:

> "I have twin girls who just turned twelve. While they can be a chore sometimes, I love them dearly. They don't rule my life, but they are an important part of it."

The four SMCs quoted here obviously love and are proud of their children. Let this show through to an SMC who will appreciate and understand your feelings. At the same time, you will fend off SMCs who do not cotton to children.

Get the bait right. Worms won't do much to further your deep-sea fishing efforts. Trout will turn up their nose at chunks of bread. So put appropriate bait on your hook. Compare the profiles of two thirty-two-year-old men:

Peter, in Honolulu:

> "I love swimming, writing poetry, playing computer games, dancing and music....I work as an accountant, and I am a single parent....If you want to know more about me,...write to me! Hope to hear from you soon!"

Ed, in Oakland:

> "I really enjoy good light conversation; no politics or world affairs please. I just like being able to connect with another person in a relaxed tone. Education is a plus but not a necessity, although intelligence is mandatory. I would also like to meet someone who is fit and at least has healthy eating on her priority list. I would love to have two or three kids someday so that is also a positive attribute I look for."

Peter listed a few interests. Ed went beyond that by describing more of his feelings, likes, and plans for the future. His actual profile, all of which he put to good use, was also three times as long as Peter's.

Weigh your reactions to the following women:

Ruby, sixty, in Flagstaff:

> "If you have an interest in the Civil War I might be just the woman for you!" [*That's all she wrote—the entire profile!*]

Veronica, fifty-five, in Boston:

> "A slim INTJ night owl with a passport, book bag, kayak, and dancing shoes, I seek as a life mate a man with a generous heart, an inquisitive mind and an intuitive and adventurous spirit. We are both at peace with our pasts and desirous of finding a soul mate to share the days, months, and years ahead."

Can we agree that Ruby has narrowed her prospects to a sliver? Veronica, even with an abbreviated profile, will attract some men. She radiates vivacity. In addition, through her well-chosen words we can gather that Veronica is athletic, reads, loves to dance, and travels abroad. As she writes well, another one hundred words or more would have been welcome. She could have explained where she has traveled and what was on her itinerary. She also could have let us know which of the multitude of musical scenarios urge her to strap on the dancing shoes.

Be careful about trying to be funny. There's a fine line between humor and sarcasm. If you step over that line you will come across as arrogant. At best, you may be seen as a smart aleck. Compare the following two profile excerpts:

Darin, forty-nine, in Cincinnati:

> "To be charitable, my looks are average. My only hope in a male beauty contest would be one where the votes are tallied by Braille."

Harry, thirty-one, in Rochester:

> "Who is this 'me' I speak of?...He is romantic like Tom Cruise WISHES he was. Ha! That putz!"

You can never go wrong by placing yourself at the receiving end of humor. Darin does that. Harry's put-down falls flat.

Refrain from directing people to "(smile)." Also avoid peppering your sentences with ("ha ha *or* he he he)." This equates to poking a listener in the ribs after telling a joke and saying, "Get it? Get it?" If your humor can't be understood without prompts, it is ineffective.

Harry, fifty-five, in Memphis:

> "I enjoy life and like to have fun. I will try just about anything once, but no sky diving.[smile] I'm a normal, healthy, fun-loving, dirty old man. [smile] Really I would like…"

No need to hold up the laugh card.

Don't hesitate to list activities, even if you don't do them well. If your ability is less than world-class, give a clue:

Sally, forty-one, in Montgomery:

> "On a good day, I'm only a D tennis player, but I enjoy just hitting the ball around."

DO TALK ABOUT THE ACTIVITIES YOU ENGAGE IN NOW

You are inviting a person to share your life. Give your SMC a decent hint of what living with you will entail. If you enjoy sports, which ones? Distinguish, for example, between downhill and cross-country skiing; deep-sea, scuba, or au natural diving; ballroom or disco dancing.

David, fifty-four, in Marietta, Ohio:

> "I can ballroom dance without causing snickers, but am hopeless at the non-contact varieties of this sport. My idea of dancing is where you get to hold your partner."

Phyllis, thirty-seven, in St. Petersburg:

> "I enjoy ocean swimming, but am not one for lying around on the beach just to get sunburned."

David rules out the disco as a playground, while Phyllis feels that passive beaching is not for her. If one term can encompass different meanings, clear up any possible misunderstanding.

Forget about activities that you did in school, or at any time in the past, if they don't help to explain who you are and what is important to you right now. Ditto if you don't do them now. Who cares if you were a quarterback if your only present exercise is clicking the remote? Describe what you do and how often you do it. Don't just list activities. Describe what the more important ones mean to you, and tell how often you do them:

Charles, thirty-six, in San Antonio:

> "I go through one or two books a week, from Austen to Zeno, Bill Bryson to Bill Moyers."

Nancy, forty-five, in Seattle:

> "Every weekend finds me out on the slopes in wintertime, skiing or snowshoeing. In the summertime I'm off for alpine hiking. I get almost a spiritual feeling when I am outdoors like this."

Daryl, twenty-eight, in Nashua:

> "Every morning before I start my job as a programmer, I take a walk through a small forest area."

Norman, fifty-two, in Duluth:

> "On weekend nights, I get out my telescope to watch the stars, galaxies, and planets...and marvel at the vastness of space."

Jenny, sixty-five, in Bridgeport:

> "On any given day you will find me out by the pond watching the ducks. This lets me relax and ready myself for the first day of the rest of my life."

Lou, forty-four, in Los Angeles:

> "I catch the Dodgers whenever I can....It's almost like I'm patriotic about them."

All of these half-dozen SMCs have opened their soul-windows a bit more than the average candidate does. This gives each a lead on the competition; every yard counts.

DO LIST THE ACTIVITIES YOU WOULD BE WILLING TO TRY

Similarly, list pursuits you are interested in exploring. Maybe you have an urge to try scuba diving or take a stroll through the Smithsonian. You can never tell what will ring your SMC's bell.

Your SMC may be looking for a dancing partner, a sailing mate, or a gardening buddy. So if you have inclinations you have yet to pursue, advertise your willingness:

Janet, thirty-one, in Tucson:

> "I'd like to take swing lessons if I had a partner to go with me."

Tom, thirty-three, in Sacramento:

> "I've had a yen to start my own garden, but don't have the room where I am now."

Barbara, twenty-five, in Santa Barbara:

> "I went scuba diving once and loved it. I'd like to do more."

Each has opened up possibilities, at the same time broadcasting his or her willingness to travel new avenues. One of my criteria for a partner was someone who would be willing to go backpacking. So what I looked for in a profile was at least some indication of an interest in hiking or camping. Don't let an SMC get away simply because you fail to mention the SMC's favorite activity as one you would like to try.

DO EXPAND ON ONE OR TWO
SPECIAL INTERESTS OR ACTIVITIES

You may volunteer in a home for abused women or in a hospital. You may be the lodge secretary or belong to the Sierra Club. Such an activity makes you just a bit different than most people, so capitalize on it. You may find a kindred spirit, or you may strike just the right note with an SMC.

Colin, forty-seven, in Mobile:

> "I love kids and sports. I have been a Little League umpire for three years."

Samantha, thirty-eight, in San Bernardino:

> "I enjoy young kids and volunteer as a CASA (Court Appointed Special Advocate) for children who have been placed in foster homes."

Both of these SMCs like young people and go one step further. "I like kids" flows easily; obviously these SMCs are offering more than just lip service to this statement.

DO DESCRIBE WHAT YOU ARE
LOOKING FOR IN A RELATIONSHIP

Just listing your activities is not enough. Do you want full participation from a partner, or will mere interest or accompaniment suffice?

Maryanne, fifty-four, in Ft. Worth:

> "I swim every day of the week. While I would like someone who could join me, I'd be happy with a partner who would just sit by the pool or read his newspaper at the beach with me."

Bill, forty-seven, in Cleveland:

> "I'd like a partner who plays a musical instrument, though that is not a must. It would be enough if she would enjoy my playing my clarinet."

Marisa, twenty-five, in New York City:

> "[I am looking for] an intelligent secure man [who is] independent and allows me to be myself, a man who is looking for adventure, is always learning new things, and who enjoys sharing his dreams with an equal."

Ellen, fifty-nine, in Salt Lake City:

> "I spent most of my life in the Midwest where I was raised with a strong work ethic, living by the Golden Rule, being forthright, and I expect the same in a man."

Each of these people sheds some light on particular stripes he or she looks for in an SMC. At the same time, each one offers tips as to particular factors that will make them happy.

DO INCLUDE POEMS OR QUOTES IF THAT IS YOUR STYLE

Add a particular verse or quote if it helps to explain you. "Life is a hundred times too short for us to bore ourselves" summed up an Alabama woman's outlook. Another included a short love poem her uncle had written to her aunt. A Canadian man modified an epigram by Woody Allen:

> "I don't mind getting old; I just don't want to be there when it happens."
> [The actual quote is: "I'm not afraid of dying; I just don't, and so forth."]

Such an addition bears subtle witness to the workings of your mental processes. Here's a unique approach I came across:

Danielle, fifty-seven, in Hartford:

> "Dear man of my dreams. I hear your passionate eloquence, your love of life expressed in metaphor and in deeds, and I was drawn to you as deeply as to my own soul's cry. We are meant to soar with the sun-dappled clouds. You must love me as...OK, now your turn—finish the thought."

As I found out later, Danielle took these words in the first part of the paragraph from a love letter her mother wrote to her father before they wed.

DO PUT YOUR PICTURE WITH YOUR PROFILE

More than 130 years ago the Russian novelist Ivan Turgenev said, "A picture shows me at a glance what it takes a dozen pages of a book to expound." In 1921 an otherwise undistinguished gentleman by the name of Fred Barnard said, "One look is worth a thousand words." Six years later he changed it to "One picture is worth a thousand words," and called it "a Chinese proverb so that people would take it seriously." Nobody has ever claimed that Ivan or Fred was wrong!

Don't try to explain your looks. You can describe yourself to your heart's content, but why? You can report on what your friends, relatives, neighbors, mother, and even the local butcher thinks of your looks. An SMC doesn't give a fig what all those people think. It is the SMC, not your gardener or local bank teller, who will decide whether to appear in public with you. You are wasting your time describing your physical attributes instead of showing them. Worse, you are letting the competition get ahead of you. Remember that a good percentage of SMCs will search only those profiles with a picture attached.

Let a picture do your work. Beauty is in the eye of the looker, not the lookee. SMCs tend to get carried away with their own charm. The problem is particularly widespread. Multitudes of SMCs cannot resist the urge to depict the indescribable:

"My friends say that I am attractive."

"I am attractive [sexy, gorgeous, good-looking, ripped, or whatever]."

"I look a lot like [any number of good-looking movie stars]."

"I'm forty-six, but could pass for thirty-six. I'm told I'm handsome (recently referred to as a 'hottie')."

Stop! Why try to tell complete strangers what you or others imagine you look like? Why not let the SMC decide by putting up your picture? Can this be any simpler? Pascal, a seventeenth-century philosopher said, "If you want people to speak well of you, don't speak well of yourself."

Why not tip the odds in your favor? The two leading matchmaking sites, Match.com and AmericanSingles.com, both claim that members with photos accompanying their profiles get *eight times* as many responses as those who do not include pictures. Hark ye!

I once agreed to meet a woman I had come across through a newspaper personal ad. She described herself as "very attractive." Our opinions on this subject differed; undoubtedly someone else would find her so, but she was not my cup of tea, nor was I hers. Both of us could have made better use of the short time we spent together.

Although looks aren't everything, they are on everyone's list someplace. And sooner or later you will come face-to-face with an SMC who shares your interests. Make it easy on both of you. If you can put up only one picture, make it a head shot, or a half-body at the most. Full-body pictures are too small when cut down to profile size. Some sites allow you to post up to five pictures; take advantage! Who knows which one(s) will appeal to your soul mate? Your primary picture should be of you alone. Save the pictures of you and your children or pets for later pictures. If you post your picture, the SMC who thinks you are the most wonderful creature on earth will have a better chance of finding you.

As an example, when I was searching for my soul mate, I constantly came across profiles that were borderline. Or the SMC was a bit outside the range I had in mind (lived on the East Coast, for example). If I was undecided, I would always look at a picture if one was available. If there was no picture, I would simply skip to the next profile. Your SMC may be a hairsbreadth away from catching your act; your picture could very well do the trick.

Use a current picture. I once met a woman in L.A. who had a stunning picture attached to her profile. In the flesh, she wasn't the same woman. The picture was of her "a few years ago," in her own words. At least ten...and when she was much slimmer. I had a similar experience in San Diego. Both meetings were wasted for each of us. Each woman was attractive, but neither was what I was looking for. The sad part is that these women were missing out on the men who would have drooled over their true pictures. You'll have enough on your mind when you first meet an SMC in person without having to dance around the fact that your picture is ancient history. Why start out on a dishonest note?

Don't choose a picture in which you hide behind sunglasses. Your eyes and your smile are crucial to your charm. And don't try to be Ms. or Mr. Cool. Pick a photo that shows a person who is enjoyable to be around.

Now let's take a look at the nine excuses for not putting a picture with a profile, and why you should ignore all of them:

1. *"I'm too good-looking and will get too many responses."* This is a problem most SMCs don't experience. I certainly didn't. Having too many emails to answer certainly beats having none. If this is *your* excuse, ask yourself whether the real reason that you don't have your picture up is fear of rejection—fear that you *won't* get an overwhelming response. Be honest with yourself. If you have too much mail coming in, you can always delete in bunches to whittle it down.

2. *"There are too many weirdos out there."* Whether you do the bar scene, or the church bazaar, you can run into crazies. You have more protection from the undesirables on the Internet than anyplace else. Swarms of men and women post pictures with their profiles. The worst that can happen is that you may be bombarded with emails from an ardent admirer whose elevator does not go to the top. Ignore such loosely wrapped characters. It takes no effort at all to delete their entreaties unread. Then just change your email address, your handle, or both if you must.

CHAILING

The Internet has spawned a multitude of new words that are now part of our everyday vocabulary: "browser," "email," "voice mail," "online," and the like. There has been no particular word to describe the business of sending email back and forth between persons. It is not quite chatting: that is done in person or over a phone line. Further, chatting in a "chat room" carries a different connotation: that of instantaneous give-and-take. And although email is written, neither is it exactly correspondence.

In a sense, you are chatting but using email as your means of communication. But it is awkward to continually say "we chatted by email," or even "we corresponded by email." In hopes of solving the dilemma, I've coined the word "chail"—to *Ch*at by em*ail*. If someone comes up with a better word, great. But for now, I'll have to ask you to bear with my coinage.

Once I chatted briefly with a woman in San Francisco. At one point I told her about the three loves of my life and my six children. She returned a wild message accusing me of either being "a liar or not very good with women." I wrote back, "Clearly our karmas are not destined to intertwine." She next sent back a message insisting vehemently that our karmas *were* destined to mingle. I ignored it and the dozen messages that followed over the next few days.

3. *"A picture is too revealing of age."* You are what you are. Is a picture going to reveal more of your age than you will in person? By hiding behind a blank screen you are doing a disservice to yourself and quite possibly to your SMC. You are only as old as you appear to an SMC, so lay it all out. That way there are no unpleasant surprises. Only once did I meet with an SMC who had declined to send a picture. She was quite nice and attractive in her own way, but not at all what I had envisioned.

    If you attach a picture to your profile, you gain a tremendous advantage over your competitors who do not. The vast majority of SMCs who come across your picture will look at it! If they like what they see, it will induce them to read your profile, and even send emails. And those for whom your picture holds no appeal will be eliminating themselves. You won't have to invest any time of your own weeding them out.

4. *"Pictures show only the physical."* True. But it is only natural to look to the physical first. You cannot get around this fact, but you *can* meet it head-on by keeping in mind that one woman's Apollo is another woman's Phantom. One man's bufferilla may be another's dumpling. And there is an amazing range of opinion as to what constitutes "good-looking," which is to everyone's benefit.

5. *"I'm not photogenic."* Nonsense! If you don't show up well in pictures it's because you are too self-conscious, you don't smile, you frown, or you do any of such things that kill a picture. To overcome this, buy a disposable camera and treat yourself to a whole roll of thirty-six pictures. Have a friend take them. The whole roll. Include your children, your dog, your goldfish, or whatever is important to you.

    Have a glass of wine beforehand to relax if necessary. Put on different outfits you look good in. Go to the park for some, or to the beach. Smile in every picture. Big! Look as if you are a fun person. With the right SMC, you will be—and you know it! Then pick out one or more of the better shots. It doesn't have to be your best picture, but pick one that truly reflects today's You.

In fact, consider showing a picture that is not necessarily your best one. Why? For two reasons. First, you don't want an SMC warming up to you strictly for your looks. More important, when you finally meet, you want the SMC to be pleasantly surprised that you are better-looking than he or she anticipated!

6. *"SMCs are looking for someone younger."* Women voice this complaint more often than men do. And rightly so in many cases. My research turned up male after male in his early to mid-forties searching for a mate in the range of nineteen to forty. No, no. Such a man is *not* looking for someone forty years old. He is looking for a teenager. Good luck to both if he finds one. Your recent picture will weed out males who suffer such arrested development.

   Similarly, women who typically date younger men may have difficulty relating to the more mature of the species. You don't need them.

7. *"My looks are just average."* Wrong! There is no such thing. Your exterior is unique. You look like no other person in the entire world! Tens of millions of singles are looking for a partner in the United States alone. Get your picture out there for the ones who are looking for just what you have to offer! Average, schmaverage; get in the ball game.

8. *"I have to lose a little weight first."* No matter where you fall on the spectrums of tall-short and fat-thin, athletic–couch potato, you will have great appeal for somebody—lots of somebodies. So don't agonize over being ten or fifteen (or many more) pounds overweight. Or having wrinkles, or a sagging chin, or a bent nose, or plain features (all of which describe me to a T, by the way). Right this moment you have exactly what an SMC is looking for. If you don't display it, a great SMC may never find out.

   Waiting until you change yourself physically is not an excuse for not attaching a picture to your profile. If you are truly going to lose forty pounds, do so before you begin searching. Alternatively, put a picture up immediately. If you don't, you may just miss the SMC who would love you just the way you are now. When you truly shed the forty pounds, replace the picture with the new you.

   So show your picture, and let your SMCs think you are their idea of gorgeous—no matter how you judge your own looks.

9. *"I have a fear of rejection."* Rejection goes along with the exercise. But don't take it personally. You will be rejected countless times. And you will be doing the rejecting on many an occasion. Are you being rejected because

you are a bad person? Or a dull one? Or a dumb one? Of course not! You are being rejected because you are a round peg that doesn't fit into the square hole that an SMC has determined must be filled by his or her needs. That's all. This is the Internet. It's perfectly OK if an SMC says, "Not for me." He or she just did part of your work for you.

I once dated a woman who was charming, outgoing, intelligent, attractive, witty, vivacious, and well-to-do. I owned a new red Ferrari, dressed well, and was lavish in my attention and affections. It didn't work. Why not? Because sleeping on the ground out in the mountains at night was not her idea of fun, as it was mine. So we both agreed to go our separate ways.

Rejection is a natural part of the selection process. Matching the panoply of likes and dislikes of two persons is a complex process, not one to be hurried. Too many couples have rushed into "love" and subsequently marriage without examining the multiple facets of a relationship. Bitterness and divorce follow like clockwork. You are far ahead of the game if an SMC with definite preferences rejects you. Better that than trying to team up with an SMC who has but vague notions of what he or she wants in a partner. In the latter case, you are just trusting to luck that you and your partner will develop similar interests.

Be thankful therefore that SMCs are rejecting you, and that you have the intelligence to reject others yourself. This elimination process weeds out potentially unsuitable matches. And when your soul mate finally rolls along, you will appreciate him or her all the more. Bear in mind the axiom "The harder you work, the luckier you get."

So, in short, put up your photo. If you meet an SMC and both of you know what the other looks like, you are 90 percent over the "looks" hurdle. Certainly there will be more to both of you than in your pictures, and invariably your real presence will be a vast improvement over the two-dimensional You. A picture cannot laugh, be witty, charm, and do all those other things you will whip out of your toolbag to impress your SMC. But it can help get you to the stage.

DO USE PROPER SPELLING, GRAMMAR, AND PUNCTUATION

Consistent mistakes in spelling, grammar, or punctuation can be a turnoff to many SMCs. Always run spellcheck before you send out an email. In some email programs you can set an option that automatically examines your spelling before you send the message. I once had a response that was so poorly written that I asked the SMC, a woman in Australia who had been born in England, about her native language. To my dismay, and the quick end of our correspondence, it was English.

A twenty-six-year-old in Toledo complained: "I HATE asperagus, broccoli, brussel sprouts, cauliflour, spiders and snakes!" Three misspellings in the same line, to go along with the others sprinkled throughout the rest of this woman's profile. That alone could cause a potential SMC to head for the exit. Further, use your territory to address traits of a partner, rather than your distaste for specific foods and creepy crawlies.

Also avoid long, complicated, or incoherent sentences.

John, twenty-eight, in Dayton:

"...or if roses—like a friend—simply remind us of growing up and going on to do great things, and if a rose were ever chosen for its power, without a friend to give it to or to bear witness of its delicate aroma."

Sarah, thirty-five, in Shreveport:

"I have an unusual independence of mind, freeing me of the constraints of authority/convention/sentiment for its own sake. I am not, however, 'open' with respect to my personal physical/psychological space; I eschew closeness/proximity to anyone who isn't an intimate, or at least a favored close relative, and dislike still more having my personal and/or private life intruded upon in any way."

Each of these SMCs is trying to convey a particular thought, but the message gets lost in the welter of surrounding words. As a rule of thumb, if your sentence runs over twenty words, shorten it. Ask yourself, "What am I really trying to say here?" How would you get the point across to a friend, to your mother, or to your ten-year-old son?

DO REFINE YOUR PROFILE PRESENTATION

Don't skimp on words in the first draft of your profile. Longer is better; by now you should have been able to pump out hundreds of words about yourself onto paper or into your computer. At this point, set your chef d'oeuvre aside. Let it rest for a couple of days.

Then it's time to tighten up the rambly stuff. Any word processor will tally the words you have in a composition (go to your Help section and find "Word count"). Let's say you have ended up with 1,000 words instead of a projected 350. Print it out. Then read over your dissertation. Use a highlighter to mark what you think will be most interesting to an SMC. You will use those particular sections to start building a more compact profile.

Next, take out any unnecessary words. You don't even need complete sentences (though don't overdo dangling phrases). Remove excessive ellipses (series of dots). Shorten sentences. The longer the sentence, the harder it is to read. If you have a long sentence, chop it in half and make two shorter ones.

Skip most of the elaborate details. Save the in-depth stuff for later correspondence, but don't be stingy. Let everyone get a decent look at you. Jerry, twenty-seven, explained that he deliberately kept his profile short (a total of thirty-seven words) to "save something for later." Jerry needs to rethink. Whether you've lived eighteen years or seventy-eight years, you have a wealth of experiences to expand upon. There will always be material for later. For instance, I mentioned my three past relationships in four sentences:

> **"I've had three good women in my life, and married the first. Each relationship brought me closer to the ideal partner. In each case, it was my fault for the most part that the relationship ended, but I've learned from the mistakes I made. This time will be the last."**

If an SMC and I seemed to be hitting it off initially, I would at a later point in our chailing expand on describing those relationships and say:

> **"I was married for ten years to a good woman, but we had different paths to follow. I accelerated the process by stepping out foolishly. I then met a wonderful woman with whom I lived for over twenty years. When I let the romance go out of our lives, she met a man considerably younger. She and I are good friends today. Three and a half years ago I met what I thought would be the last woman in my life."**

Don't worry that describing your past life, hopes, and dreams will strip you of topics of conversation at a later date. To the contrary, the more you open the window to your true self, the more interest you will build in the right SMC.

Be succinct. If English was not your best subject in school, ask a friend to help. Here are sections of profiles and suggestions about how they could have been cut back without losing the intended effect:

Original: "Thanks for reading this, if any of it sounds interesting to you I would love to know about YOU and YOUR DREAMS!" (22 words)

Revised: Now YOU tell me about YOUR dreams! (7 words)

Original: "I have lived in Minnesota and Seattle, WA, and now in New Orleans. They are all neat places to live." (20 words)

Revised: New Orleans is neat! I've lived in, and also love, Minnesota and Seattle. (13 words)

Original: "I keep an active workout schedule to keep a balance. I really enjoy traveling to new areas of the country. I am fortunate that my profession allows me flexibility, opportunities to travel, and new ways to learn." (37 words)

Revised: I work out regularly. My profession allows me flexibility, opportunities to travel (which I really enjoy), and new ways to learn. (21 words)

You get the idea; don't make the reader work by just babbling on.

But suppose you can't get your complete message across in 350 words? Compose a separate addition that you can attach to an email. An addition that I composed and sent along with every first contact began:

"Each day I feel the need for some exercise—running, biking, or even just walking the dogs. But I'm not a fanatic, and enjoy more mundane pursuits—coffee, book, and bagel on weekend afternoons. By 'the ride of your life' I mean all this plus a healthy lifestyle with concerts, ballet, theater, travel (rubbing elbows with the natives)....Please don't apply if you are just looking to sail off into the sunset. Life is meant to be lived out loud."

Janna, thirty-five, in Baton Rouge, adds this standard language that she couldn't fit into her profile:

> "I enjoy people but do not do a lot of socializing outside the office. I prefer a one-on-one relationship with a man for the most part. An occasional party is enjoyable, but I wouldn't want a steady diet. Of course, each of us needs our respective space and private times. Jealousy has never been a part of my life."

If you do use an addition, follow the same rules as for your profile: don't ramble, but do eliminate extra words, shorten sentences, and be concise.

DO GET FEEDBACK

When you finish, run your effort past a friend who can spot mistakes. One who is also willing to critique content and understandability honestly. What you wrote may not be as crystal clear to a stranger as you think.

Your profile can be as powerful and influential as an opening statement to a jury. When I was a practicing trial lawyer, I knew that my opening statement had to communicate the key points to a jury. Predisposing them to rule in my client's favor was crucial. So I would meticulously prepare the right words to set the tone of my case. I would then invite a few non-attorney friends for coffee and donuts, people who knew absolutely nothing at all about the case. Each would receive a pad and pen to make notes. I then proceeded to strew before them the pearls of wisdom in my proposed opening statement. Invariably, the criticisms I received punctured my ego. But the comments helped immensely. They enabled me to change my opening statement to one that would be better understood and received by a jury.

Do the same with your profile. Find several friends of the same gender as the SMC you are seeking. Have them over for tea and crumpets (beer and pretzels, whatever). Ask them to read your profile and comment. Pay attention to their suggestions. Discuss them.

Look for as much help as you can get in making improvements to your profile. *Anything* can be improved. My grandmother was not a cook. She should have paid attention to the sign in a local bakery: "Pies like mother used to make, $3. Pies like mother tried to make—$5." In dishing up a delectable profile, don't be reluctant to ask for and accept help.

Now for what you *shouldn't* do.

DON'T BE NEGATIVE

You want to come across positively. Talk about interests you have and want to enjoy. Leave the bad behind. If there is a particular activity in which you have no interest, make that plain. But do so in a positive manner:

Negative: "I do cross-country skiing, but downhill is for nuts."

Positive: "I do cross-country skiing but I'm not interested in downhill."

Negative: "I like most music, but opera sucks."

Positive: "I like most music with the exception of opera."

Negatives will clip the reader right in the chops. An SMC may come to an unfavorable snap judgment about your character. If your profile is downbeat, the message may be "Not a fun person. Next!" Here are some examples of how you don't want to project yourself:

Gregory, fifty-six, in Boston:

"I'm tired of getting you-know-what upon by unfeeling women."

The rest of Gregory's profile was interesting, but how many SMCs stopped reading after the first sentence?

Rita, fifty-five, in Miami:

"NO TIME FOR GAMES, PLAYING AROUND, OR DEADBEATS."

Is it really necessary to say that you're ruling out such undesirables? Doesn't *everyone* want to avoid these no-no's?

Andrew, forty-two, in Tulsa:

> "I'm tired of women who use their femininity to get what they want. I want a woman who is not afraid of being herself so that I can be myself. No snivelers, please. I love shooting pool and then going out for pizza and beer afterwards.
>
> "So give me some SUBSTANCE in your response—tell me something more than just a couple of lines about yourself. OPEN UP a bit. I can't stand someone who hides behind anonymity, or is leery of making a commitment. If that's something you can't handle, or you're into 'post-traumatic relationship disorder,' you'd be better off looking elsewhere. Also, please be within a two-hour drive from Atlanta. I don't need pen pals, nor should my travel agent know where my love life begins and ends."

Andrew starts out with a complaint and goes on to unwind a series of don'ts: don't hold anything back; don't be anonymous; don't be afraid of a commitment; don't have post-traumatic disorder; don't live too far away. Rather than spending time setting out conditions, Andrew might better explain who he is beyond pool, pizza, and beer. It is a lot to expect a contact to "OPEN UP" when what little personal information this man has provided centers mostly on his dislikes and conditions.

Rudy, thirty-three, in New York City:

> "I'm bored, bored to tears with the materialism that absorbs most of the human race, and by the superficiality of women who seem to have lost all interest in the people around them. So this is pretty much an experiment to find out if the woman in my mind (strong of will and character and heart) actually exists. Let me know if there is any such creature out there!"

If you happen to be the strong-willed, -charactered, and -hearted woman of this man's dreams, what will you do together? Sit around and be bored with the rest of humanity?

Raoul, fifty, in Coeur D'Alene:

> "I'm an Old Fart looking for a lovely Lady. To whoever, I am fifty going on seventy-five, and sick and tired of being on my own. The truth is I have been divorced four times, and to one woman twice. Who knows who was to blame each time? I am interested in joining in a relationship with

someone who is honest and trustworthy and doesn't give me any (Bull****). I want it straight down the line. I am a working man who does thirty to forty hours of overtime a month. I've worked hard all my life, and unfortunately I don't have much to show for it, except a new camper.

"I need to lose forty pounds at least, and I suppose you could say that I'm not really a legend in bed. My reputation does not precede me in that respect. So that is me in the short version. I am lovable, caring, and honest and take care of what is mine, or what could possibly be. This should help to narrow down the field a bit. Send me some email if you think you could survive this type of a wreck. Thanks for looking. —Raoul"

True. Raoul has narrowed the field a tad. In the "short version," Raoul spends most of the real estate beating up on himself and explaining what he *doesn't* want. With a more positive approach, Raoul might find just the woman who would appreciate a hard worker who is loving, caring, honest, and who takes care of his own.

As a last note here, never mention a job that you lost. That's history and may depress potential SMCs.

DON'T WASTE WORDS

Avoid unnecessary preambles:

"I never know what to say."

"I've never done this before."

"I'm pretty shy about this."

"I'm finding it hard to believe I am even doing this."

"This is the first time I've ever..."

Don't waste words; the attention span of your SMC is short. Rather than complaining or apologizing, start right out with what you are going to say. Let's look at a couple of fast starts out of the gate.

Dale, thirty-two, in Riverside:

"I love rummaging around at swap meets and in antique stores."

Alex, fifty-three, in Philadelphia:

> "Doubles tennis is my favorite sport, and I'm looking for you as my partner."

No warm-ups; these SMCs go right from the chutes. Join them.

• *Avoid listing what everyone wants.* Words can be wasted in other ways. Men are looking for women "who like to be treated like ladies." *All* men want "a caring woman who is fun to be with." Does anybody really want one who *doesn't* care and who is a drag into the bargain? Instead put some life into these banalities:

Aaron, forty-six, in Buffalo:

> "You will delight in receiving princess-style attention."

Marilyn, forty, in Durham:

> "We will enjoy each other's company nonstop."

Many women confess to liking quiet walks on the beach (with the right person, implied), watching sunsets, holding hands in the moonlight, and so on. Is there a woman out there who does not? Turn these ho-hummers around:

> "I love walking on a beach to look for rocks and watch the sand crabs fight the waves."

> "One advantage to the smog in L.A. is that it creates such magnificently colored sunsets."

> "The moon has fascinated me since I was a kid. I would love walking about with you when it is in its full splendor."

Here are some more universal wishes that are popular space-fillers:

> "Looking for someone honest, loving, and capable of giving back."

> "Looking for someone lovely and loyal, intelligent and honest who I can love and who will love me back."

> "If you love to be pampered, snuggle for any reason, or receive bouquets of flowers out of the blue,…"

> "Looking for someone who enjoys a romantic evening by the fireplace."

Aren't we all—male and female—looking for the same? So why spend time talking about these givens? The same goes for professing to be "incurably romantic" or "hopelessly romantic." Maybe I missed something; given the chance, does the unromantic man or woman exist?

DON'T SPOUT PLATITUDES

"Life is but a short journey in time—it is here for us to share, enjoy, and pave the way for a better life for others."

Who would argue about this comment on the way the world works? But in your profile, including such drivel only adds extra words you could make better use of by telling what a fun person you are. Save metaphysics for later events. Replace such old saws with more homely philosophy if you must:

"I'd rather spend my time hiking down the canyon in back of my house with you than sitting around watching TV."

DON'T BRAG ABOUT HOW GOOD YOU LOOK

If you truly look fifteen years younger, let it be one of the surprises your SMC will enjoy when he or she meets you for the first time. The SMC may not agree, and will then be disappointed if he or she is expecting you to look thirty-five and a person who looks forty-five shows up.

"I have a young body."

What does that mean? Old head? How young? Keep that for one of the surprises when you first meet an SMC candidate.

> **"I'm pretty muscular."**

This and similar comments can be made unnecessary simply by attaching a picture with your profile.

DON'T USE INAPPROPRIATE SEXUAL INNUENDO

This profile will draw loads of attention, but not a true soul mate:

> "hi! To all u Sweet n Sexy guys, my name's suzi and i'm one hot babe from alabama. TO ALL SWEET n SEXY GUYS HIDING OUT THERE…Im 21/ female from Missouri so i can drink whatever and whenever i want…so if ur interested in a great babe like me…contact me thru icq or email me…here's my icq # xxxxxxxx GET BACK TO ME QUICK—oh one more thing here's a @**#'",%%)(and a -)))&^) *french kiss* for all YOU GUYS WHO ARE GONNA CONTACT ME. i love all of you."

At least be a bit more subtle like this SMC:

Don, twenty-nine, in Carlsbad:

> "Do you feel like there's a path to somewhere and you want to find it?…You show me your path and I'll show you mine."

And some humor that works well:

Grace, sixty-one, in Newport Beach:

> "The two most important rooms in the house? Easy. The bedroom and the kitchen; I can cook in both. Conservative Lois Lane–type girl next door until the doors close."

Save the stark sex talk for later emails when you and your SMC become more comfortable with one another. What you intend as a cute remark may inadvertently be taken the wrong way. Why start off on the wrong foot unintentionally?

DON'T SHOUT (USE ALL CAPITAL LETTERS)

Using all capital letters is tough on the eyes and will annoy most readers. Many SMCs won't struggle for long with this type of message. Take the read test yourself if you disagree. Following is a profile as written, with seven typos and punctuation in disarray, in all capital letters. Below it, I show the same profile with upper- and lowercase letters and the spelling and grammar dressed up.

> "HI, I AM A VERY UP PERSON, SLIM, TRIM, AND ACTIVE, UNINCUM-BERED PHYSICALLY, MENTALLY, AND FINANCIALLY. TWO HAPPILY MARRIED CHILDRED LIVING FAR AWAY, WHOM I LOVE VERY MUCH, BUT THEY ARE NOT MY LIFE. LOTS MORE TO SAY, BUT WILL TELL YOU LATER. I HHAVE LIVED IN FLORIDA TWENTY YEARS, AND LOVE EVERY MINUETE OF IT, LIKET THE RAIN, PRE-FERR THE SUN. VERY ADVENTURES, AND WILLING TO TRY ANYTHING."

> "Hi. I am a very up person, slim, trim, and active; unencumbered physi-cally, mentally, and financially. Two happily married children living far away, whom I love very much, but they are not my life. Lots more to say, but will tell you later. I have lived in Florida twenty years and love every minute of it. Like the rain; prefer the sun. Very adventurous and willing to try anything."

DON'T TRY TO USE WORDS THAT ARE UNFAMILIAR TO YOU

Make your profile easy to read. Don't try to show off a vocabulary you don't have. Too often I would receive a message from a woman saying that my pro-file had "peeked" or "peaked" her interest. Neither is correct; the term is "piqued," meaning "to excite." Better to have said, "caught my interest."

Here are two other boo-boos:

"like a symphony of stars *elumniated* by the moon" [illuminated]

"These are the *tenants* I live by." [tenets]

If you have the slightest hesitancy about using a word, either look it up in the dictionary to be sure of its correct usage and spelling or find a more familiar synonym.

DON'T USE ACRONYMS
UNLESS THEY ARE UNIVERSALLY UNDERSTOOD

USA is familiar to anyone over the age of six. So is IRS to anyone over fifteen. But what about ICQ? Or ILN? Perhaps BCDA? INTJ? LOL? LVN? For most people, these are words straight from a foreign language. If it is important that the reader understand what an abbreviation means, explain it in parentheses. Otherwise, spell it out or leave it out.

DON'T USE UNNECESSARY ABBREVIATIONS

Inserting SWF (single white female) is not necessary. When you join any site, you generally identify your race and gender. Whenever an SMC calls up your profile, it will automatically identify you as a female Caucasian. Some sites will also classify your marital status. For those that do not, a plain "I've been divorced for four years" tells the story.

DON'T DISPARAGE PREVIOUS RELATIONSHIPS

Practically everyone you will run across has had a relationship that went down the tubes for some reason. As with surgical operations, nobody really wants to hear the gory details. And don't whine about what you didn't get out of the last relationship.

Marilyn, forty-four, in Chicago:

> "My husband was a drunk. I could have handled that, but he also ran around. The combination was too much for me. So I don't want to go through this again."

Max, twenty-eight, in New Orleans:

> "My ex-girlfriend just never gave me any space. I couldn't go anywhere on my own hardly. She nearly suffocated me. If you aren't into each person having their own private times, don't bother."

This is all history. Regurgitation only detracts. Your best bet is to avoid these bêtes noires: ask the right questions; pay attention to the answers. We'll cover all this in depth in the next chapter.

In Summary

The lantern fish lives in the darkness of the Sargasso Sea. To attract a mate, he turns on sequences of phosphorescent lights that run under his belly. Wrong sequence—no mate. After you let your profile set for a few days, read it over to see if your message shines through. Take a lesson from the lantern fish. Let your profile flash the right signals; your SMCs will come swimming in your direction.

Come up with a handle that reflects either your personality or your imagination. Do the same with your headline. Take your time; be creative. These are the first impressions you make on an actively searching SMC; make them good ones.

Prepare your profile with the same care and precision that a sculptor devotes to working his marble. Take your time. This is the window to that singular individual who is You. Make sure the window is clear, open, and that there is a distinctive You for an SMC to discover. Let your exciting uniqueness shine through.

Now let's talk about getting set up to handle the SMCs who come calling.

4

Gathering Your Tools
for the Hunt

There are no secrets to success. It is the result of preparation, hard work, learning from failure.

—Colin L. Powell

If at first you don't succeed, you are running about average.

—M. H. Alderson

Right now you know far more than I did when I began cruising online to find a soul mate. The first day I found what ultimately became my favorite matchmaking site, I bundled emails off to women right and left. I didn't even know what I was looking for, but off I sailed. No organization, no checklist, a barebones profile, and no artfulness. My opener was along the lines of "I like what I see; tell me more about yourself." One SMC brought me up short by pointing out that etiquette called for a little more finesse. I had assumed that once I made contact, women would fall all over themselves to respond. This SMC suggested that this might more readily come to pass if I would first invite the recipient to look at my profile. Chastened, I began using this more modest approach.

Getting Organized for a Smooth Search

Hard work most often rides shotgun with Success. Hard work's partner is Preparation. Yes, yes, I know this sounds preachy, but it is so true. To be a winner, you must spend hours in preparation. Before you go waltzing onto the Internet, flashing your new profile in all directions, do your homework. You will be asking a lot of questions and ladling out different scoops of information about yourself. The odds that you will connect with your soul

mate on the first try are slim. Also, even when you finally enter the initial stages of communicating with "the One," undoubtedly you will still be conducting electronic courtship with others.

Two questions naturally arise: Should I chase down every SMC who seems to have a little potential? Or should I instead work with just my one or two top choices? Millie, forty-five, in St. Louis explains her preference:

> "I spent two months doing some heavy-duty email with a man who was in my field. We also had a lot of other things in common. Suddenly there was no response at all—nothing. I must have sent six or eight emails. Then out of the blue he sent me a one-liner saying he had met someone else, and good luck in my search. I was devastated, as I thought we really had something going. I even quit looking for a couple of weeks.
>
> "I finally went back online and found thirty-five profiles that interested me. Over about a month's time I contacted most of them, and have some good stuff going back and forth with six. No more of this one-at-a-time—too tough on the emotions."

On the other hand, Carla, forty-one, of Toronto writes:

> "I can't get my heart into writing to more than one man at a time. Each time I strike up a correspondence, I put a lot of effort and emotion into it. Plus I don't want to have to keep track of what I am saying to whom. If it doesn't work out, I just take a breather for a while, and then look for another one. There are always plenty to pick from."

The choice is yours. I favored putting out as many feelers as I could handle at once. But whether you are going to chail with one or many, there are five steps to preparing for a smooth and successful search:

1. Keep track of the info you exchange.

2. Prepare the key questions you intend to ask SMCs.

3. Set out the information you want the SMCs to know about you.

4. Organize your email.

5. Set up your search guidelines.

Now let's take a look at some more details in each category.

KEEP TRACK OF INFO YOU EXCHANGE

Early in my search I asked a woman for more facts about her two sons. She replied frostily: "I've never been married. You must have me confused with someone else." I then devised the following Ask-and-Tell (A&T) worksheet to keep my information flow organized and quickly accessible.

I prepared a separate worksheet for each SMC to gather the various bits of information I received in the course of our contact. In the example that follows, the first three columns refer to the information provided by the SMC, Lumi in this case. I did the table in Excel, because I could create tabs for each SMC; those familiar with the software will understand. Otherwise a simple table in your word processing program will suffice nicely. Even a ruled piece of paper will do the trick.

Next to the topics in the left-hand column I filled in the answers as I received them from Lumi. In the right-hand column, I checked off particular pieces of information about me as I gave them out. For instance, when I explained to Lumi about my six children, I put an "X" next to the column item "six kids." When I described the "trip to Mt. Whitney with V," I put an "X" beside that topic, and so forth. This way I could see at a glance which of the listed topics about myself I had discussed already with Lumi, to avoid repeating myself. An understanding of each entry isn't necessary.

ASK & TELL (A&T) WORKSHEET

		About Her	About Me	
Name		Lumi Workman, nee Valerio	raised in Boston	X
Ethnicity		Filipino	3 women in life	X
Address		548 Crass, San Jose 94539	agnosticism	X
Age		56	fell off bike	
Height		5'5"	live in Chula Vista, dogwalk	
Phone		510-111-0000	house for sale	
Picture?	yes	11/15 requested		
Own Home	yes		sold BHC, rest, Ms2000	
			taught myself computer	
Marriage and kids?		2 sons	was stockbroker	
Type of work		Bio-medical Engineer	skiing not for me	
College		MBA	backpacking, B's attitude	X
Backpack?	yes		fell off bike	
Run?	no		trip to Whitney with V.	X
Bicycle?		wants to buy a bike	six kids	X
Sports		ski, tennis, racquetball, golf	my authors	X
Religion		spiritual	own/sold company	
Cooking		Italian, Mexican, Chinese	sent picture	X
Reader?	yes		bought TV for Ma	
Relationships		2 yr. Married twice, 11, 4	my run/race schedule	
Irritate in man?		possessive	political orientation	X
House state neat/messy		bad weather		
Try something new			vitamins	X
Plants in house				
Sleep bed window open				
Bad weather		doesn't bother		
Vitamins	yes			
Health	yes			
Healthy eater	yes			

		About Her	About Me	
Travel		Orient, Africa		
TV				
Spontaneous				
Time available				
Ballroom dance				
Weaknesses		perfectionist		
Morning or night person	yes			
Financially secure	yes			
Shower in A.M. or evening				
Sleep in pajamas				
Good sense of humor	yes			
Reader/authors	yes	Stephen King, Danielle Steele		
Have a pet?		wants one		
Computer literate?	yes			
TV amount?		news only		

Notes: Makes great salads, gym in house, works out every day, lots of hiking in summer, quick-witted on phone, staunch Republican

If the profile came sans picture, I would put the date(s) requested until it arrived. A lack of results after three requests would nudge me on to the next SMC.

Many SMCs won't bother to respond to your first email. Of those who do, some will put you off with their first email for one reason or another. So you won't need to get into a worksheet. But you should make one up for each SMC with whom you get beyond preliminary skirmishing. Glean whatever nuggets you find in the SMC's profile. Examine each email response for information you can add to the left-hand column of your worksheet.

Before I developed this system, I stepped into embarrassments right and left. Two comments that came along with regularity were "You told me that already," and "You asked me that before, and I answered you." There's not much of a zippy comeback to either.

As I was normally in touch with multiple SMCs, I also kept a separate sheet to give me an overview of those who were still in the running.

SMC SUMMARY

NAME	LOCATION	AGE	FS*	PICTURE	WORK
Cecile	Kauai	55	OK	**yes**	sales
Lumi	San Jose	56	yes	**yes**	biomedical engineer
Susan	New Guinea	53	prob.	**yes**	teacher
Diane	Brea	61	yes		medical rschr.
Harriet	Boston	57	?	mail 9/15	corp. officer
Sheri	San Diego	53	prob.	**yes**	CPA
Sandy	Bay Area	54	?	**yes**	financial planner

*Financially Secure

PREPARE THE KEY QUESTIONS YOU INTEND TO ASK SMCS

As you range from SMC to SMC, you will be asking the same initial questions. First determine what those questions will be. (In the next chapter we'll get down to specifics.) Then take time to phrase each one to suit yourself exactly. Do this in your word processing program (Microsoft Word, WordPerfect, and so forth). Save all the questions in one file so that you can copy and paste them (see following Side Note) into your email message. This saves excessive typing. I called this file *Ask*. Posing all the questions you want answered in the first email volley may be overwhelming, so break your list of questions into three or four sets. Send one set at a time to your SMCs. Track the particular set you sent by titling your email message accordingly.

My initial exploratory email to an SMC was titled "You Sound Delightful." There was no interrogation with this one; I was just making contact (all the details follow in the next chapter). When I got a positive response to this communication, there were certain questions I would then ask of most SMCs. The questions broke down into four sets, with the more important ones at the beginning. My first set would go out with the email subject line "You"; my second set, "More About You"; my third set, "Details"; and the last set, "More Details." Thus just by looking at the title of my email messages, I knew which of the first four sets of questions I had sent. In Chapter Six, I'll go into detail about these sets of questions, and how to tailor them for your own use.

CUTTING AND PASTING

In every word processing program there is a way to copy things (text, pictures, sounds, and so forth) from one document to another. You can even copy material from one program to another; Microsoft Word to WordPerfect, or vice versa, for example.

Your *cursor* is the short vertical (though occasionally horizontal) line that blinks on the screen to show where you are if you start to type. Yes, yes, I know that's pretty elementary to most, but not all, of you.

The following steps tell you how to copy in either Word or WordPerfect. If you have a different word processing program, the steps may be very similar. If not, click on Help (usually at the top left or right of your screen) and see what you can find under "Copy." If all else fails, bring in one of the neighborhood teenagers.

1. Highlight the text that you want to copy. Do this by putting the cursor at the beginning of the text you want to copy. Hold down the left button on your mouse, and drag the cursor across or down the page until you get to the end of the text you want to copy.

2. Release the mouse button (take your finger off).

3. At the top of the screen are the commands <u>F</u>ile, <u>E</u>dit, <u>V</u>iew, and so forth. Click once on the word <u>E</u>dit, and a box drops down with a bunch of commands, among which are Cu<u>t</u>, <u>C</u>opy, and <u>P</u>aste.

4. Click once on <u>C</u>opy. The drop-down box disappears, and the text has been copied.

5. Go into the screen where you want to paste the copied text. This might be another Word file, or an email. Put the cursor where you want the text to appear.

6. Click on <u>E</u>dit again. This time when the box comes down, click once on <u>P</u>aste. The text you copied will pop up.

If you copied too much text, just delete the portions you don't want. If you finished up a bit short, type in whatever is missing. There are other faster ways of copying text that are beyond the scope of this book. You'll have to ask friends and teens.

PREPARE INFORMATION ABOUT YOURSELF

Just as you will want to prepare certain questions to ask, you will also want to prepare blocks of information to send off to an SMC. Save these info blocks in a file. I titled my file *Tell*. I typed up paragraphs of information that I knew an SMC would want to know about me. Was I clairvoyant? No, I simply put myself in the place of my soul mate and decided what it was she would want to see in *her* soul mate. From time to time I would receive a question that I guessed I was likely to receive again. After writing the answer, I copied it and added it to my *Tell* file. When another SMC later asked the same question, or a similar one, I already had the answer. I would go into the *Tell* file, copy that answer, and then paste it into the email. I might do a speck of retouching but no major typing.

Once you have the blocks of information, make reference to each on your A&T worksheet and give them names, at least in your mind. For instance, let's say you have an amusing anecdote to pass along about your dog Furball at the beach. You might think of this as the "Furball at the beach" paragraph, and make that a line item on your A&T worksheet. When you send the paragraph off to an SMC, put an X beside the line "Furball at the beach" on the worksheet for that SMC. Do the same with every such tidbit that you are going to use more than once. That way you won't say the same thing twice to the same SMC. For instance, there is a check next to the entry "raised in Boston" on the Sample A&T Worksheet (see page XX) under the "About Me" column. This meant that I had sent off to Lumi a one-paragraph block about my early life. Now the SMC may suspect that you have certain paragraphs prewritten. If you send along the same elaborately worded paragraph(s) in successive emails, you will remove all doubt. Working with the A&T worksheet as I have described will help you to avoid such mishaps.

Also, personalizing your messages adds tang. You can take a block of information, insert the SMC's name occasionally, and massage it just a bit. That way you will avoid having your email sound like mimeographed Christmas letters that recap the family's year of activity.

In the next chapter we'll talk more about what to disclose about yourself and how to do it.

ORGANIZE YOUR EMAIL

There's no need to rush into creating either a paper or computer folder to hold correspondence with a particular SMC. Spend a bit of time getting to know the person, and making sure that the correspondence is apt to continue. Otherwise you will go to a lot of trouble for nothing in most cases. So when responses from SMCs start flowing in, set up two folders, "New SMCs" and "Respond."

MAKING EMAIL FOLDERS

There are many different email programs. The directions below work with Outlook Express version 5.5. Even if you have a different program, the explanation might be enough to lead you in the right direction. Making a new folder requires seven steps.

1. Bring up the program by clicking on the Outlook Express icon.

2. In the upper left-hand corner, click on File.

3. When the drop-down box appears, highlight New.

4. A second drop-down box will appear to the right. Click on Folder.

5. A window shows up with the title "Create Folder."

6. The cursor is blinking in the box at the top. Type in the name of the new folder, "Respond," for example.

7. Click on OK. A new folder with the title you typed shows up.

Don't despair if this degree of organizational work exceeds your expertise and that of your friends. As a last resort, print your emails (both the ones you send and the ones you receive) and put them into real-world manila folders with an SMC's name on each tab.

As emails arrive, you may decide immediately, "Thanks, but no thanks." In that case, be courteous enough to go back with a short, "Thanks for your interest, but I have someone I'm pretty interested in right now," or something comparable, and delete the message. But let's say you get one from someone named Brenda in whom you see a bit of promise. No need to answer immediately, so file it in "Respond."

MOVING MESSAGES

Let's assume you have created a "Respond" folder and want to move a message into it from the In Box folder.

1. Highlight the message you want to move by clicking on it once.

2. In Outlook Express, you should have a left window entitled "Folders." If you don't find the window, click on <u>V</u>iew at the top of the screen. When the drop-down box appears, click on <u>L</u>ayout.

3. A separate window will come up, entitled "Window Layout Properties."

4. Under the "Basic" section, put a check in the box next to "Fol<u>d</u>er list." Make the check by clicking in the empty box. Click on OK.

5. The Folder window will now be on your screen, showing all the folders you currently have.

6. Click on the message you want to move and keep your finger on the mouse button.

7. Move the mouse so that the arrow goes over the "Respond" folder, which will highlight that folder.

8. Release the mouse button. The message is now in the "Respond" folder. Bravo!

If you later decide to get back to Brenda, move the email message to the folder called "New SMCs." Chailing with Brenda may carry on for a few more emails. Each time you receive one from her, stick it in the "Respond" file. Once you answer, move it to "New SMCs." At some point you decide either to call it quits with Brenda or become more charming. If Brenda falls by the wayside, delete all of her messages from the "New SMCs" file. On the other hand, let's assume that things seem to be going in the right direction for both of you. Then you will want to make a special folder just for her and transfer all previous email into it. Also go into your Sent folder and move all the messages you have sent her into Brenda's folder. Now you have all the emails from both of you in one place, available at a single glance. If you don't want all these messages cluttering up your computer, make the folders up in a floppy disk, and do all the saving to the disk.

Making up a real-world paper folder for Brenda is a bit more work, and not necessary in most cases. But if you opt for this method, print out the messages that each of you sends. File them in the paper folder in chronological order. But remember, you can always do that at a later time when things seem to be coming along well with Brenda. Otherwise you will end up like I did at first, with a stack of printed emails a foot high from a group of eliminated SMCs!

SET UP YOUR SEARCH GUIDELINES

Let's go through the steps of filling out the sign-up form to put your profile on a popular site, Match.com. The principles apply to data you may enter on *any* matchmaking site. As you probably realize from reading Chapter 2, the better sites ask for pretty much the same information one way or another.

At Match.com, to make up your profile, you must first give some information about yourself and the match that you want. Much of this information is in the no-brainer category. Once you complete your own profile, the matchmaking site's computer will search its database for anyone whose profile seems to harmonize with your wish list. Some of the questions require that you assign a number value (1–5) according to how important that issue is to you. Be careful in this respect. Assigning the number 5 means that any potential matches must *also* have assigned a number 5 to this same category. So deal your 5s sparingly; use them only for red-flag-type items such as smoking.

Here are some pointers:

• *Your birthdate.* Insert the full year in which you were born, "11-06-1964," for example. On some sites, if you put "11-05-64," you will get a message telling you that you are too young to use the site.

• *"Distance to search."* It would be nice to find a soul mate just around the corner. And undoubtedly there *are* one or more candidates shooting pool or having their hair done nearby. But how do you locate them if they are not on the Internet? So why limit yourself? One of my correspondents was located in New Guinea of all places, more than 7,500 miles away. She was an American woman teaching for an oil company, and she was ready to come back to Southern California in the next two months.

I also chatted briefly with a woman in South Carolina. She planned a move West to within twenty-five miles of my home. Another woman from Boston, ready to retire, was deciding between the West Coast and South

Carolina. I also found a lot in common with Ane in Denmark. When I finally came across my soul mate, she was living in Honolulu; I was in L.A. We subsequently moved to San Diego together.

The point? Select the furthest distance possible as the distance to search. On Match.com, this is "12,500" miles. That pretty much wraps up the whole globe, no matter which way you drag the string. Whatever site you visit, cast the widest possible net.

The location search mode on Match.com has its minor drawbacks. If you want to change the area you search, you have only two choices. First, you can search within a certain number of miles from you. If this is unproductive, go to "New Search," where you can change any of the criteria you set, including distance. Under "New Search" you are also offered the alternative of searching by city. First select the state that interests you, and then a city within the state. There is no way to search an entire state, except city by city, or by using the mileage figure. For instance, as I am in San Diego, if I used 300 miles, that would get me everyone in Southern California from Santa Barbara on down. If I used 1,000 miles, the approximate span to the Oregon border, I could sweep everyone in California into my net, and a considerable number of citizens in adjoining states in the bargain.

If you want to search outside the United States, you are again limited to particular cities. Assume that you intend to take up residence in France and wish to test the waters for the availability of local talent. You would have to go city by city in France.

When your matches show up, you can skip over those in areas that are not of interest. For instance, early in my search I sensed a strong defensiveness in women in a certain urban area. I chailed for a couple of months with a woman smack in the middle of this metropolis. We exchanged views and pictures. Much was coming together. I finally made arrangements to spend a weekend in her company. We discussed which was the best airport to fly into. Since I was to arrive on a weekday, she gave me detailed directions to her office. After setting up plane, motel, and car reservations, I gave her times and locations. She immediately responded,

> "First, you should know that where you are planning to stay is in a high crime area. Also, if you are going to rent a car, parking in the city is horrendous and expensive. But most important, Eric, I only planned on having lunch or dinner with you on that Friday. I really don't know you well enough to assume anything more than that. The emails back and forth were safe. You were a 'million miles' away in San Diego, so no harm done....If I feel comfortable with you on Friday, then maybe I can meet

you in the city again on the weekend. But it will be out in the open and safe for me. So plan on doing things on your own."

For both our sakes, I canceled the trip. I had no intention of wandering alone and unarmed in that particular town on a weekend. But I learned from that experience. We hadn't discussed what was to happen once I hit town. I should have told her, "You understand I'm coming to spend time with you, rather than sight-seeing in [hometown]," and then gone on to discuss what types of activities we might both enjoy. She, in turn, might have asked earlier on, "What did you have in mind when you get here?" She might also have dropped a clue about neighborhoods to avoid.

• *Age range.* Whatever range you put in will show on your profile. Be a bit conservative here, say five years on either side of your age. You may be fifty-five, look forty-five, and feel twenty-five. If so, go for whatever age range you want in making your search (twenty-five to fifty, say), but leave your profile to read that you are looking in the range of fifty to sixty. An SMC first alighting on your profile may well be turned off by an indication that you are looking for someone from your offspring's generation. Whenever I spotted a profile where a woman seemed interested in much younger men, I stopped at the threshhold. What I'm trying to get across here is that if you have a yearning for the younger set, don't make it apparent. Otherwise you may turn off someone older who could very well turn out to have the Right Stuff. You'll still have to use your imagination in deciding how to explain your interest in someone half your age if *you* make the first contact.

The joke of listing an age range of two to ninety-nine on profiles falls flat—the impression is more one of desperation. The same goes for specifying height ranges of four feet to seven feet seven.

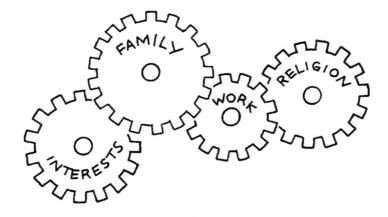

- *Religion.* You will fall into one of four broad groups of individuals:

1. those with strong religious inclinations who want an SMC of the same persuasion;

2. those with strong inclinations but who are willing to consider an SMC with a different religious viewpoint;

3. those whose inclinations fall more into the "spiritual" area, and

4. those for whom religion is not a significant factor in their life.

If you are in the first category, by all means check off the appropriate box and assign an importance factor of 5.

Those of you who are in the second category should check "any/no preference"—even if there is a particular religion that doesn't strike your fancy—for two reasons. First, Match.com allows you to go through and check off those religions that you would find acceptable in a partner, while leaving some blank. You'll be better off weeding out SMCs as they pop up, rather than making it obvious which religions you don't cotton to. Second, you will find that people who declare a particular persuasion often do so because it was their religion of upbringing. They may no longer be church-oriented. If you elect "any/no preference," it seems to make no difference what number value (1–5) you assign.

Now assume that you are in the second category. You will want to indicate the extent of your religious tendencies. This in itself will tend to weed out incompatible SMCs. You can do this in the "Additional Spirituality" description box. Alternatively, stick this text in the "Personal Descriptions" section a little later in the process. For instance, I am halfway between categories 3 and 4. An SMC who would want to talk earnestly about her religious commitment was not a likely match for me.

Corinne, thirty, in Minneapolis:

> **"I am interested in someone who shares my core values: God, family, and work (in that order)."**

If you are in either the third or the fourth category, go for "any/no preference" and assign a number value of 1.

- *Ethnic group.* Here you can choose more than one box. Help yourself.

• *Eye color, hair shade.* To me, these seem to be somewhat useless categories. Check whatever you want for yourself, "Any" for your match (unless, of course, you have a compulsion to be matched with a green-eyed redhead, or a brown-eyed blond, and so forth). There was no category for my type of hair: "fringe on top only visible at close proximity."

• *Height range.* When I stand up straight, I'm five feet eight. I do this on occasion when prompted. One of my first real-world "meets" was a woman who was exactly my height in inches. She wore heels and had a bouffant hairdo. The combo capped her out at a bit over six feet. I lowered my search range maximum to five feet six.

• *Body types.* From my own experience, and that of others, I offer the following interpretation of the body types some people claim to be blessed with. You will develop your own sixth sense as you go along; this list may help at the inception of your search. Select accordingly.

Slim/slender	True 80 percent of the time
Average	Usually five to ten pounds overweight
Athletic	True, but a strong person can also be overweight, *and is,* 25 percent of the time
A few extra pounds	A *lot* of extra pounds
Large	True
Other	What's left? Plenty! Here's what I found from time to time: "Tall and slender," "Not perfect, but who is?" "Athletic and a few extra pounds," "Broad of chest, legs to kill for," "Pre-Raphaelite," "Like looking in a wacky mirror," "Full-figured/very huggable," "Big, but nice guy take a chance!" "Athletic: a little on the husky side" "200 lbs. [with a six-feet-two male frame]," "THICK," "'Jane Russell' type," "Lush & lovely they say! BBW," "Old and used, but still in shape [fifty-two-year-old]," "Voluptuous, round, Delta Burkeish," "Getting Ancient [sixty-three-year-old]," "I'M BROAD BUT NOT FAT"

• *Bottom line: no matter what other category(ies) you choose, also check off "Other."* If you fail to do so, you could very well miss your soul mate by a sliver. All because he/she exhibited a bit of creativity in the "Body Type" section.

• *Diet.* For most people, this will be like trying to fit two pounds of sugar into a one-pound container. I enjoy a lot of fruits and vegetables, chicken and fish with a bare sliver of red meat now and then, and I am a sucker for sweets. That is not one of the categories. If your tastes run to something other than a food combo listed, describe it in the "Additional Diet" description box and check "Other."

• *Smoking and drinking habits.* State your preference. Don't figure on changing anyone else.

• *Living status.* For yourself, tell it like it is. If your situation changes, go back and modify your profile. I once corresponded, and occasionally saw, a woman in San Jose. She billed herself as being divorced. She later admitted to being "near the end" of a divorce. Six months later the finish line seemed to be no closer.

• *Presence of children.* This is a particularly important area, no matter what your age. For example, perhaps you are not interested in someone with children because you would prefer to raise a family from scratch. If you choose "No children," you could very well fail to meet an SMC who has a child but has just agreed to letting the spouse have custody. Or you may miss out on one who has joint custody a small portion of the time, which you feel you might be able to live with. Rather than rule out SMCs at this stage, consider taking all comers; elect "No preference." We'll discuss this issue in more depth in Chapter Seven.

• *Do you want children in the future?* Your call, but be sure to indicate strong feelings one way or the other. This is definitely an area in which you don't want surprises down the line.

• *Education and income.* If you don't want to disclose your income, check "Prefer not to say." Otherwise, tell it for real even if your income is modest. If your income is high, "Prefer not to say" will minimize the possibility of visits from scam artists.

• *Personality questions.* The prompt asks you to select five activities you enjoy. Don't limit yourself to that number. All that you select will show up. Indicate whatever is applicable and add more in the additional box right below if necessary. A bit further down in the sign-up form you will have a chance to describe yourself. Make certain that all your pleasure pursuits are mentioned in one place or another.

Don't get carried away with checking boxes under "My friends might best describe me as..." and "I value someone who is..." Instead put these values in your own words in the appropriate boxes under the "Personal Descriptions" section of the form.

• *Personal descriptions.* Start by filling in the captivating headline you came up with in the last chapter.

You'll see "Tell us a little about yourself. Be creative." The latter suggestion means "be colorful," rather than "invent." Start by inserting the profile you have created. You have about 350 words to work with, and another 350 words under "Tell us a little about who you are looking for." You can talk about yourself and your soul mate under either or both headings.

Security and Privacy

So now you have the formula for organizing a smooth search. Ready to hit the Internet? Not quite. Before you take the matchmaking world by storm, let's talk about the ding-a-lings and scam artists you might attract, and how to handle them.

Be cautious about the type of information you give out to strangers on the Internet. No matter where you look for a soul mate—church socials, bars, dance classes, wherever—you must always watch for the screwballs and lamebrains. Occasionally you may run into those who won't take no for an answer when you decide to call it quits. The same goes for finding an SMC on the Internet.

Most of us looking for an SMC are lonely to some degree. Through the Internet, you can meet fascinating people. Occasionally, one of these fascinating people is a psycho; others may be cons and thieves. You must be careful that the attention and kindness such people may show to you does not undermine your common sense. So be cautious and maintain your privacy. There are two key rules: Keep your email anonymous, and don't give out vital information prematurely. Let's look at each one in some depth.

KEEP YOUR EMAIL ANONYMOUS

Most match sites arrange to send along your email to prospective candidates anonymously. They give you a special mailbox on their site through which others can contact you. For instance, let's assume that your true email address is *linda@aol.com*, and your handle at *Match.com* is *LuckyYou*. If I want to send you an email message, I address it to *anon.LuckyYou@match.com*. The Match.com program is set up to automatically ricochet my message to your *linda@aol.com* address. I cannot determine your true email address.

You can inadvertently disclose your true address, however, if you are careless in responding. Let's assume that you're Linda and I send you a message through Match.com addressed to *anon.LuckyYou@match.com*. Match.com in turn forwards the message to you, and it shows up in your *linda@aol.com* mailbox. You look up my profile on *Match.com* and decide to respond. You can do this one of three ways.

1. Below my profile you click on the Email button and send a message on the email form that comes up,

2. You go back into your AOL email and click on New Message, or

3. In your own email you click on Reply to Sender.

If you do what is outlined in item 1, you keep your email address a secret. If you do what is described in item 2 or 3, your true email address will come zipping along to me. An SMC was astonished to find that I called her by name on the second email given that she hadn't disclosed her real name in her message. Her real email address was along the lines of *janesmith@aol.com*. She had thought for some reason that AOL would shield her from such a revelation. Before you sign up or send email through any site, be clear in your mind about the extent of anonymity you can expect. Contact the site if you are unsure.

DON'T GIVE OUT VITAL INFORMATION PREMATURELY

It's important that you choose an appropriate time to give out information about yourself. This should come only when you have confidence that your SMC is a person whom you can trust. Consider that you really don't know this SMC. He or she may come across well enough in your correspondence that you begin to become comfortable. But wait until you have a really good feeling before giving the store away.

Nydia C., thirty-four, in Atlanta, put it this way:

"I pay a lot of attention to little details in the first few emails. If I see any contradictions at all, no matter how slight, I'm out of there. I don't even bother asking about them; it's enough that the guy is not being completely candid with me. Been there; done that."

Sylvia P., fifty-four, in Boston, volunteered:

"I have to feel good about someone before I give out my phone number. A 'good feeling' for me was that a man might come back with a compliment, maybe a remark like 'good comment' and there were no put-downs. I also like it when somebody responds with further meaningful thoughts, especially when I give of myself and let my hair down a little.

"Once I told someone that I wasn't a very good housekeeper. He said, 'That just means that you spend your time more intelligently than doing windows.' I liked that. It made me feel good about myself and about him too."

• *Your phone number.* Don't give out your home phone number immediately. When you get to the stage of wanting to talk with each other, ask the SMC for his/her phone number so that *you* can initiate the call. See how the conversation goes before giving out *your* phone number. If there is the slightest doubt, err on the safe side. If you can, give out a cellular number or a pager for starters.

You could run into the situation where neither of you wants to be the first to give out a phone number. Fine. Keep chailing until either one or both of you loses that reserve, or you decide it isn't worth the effort.

Don't call anyone collect! Your phone number will show up on their monthly bill. This is also true for 800 and 888 numbers. If you have Caller ID, activate the blocking feature before you call.

• *Your real-world address.* Be slow to give out your address. If you mail something to an SMC, such as your photograph, do not put a return address on the envelope. Consider getting a post office box, or use one of the Mail-Boxes-Are-Us arrangements for SMC communications. Expect to pay $10–$12 a month. P.O. boxes can be a lot cheaper, but are not always available for that very reason.

If you live in a small town, you can always mail something from a neighboring town. Or send a letter to a faraway friend or relative and ask him or her to post it for you. You can also ask your post office to cancel your stamp without office identification.

When you are giving geographical information in your profile, if you live in a small town, specify the county only, or say that you are "close to" a nearby larger city. Similarly, go slow in giving out the name of the company you work for unless it is in a big city and is a large outfit.

• *Your name.* Give out your first name only. It's a bit awkward addressing someone with a handle of CrepesSuzette, for example. If you are really fearful, use your nickname, or make up a name. Don't give out your real last name or initial.

• *Your email address.* Be careful about passing along your true email address if it includes your last name or initial. Mine, for example, starts with ericff. That includes my first name, as well as my middle and last initials. I've seen many emails that have the owner's entire first and last name. An email that reads *paulkelly@friendlyisp.com* most likely belongs to someone named Paul Kelly. Not always, however. One clever SMC had set up a mailbox beginning with "BettyG"; her real name turned out to be Connie L.

To be even more cautious, set up a separate email account with one of the free mailbox services as described in Chapter Two. Generate a false name, and use this email account only for Internet searching.

In most cases, you cannot attach anything to email sent from a free mailbox site. Instead, you'll need to copy the text and paste it directly into your message. If you want to be able to include attachments, you'll need to use the email provided by your own ISP.

The chances are slim that you will end up with a pest. If you do, you can always change your handle to get a new site mailbox. If your handle is Big Mama, for instance, your site mailbox will be *anon.bigmama@site.com*. If you change your handle to Big Lucy, your mailbox will also change to *anon.biglucy@site com*. After the change, any emails sent to Big Mama will be returned to the sender as undeliverable. But what about someone who has your personal mailbox and won't go away? The Delete key is made to order for such problems, though I personally had only one such encounter and a minor one at that.

• *Your assets.* Don't invite a scam artist who is looking for money and valuables to take advantage of you. There is no need to mention that you own your own home, a boat, or other valuables. If you describe a life full of frequent exotic vacations, you'll communicate that you are wealthy (whether you are or aren't). If you are employed, don't play up the financial aspects of your job.

From Jennifer, fifty-seven, in Houston, with whom I had exchanged four messages, came this information:

> "The greatest thing abt Maui was being able to see the whales, & hear them the whole time I was snorkeling/scuba diving. Also the bike ride frm the top of the volcano to sea level was fun, fun. I was able to ski w/my daughter & my grandchildren & many of my friends the next wk at Aspen. I'm off to Las Vegas next week."

Vacation weeks back-to-back in three different locales indicates that Jennifer has lots of money to travel, at least. If Jennifer had left out the timeline, her circumstances would have been a bit less revealing. For example, she could have said:

> "The greatest thing abt Maui was being able to see the whales, & hear them the whole time I was snorkeling/scuba diving. Also the bike ride frm the top of the volcano to sea level was fun, fun. *Almost as much fun as being able to* ski w/my daughter & my grandchildren ~~& many of my friends~~ *when I vacation with them* at Aspen. *I also have in mind a trip up to Las Vegas one of these days.*

From Lucille, fifty-five, in Roanoke, in her second email to me:

> "Since spring is here, I felt compelled to go down to Memphis this past weekend to get my "spring fix" of good old southern blues. The weather was wonderful, and Beale Street was fun, as always! The daughter of a friend is finishing up a six-month stint with one of the regional theater groups, and we wanted to catch her Friday night show. The rest of the weekend was devoted to fun, visitor type things."

The tone was that of a woman who regularly patronizes this area, not just at vacation time. Note how just a couple of slight changes can make this a safer message, without losing the flavor:

> "Since spring is here, I felt compelled to go down to Memphis this past weekend for ~~my~~ *a* "spring fix" of good old southern blues. The weather was wonderful, and Beale Street was fun. ~~as always!~~ The daughter of a friend is finishing up a six-month stint with one of the regional theater

groups, and we wanted to catch her Friday night show. The rest of the weekend, ~~was devoted to fun, visitor type things~~ *I was your typical tourist.*"

Yet another, Cynthia, fifty-seven, in Detroit, in her first email, imprudently asked me:

"How do you feel about the north woods, or more specifically, central Michigan? I'm looking to build a house on a lake there as a home base and move from the Cities."

The ability to build one's own home implies a certain amount of financial dexterity. The second sentence could have read:

"I'd like to move from the Cities; a home somewhere near a lake would really appeal to me."

Yet another SMC did not disclose income in her profile. But the service she was using allowed her to indicate the minimum income she would accept in a suitor. She selected the highest, "over $100,000." It would have been safer for her to express no opinion, and then winnow the SMCs according to her taste.

A good rule of thumb: Think carefully about the information you are about to disclose to an email acquaintance. Would you advise your son or daughter or your best friend to reveal the same type of information to a person he or she had never met? If in doubt, ask your offspring or your parent. Pay attention to the answer. Over the thirty-five delightful years I knew him, I ignored much advice passed along by my father, virtually always to my detriment.

In Summary

Put time into your preparation. Organize your email. Be specific about what you are looking for, and where. Think through the questions you may be asked by a matchmaking site to ensure that your responses correctly reflect your thoughts. Whenever the occasion warrants, update the information you have provided to the site.

Be cautious about giving out personal information to strangers on the Internet. Once you give it out, you can't get it back. Disclose phone numbers and addresses only when you have a significant measure of confidence about your SMC. Err on the conservative side. Don't give out finance-related information that might attract social sharks and would-be swindlers.

So now that you're ready to jump on the Net, let's come up with some dazzling email openers that will bring results.

5 Contact!

You can do what you have to do, and sometimes you can do it even better than you think you can.

—JIMMY CARTER

Anything I've ever done that ultimately was worthwhile…initially scared me to death.

—BETTY BENDER

If you think back to Chapter One, you'll remember that you don't want to take up with someone like a dud from your past. So let's start sifting through SMC profiles to find ones worth running through the filter twice. As you do, you'll be noting red flags, scrutinizing yellow flags, and welcoming green ones. Red flags will eliminate an SMC. Yellow flags will call for closer looks. Green flags will warm your heart.

Let me emphasize again that with a bit of patience you can snag exactly the SMC you want. So don't get discouraged if you have to throw a lot of them back. *Don't compromise!* Once you have thought through your A, B, and C lists, don't start making exceptions. If a red flag pops up, head for the exit. The same goes for a yellow flag that turns crimson after investigation. Ignore those friends who claim that you are being too picky. Stick to your guns; you'll be rewarded in the end.

Red Flags

You can filter out many red flags by setting your search criteria accordingly. If you want nothing to do with an SMC who smokes, or drinks, or has children, that's easy. Check the boxes that say "don't smoke," "don't drink," and "no children" as explained in the last chapter. But you will have to dig deeper to

catch sight of many red flags. Some won't show up until you actually meet the SMC. Even then, you must keep your antenna raised.

Look closely at an SMC's profile for immediate red flags. These are signs that point to aspects that will leave you cold. In addition, you will have to probe for many that will not be apparent from the profile itself, for instance, the extent of an SMC's involvement in religious activities. If you and the SMC are not simpatico, best to find out early on.

Let's scan some red flags supplied by different individuals.

Maya, thirty-one, in Seattle, wants to avoid workaholics, engineers, attorneys, couch potatoes, and men who are financially insecure, have been divorced less than a year, have children living at home, or have been married more than once.

Betsy, forty-nine, in Santa Barbara, is concerned with cultural flexibility and sophistication. Thus she looks to an SMC's political awareness and his grasp of world history and art. She inquires about the books he has read to determine his breadth of knowledge. "No provincials, please," as she puts it. She has to dig for the answers to these broad issues.

Larry, forty-two, in Akron, stays away from women who are sun lovers, boat-oriented, ride horses, play Scrabble or bridge, or downhill ski. The minute one of these interests pops up as a candidate's preference, Dan is on to the next SMC.

Mike, forty-four, in Los Angeles, wants an SMC who enjoys the arts. Also, the extremes—too athletic, or not athletic at all—are his particular red flags.

Debbie, thirty-eight, in Phoenix, steers away from anyone who does not read much and/or prefers watching TV to reading. She feels that poor spelling and grammar indicate such a flaw.

Nicole, forty-nine, in Santa Barbara, declines a man who is rich, is unwilling to respond to her questions, doesn't like animals, and/or is a hunter. She also scratches anyone with rigid opinions who declines to consider varying viewpoints.

When you receive a bite from an SMC, read it closely. Look for the obvious, such as an SMC who expresses doubt that you have enough in common. Or one who loves an activity you don't. Whenever an SMC would mention to me that she was looking forward to downhill slopes or lying out on the beach, it was all over. On the other hand, one who mentioned that the previous week she had finished up a 350-mile bike ride from Seattle to someplace boosted her rating immediately. A third mentioned that she never had a dog because she couldn't envision leaving it (the pronoun was a clue in itself) alone all day while she worked.

So with every response, try to match up some criteria on your lists of must-have, would-be-nice-to-have, and no-way yardsticks. If you come across something that turns you off, head for the next SMC.

Often a turn of phrase will catch your eye (or your black marker). If there is any doubt in your mind about something, go back with a question:

"You mentioned that your last boyfriend had a 'wild streak.' I'm curious—can you expand on that a bit for me?"

"You said, 'I want a substantial fun-lover at my side when I party.' Fill me in a bit more, as I'm not sure exactly what you mean."

"When you wrote, 'Put the kids in the closet,' did you mean that literally? Are there any circumstances where you might have a different opinion?"

If the next response isn't any more enlightening, try again. Persist until the point is cleared up. If your SMC continues to waffle, perhaps that in itself is the answer.

Most SMCs will not admit to the following red flags. You must read, listen, and observe carefully to find hints that a candidate may exhibit the characteristics that follow. Ask the questions like the ones I suggest:

• *Extreme jealousy.* "How do you feel about spouses dancing with others at a party?"

• *Unwillingness to take any blame for the outcome of past relationships.* "What brought your last relationship(s) to an end?"

• *Easily angered.* "How do you feel about drivers who cut in front of you on the freeway?" or "What makes you angry or upset?"

• *Unpunctual.* "How important is it to you to be on time for everything?" At an in-person meeting, does the SMC show up on time?

• *"The glass is half-empty" attitude toward life.* "What major events have you had in your life, and how did they affect you?" Does the SMC prefer to discuss negatives or positives?

• *Prejudiced against minorities.* "What are your thoughts about [some particular news item such as a hate crime]?"

• *Conceited.* Comment on the SMC's work, hobby, and so forth. "It sounds like you are pretty good at this," or ask, "What things do you do best?" At an in-person meeting, does the SMC want to talk mostly about him- or herself?

• *Abusive.* There is sometimes a correlation between animal abuse and physical or verbal abuse of a partner. Ask, "What do you feel is the best way to housebreak a puppy [kitten]?" or, "How do you feel pets should be disciplined?" Also try, "How do you feel children should be disciplined? An eight-year old who begins stealing change or starts lying, for example."

• *On the rebound.* Time heals; find out how long since the last relationship ended, and why. At an in-person meeting, does the SMC continually refer to a past partner?

• *Noncommitting.* Clues will lie in past relationships. "During the *x* years you went with [past partner], did you live together?" Also, the question "Did you ever talk of marriage?" can be revealing, but the timing has to be right. Avoid sounding as if that topic is next on your "Why-don't-we…" list.

• *Health problems.* "Any health problems?" or "When was your last operation?"

• *Poor social skills.* "Do you like meeting new people at a gathering?" or "What kind of events do you enjoy dressing up for?"

Further, be on the lookout for signs of alcoholics or SMCs who use drugs, people pretending to be of the opposite sex, those interested in your money, and those who are married. A Virginia man dated a woman steadily for two months—until her husband's ship returned to port.

Let's take a look at some profile excerpts to see what can be gleaned.

Carla, twenty-five, in Milwaukee:

> **"For quieter evening times, I like to be with friends (I'm rich with an eclectic base of friends) to go dancing, play bridge…."**

Don't expect this SMC to give up her horde of friends. Socializing is part of the package.

Mary Ellen, fifty-four, in Eugene:

> **"Moved back to Oregon recently and love it here."**

This SMC may be permanently planted in Oregon. Make sure you could handle the weather.

Dan, thirty-two, in Canberra:

> **"I am self-motivated, but not overly ambitious. I enjoy work, but friends and family are more important….I'm generally upbeat, sometimes sarcastic. I am a down-to-earth guy and am looking for someone similar. I'm here because I'm working too many hours (medical consulting)."**

Will Dan be a consistent provider? Will he be sarcastic with you? Can you handle that if he is? Will his overtime at work continue, or does he have plans for cutting back his hours?

Phil, forty-five, in Dayton:

> "I'm forty-five, but both my exes say I still have the best butt they've ever seen. Looking for an eighteen- to forty-five-year-old female."

Men or women looking in an age range beginning much lower than theirs may have difficulty having a relationship with someone close to their own age. The age of past partners and the duration of relationships would give some insight into whether this SMC is ready for a mature liaison.

Lesley, forty-four, in Bangor:

> "Tired of the singles scenes. I enjoy watching movies and listening to music. ...I want a responsible person who just likes to have fun! I don't care what your job is...just have one! I live on the coast and LOVE lying out on the beach! I'm a VERY young forty-four so need someone who is able to keep up with me....[I] have pretty much always dated younger guys just because we seem to have much more in common....Let me hear from you!"

What is it that Lesley has in common seemingly with only younger men? The only interests she admits to are movies, music, and the beach. None of these require a lot of stamina or attention span.

Rita, sixty-one, in Des Moines:

> "I have a caring and nurturing nature. I can handle many situations and with years of experience am considered by others as a problem solver....I have a reputation for helping others, so those of you eligible bachelors out there who are interested will have lots of ways of getting to know of and about me."

This woman gives a lot of herself to others. Will this demand on her time detract from your togetherness? What did she spend the "years of experience" doing? Has she been prone to picking men who were problems that needed solving?

Cynthia, fifty-seven, in Freeport:

> "I want a man who is tall and slim-average, who will envelope me in his embrace. I want a man who will be attentive to only me and treat me like a queen. After all these years of raising a family and building a future, it's time to retire. My family and all my friends insist that I deserve all my wishes granted at this time in my life. Love to travel. Find out for yourself what a true diamond I am."

What does Cynthia have in mind for her retirement years? The slight clue is "travel," but domestically? Internationally? By motor home? By motorcycle? We need more details from her as to why she is such a gem.

Charles, fifty-eight, hometown undisclosed:

> "Now I have a job that has me roaming the entire country....I don't mind giving back at least as much as I receive, but I do love to receive. That is something that I never got in my marriage. That's one of the many reasons I am divorced. I want to find the love of my life, but I would also like to meet nice women while I travel. I can't guarantee that we will or will not hit it off. If not then we will have a great time. If we do then I will do my best to keep coming out there and see where things lead."

First you'd want to get down to some details about his job. What does he do, how often does he do it, and how long is he gone each time? Why didn't Charlie receive; did he do any giving? What were the other reasons for the divorce? Let's see if we can get this straight: if you *don't* hit it off, you will have a great time. If you *do* hit it off, he will "do my best to keep coming out there." What does all that mean exactly? Is Charlie ready for one woman? Or is he trying to line up friendly bunkmates in every port? Would you get to travel with him?

Randall, thirty-nine, in Birmingham:

> "Age now thirty-nine...my picture is when I was age twenty-eight."

Whoa! What does thirty-nine look like?

Yellow Flags

Yellow is a warning color. Unlike traffic lights, a yellow flag may lead to either a green or a red one. Pay attention when you have a vague sense that some of an SMC's information may not be quite right for you.

Here are some yellow flags:

Steve, thirty-nine, in Los Angeles:

> "I'm ambivalent about teachers. I was married to one for eleven years."

Fred, fifty-nine, in Duluth:

> "I stepped careful with women who still had grown kids living at home."

Olivia, twenty-eight, in San Diego:

> "Any man with a daughter over ten living with him was a potential rival. I didn't feel I could get too involved until I had met the daughter."

Teachers value the stability their profession brings, and generally they are not interested in career or financial risks. On the other hand, an SMC who is presently a teacher may very well be on the way to a new career in computers. The grown children may be on the wing to their own nest imminently. The live-in daughter may prove delightful.

Let's extract some yellow flags from more profiles:

Phil, fifty, in Tacoma, writes of himself:

> "My quick wit gets me in trouble sometimes but has come in handy on occasion....I am a graphic artist, singer, know-it-all....I am looking for someone who will...not be afraid to slap me upside the head when I've been bad."

Phil is forthright. Further investigation will tell you if you might be dealing with a potential ego problem. The "when I've been bad" part might extend to the bedroom; who knows? Find out.

Gilbert, thirty-one, in Philadelphia:

> "I'm [looking for] a woman who enjoys...AND understands how to honor another's space. I enjoy riding my Honda gliding in the hills around the county, golf, pool, a little fishing."

The "AND" seems to stress that by golly you'd better give Gilbert his space. Further, does he want his space with the Honda, the golf, the pool, *and* the fishing? Or just one or two of the above? This would call for some follow-up:

> "You are looking for someone who respects your space. Can you be more specific? Have you had a problem with a partner in the past about this?"

Sal, fifty-five, in Trenton, promised:

> "We will take on whatever comes down the road."

Has life been a constant struggle? Does Sal do a particular kind of work that might cause or require an aggressive attitude? Or is he just an optimist? Or perhaps a patient realist? A natural follow-up might be "You say, 'We will take on whatever comes down the road.' Tell me more about that."

Lillian, forty-two, in Lake Tahoe:

> "I am a professional....For the spontaneous child within, I know that until I finally set eyes on you, I will be missing the richest of riches. In the world, you are an integrous, successful, imaginative, and respected leader. As a lover, you have known the rare honesty of commitment until 'death do us part,...' your first love taken too soon from your life. And, as now the grief softens, and the longing to love consciously again begins to waken you in the night, and haunt you in the day, the time for us is near. It would seem that until each of us finds the other, life is empty."

There was more to Lillian's profile, all in the same spirit. Although her profile is well-written and emotionally appealing, we have no idea what Lillian does in off hours. Also, need only widowers apply? What if your first love has been taken by decree of a judge in a divorce proceeding; does that qualify you? She guessed at "integrous," which isn't a word. Spellcheck would have alerted her.

Kathleen, twenty-six, in Sacramento:

> "I love the outdoors, exploring new and interesting sites, box lunches, and easy hiking."

By "easy hiking" does she mean one mile? Ten? Four hours? Two hundred yards? What is a "new and interesting site"? How does she explore—via Range Rover or on foot? Is dinner apt to show up in a box too?

Cheryl, thirty-five, in Las Vegas:

> "I've been divorced for five years and have certainly been enjoying being a whole person by myself instead of part of a couple. Sometimes I miss that commitment though,...so as you can tell I'm wavering on where I want to go! I hope that meeting the right person will help me decide."

Cheryl is right up front: she doesn't know whether she wants a relationship or not. What was it about her marriage that made her feel like less than a whole person? The commitment she misses was a commitment to what?

Jerry, thirty-five, in Oakland:

> "I purchased a cute Victorian home a few years ago and enjoy the occasional weekend 'fix-it' projects; I'm handy that way. I also enjoy a bit of gardening. I have potted plants all over my backyard."

Victorian homes, by their nature, often require lots of TLC. You might want to ask Jerry what his fix-its were for the last year. Will he expect you to pitch in alongside? How much time does he spend gardening and repairing? If he goes on vacation, who tends the potted plants? Will he have enough spare time to do things you enjoy?

Carole, fifty-one, in Seattle:

> "I am looking for someone who wants to share life's emotions, feelings, tears, and laughter. I am a romantic and love to be spoiled. A good relationship is a blending of two imperfect individuals into stronger, better people who laugh, cry, and work together."

The last two sentences are faintly oxymoronic. It would be natural to ask: "In what ways do you like to be spoiled?"

So don't rule out an SMC because of a yellow flag. If it shows up, and the SMC is otherwise of interest to you, ask some questions. Chase yellow flags down until they turn either green or red. Keep looking at your list of greens and reds until you are certain the yellow goes one way or the other.

YOUR SMC'S PICTURE(S)

You come across an interesting profile, but there is no picture. This is a yellow flag. It doesn't necessarily mean that there is a problem, however. Several women with no pictures in their original profile sent photos of quite attractive ladies (at least I thought they were attractive; it's all subjective, remember).

Don't demand a picture in the first exchange of information, or it will appear that you are putting too much emphasis on looks. I would generally tack my request at the end of the second email, as sort of an afterthought.

If for some reason you do not have a picture attached to your profile, this is an opportune time to send one along. In addition to my profile picture, I had two better ones that I would send along with this second email. My expectation was that it would help the SMC to decide that I was serious about this business, that she might want to get hustling to send me her own picture.

When you make such a request, you will receive either a photo, a promise, or one of several excuses.

• *The Promise.* The promise is to send a photo. Make a note on your A&T worksheet of the date of your request. If one didn't show up with the next couple of emails to me, I would simply say at the end of a message, "You were going to send me a picture," or "How are you coming on getting me a picture?"

If one doesn't arrive one or two emails later, you are wasting your time. There is something the SMC does not wish to disclose that a current picture would reveal. Wish your SMC luck in his or her search and head on down the lane.

• *The Excuses.* One catch-all excuse is that the SMC doesn't have a scanner, doesn't know how to email pictures, or both. You can point out that most copy places now have scanning equipment. For $10 or less, they will scan your photo and put it on a floppy disk (that you provide). Attaching the image file to an email is not difficult. You might copy and paste the instructions in the following Side Trip into an email to your SMC. If the SMC still can't make it through the simple steps, he or she undoubtedly has a friend who can help.

ATTACHING PHOTOS TO EMAIL

Let's assume that one way or another, you now have a floppy disk with a file named *mypic.jpg,* that is your picture. Here is how to attach it to an email message in Outlook Express. The steps will be somewhat similar in any other email program.

1. Open your email program and click the New Mail button at the top left of the screen. This brings up the "New Message" window.

2. At the top of the "New Message" window, click on the Attach button. If you don't see anything like this, it may be because your window is not full-screen. If this is the case, click on the little square between "–" and "X" in the upper right-hand corner of the "New Message" window. The window will then go to full screen and the Attach button will show up.

3. Clicking the Attach button brings up another window that will be titled "Insert Attachment." Click the little down arrow to the right of the "Look In" box at the top.

4. In the drop-down that appears, highlight "3½" floppy [A:]" by clicking on it.

5. Your file, *"mypic.jpg,"* will show up in the large box below. If it doesn't, maybe you put the wrong floppy disk in. Make sure you are using the one with your picture copied onto it.

6. Highlight *mypic.jpg* by clicking on it.

7. Click the Attach button on the right side of the "Insert Attachment" window.

Your picture will now go along for the ride when you shoot off the email.

At times, you may not be able to open a picture attached to an SMC's email to you. Or your SMC may complain that he or she cannot open *your* attached picture. There is an easy solution: include the photo in the body of the email message.

INCLUDING A PICTURE IN THE
BODY OF YOUR EMAIL MESSAGE

1. Prepare an email to send to your SMC. You'll be doing this in a "New Message" window. Let's assume you end the message with your name. After you finish writing your name, hit the Enter button on your keyboard a couple of times. The cursor will end up jiggling around at the left, two lines below your name.

2. At the top of the "New Message" window, click on Insert.

3. Click on Picture in the drop-down box that shows up. Another window titled "Picture" appears.

4. To the right of center, click on the Browse button. A different type of box, also titled "Picture," will show up. Click the little down arrow to the right of the "Look In" box at the top.

5. In the drop-down box that appears, highlight "3½" floppy [A:]" by clicking on it.

6. Your file, "*mypic.jpg*," will show up in the large box below. If it doesn't, check to make sure you have inserted the right floppy.

7. Highlight *mypic.jpg* by clicking on it.

8. Click the Open button on the right side of the "Picture" window.

9. The second picture window will disappear. The first picture window will still be open; click OK.

Your picture will show up in the email just below your name. Send the whole works off to your SMC.

As an alternative, I have at times suggested that an SMC drop a photo in the mail to my Post Office Box address. Don't forget what we talked about in Chapter Three—being careful about mailing stuff through the USPO. This applies to being on the receiving end as well.

The other excuse is "I don't have any pictures." A serious SMC can get a disposable camera for just a few dollars, and will do so. Otherwise, the SMC is either on the fence about a relationship or has something to hide.

In short, if the SMC is not willing to cough up a recent picture within a reasonable period, shuffle along to the next SMC.

Green Flags

Green flags will lead to interests you would enjoy sharing with your soul mate, or that you could develop. Sometimes the flag is quite clear. "I'm considering bicycling in Ireland this year" in a profile caught my eye immediately, because I had the same intention. I was interested in a woman who enjoyed physical activity, indoors (dancing, and so on) and outdoors (backpacking, tennis, and so forth). So the following statements in profiles were green flags for me:

"I love to do almost anything outdoors.…[I]ntroduce me to the things you enjoy as well."

"I have a big heart for people and the environment."

"I would enjoy hiking across rural Turkey."

Headline: "Thirty-love." [reference to tennis score, not age]

The following examples are less distinct but may be going in the right direction for you:

Steve, thirty-four, in Fitchburg, says:

"I enjoy dancing, astronomy (I built my own telescope and am working on a second),…learning golf (one of my latest projects)."

This could be a man who is handy around the house and may be willing to try anything you like as well.

Don, sixty, in Richmond, claims:

> "I enjoy life and like to have fun. I don't have to be on the go all the time, but I will try just about anything once, but no bungee jumping."

At sixty, Don doesn't sound like a couch potato. Will he try things twice? Who knows? Perhaps you might ask what he has tried once and not liked. Sounds like Don is someone who wants to be part of the parade of life, rather than just watch it go by.

Ruth, forty-seven, in Dallas, writes:

> "[My SMC] would be equally comfortable just sitting by a campfire talking about life in general."

If you are outdoorsy, Ruth may just fill the bill in this respect, though there was no other indication in the profile of what she likes to do outdoors. Each of you would probably want to find out how far the other is willing to walk to get to the campfire site.

Ed, forty-three, in Milwaukee:

> "When I'm not on the freeway though, I enjoy activities like going to hear Bonnie Raitt or Boz Scaggs at the Filmore, small acoustic or vocal music concerts, Tango dancing (beginner), coffee and the paper at Starbucks, or weekend drives with someone special; it's fun to buy fresh veggies along the way, and cook 'em up when we get home.
>
> "Sunday hikes and bike rides are nice too, or an occasional run, lap swim, or even snow skiing (just past beginner) or scuba (but only in warm water!)."

Ed seems to have it all together, or most of it at least. I was fortunate he wasn't in my age range. There was more to his profile, all in a positive tone. I doubt if he remained on the market for long.

Your Turn!

You've put together a killer profile on a site that you like. You've scared up a few prospects who seem worth closer looks. Now let's talk about making the first move.

The shark, king of the sea, aggressively pursues its snacks. A two-inch sea anemone, on the other hand, sits and waits for lunch to drift within its orbit. Whether this accounts in part for the difference in the size of the two creatures, I don't know. But the shark's dinner selections, as well as its process of gathering same, must be more interesting by far.

You, similarly, have two potential approaches to using the Internet as a matching device. You can plaster your profile all over the place and wait to see what happens. Or you can go beat the bushes yourself. The latter approach is harder work, but more effective, and you will have a better chance of coming across your SMC before the competition does.

When I first began searching for a mate on the Internet, I assumed that while I was busy scouting women, various females would come across *me* in *their* search. That was correct; once every two or three weeks someone would initiate an email to me. Had I just sat back and waited for my soul mate to find *me*, I may very well have spent a few more Christmases alone. So male or female, start looking. Sharks don't wait for food to wander into their maws. Don't sit back and hope that someone will find *you*. Increase your odds. *Go for it!*

Once I came across an attractive profile of a woman living just a few miles up the coast. For some reason, I delayed making an approach for a couple of weeks. To my dismay, the response to my first contact, when I finally got it out, was "Sorry, but I just met a man yesterday with whom I seem to have a lot in common." Ouch! That was the last time I let grass grow under my feet. You needn't jump on every lead immediately, but don't let too many suns go down.

Moreover, it could very well be that your soul mate has already looked at your profile and passed. An expression of interest on your part could be the deciding factor in your soul mate's going back for a second look.

My advice about being first to extend the invitation is directed toward both genders. Victorian times and attitudes have faded (for the most part). Modern women fly airplanes for the Military, run corporations, tone by lifting heavy weights, and in general match or exceed their male counterparts in most arenas. You shouldn't even give a second thought to forging ahead on a more elemental playing field—that of searching for a mate. You may be working with a dozen or more SMCs at a time; who knows other than you? Mahatma Gandhi put it eloquently: "If you don't ask, you don't get."

Women: Your ultimate soul mate, when you find him, won't care who asked whom to dance. If a man voices concern that you are aggressive, you probably don't have a match anyway. He is just not with the times.

So get busy; start turning over rocks. Don't wait for the SMCs to flock to you. Search out the ones that seem to have promise, and make the first move. Bear in mind the Chinese proverb, "The man who waits for roast duck to fly into mouth must wait very, very long time."

WHAT TO SAY IN YOUR FIRST EMAIL

A new client once called me to tell me about her case. I listened to her patiently on the phone for thirty free-to-her minutes, as she described in exquisite detail a story of fraud. When she got to the end of the tale, I was stunned to find that she had already gone to another lawyer and settled the case! Having second thoughts about the settlement, she wanted me to go back to trial, which was impossible. I learned the hard way not to listen to a caller's case over the phone before asking a couple of questions and looking at the paperwork.

For like reasons, limit your efforts in composing the first message to an SMC. Many of the recipients will not have the courtesy to respond. So often your first email will be a wasted effort. Don't knock yourself out on it. Others will come back with varieties of "Thanks, but no thanks." So save your time and energy for an SMC whose response appeals to you, and who wants more interaction. *That* SMC will appreciate that you have not been presumptuous or overbearing right off the mark.

In a first-contact email, I would say the same thing each time. For the subject title of the email, I would compliment my correspondent in some fashion. My usual subject title for the email was "You sound delightful!" This was my genuine feeling as I responded to a profile. For women, "You sound (great, incredible, fantastic, and so forth)!" works well on a man. Anytime I got a return message with such a title the SMC and I were off to a smart start.

In that first email I would come right to the point. I liked the profile, so I would write:

> "I like your profile," or "Your profile appeals to me."

We obviously had some mutual interests. I would ask the SMC to respond if she agreed:

> "If you think we might be hitting on a sufficient number of cylinders together, get back to me so that I can find out more about you."

The "so that I can find out more about you" part also implies that you are more interested in learning about the SMC than in talking about yourself. You will be points ahead if this is true.

So that the SMC would know enough to fish around and find the attachment, I'd add:

"I'm pretty active physically, so I've attached a bit more about myself."

Usually I would try to personalize my message with an additional sentence or two.

To an SMC who lived near my hometown I wrote: "I should mention that I was born and raised in Lowell."

To a skier I said: "One question, however. Is your passion downhill or cross-country? I do too many things that require unbent, unsprained, and unbroken limbs to risk the former."

So my basic email looked like this:

"I like your profile. Take a look at mine. If you think we might be hitting on a sufficient number of cylinders together, get back to me so that I can find out more about you. I'm pretty active physically, so I've attached a bit more about myself." [And then I'd add a personal tinge, as explained just above.]

Check your spelling carefully. Consistent misspelling is the literary equivalent of a missing front tooth. Run Spellcheck, and *also read over your message*. A sentence that says, "Take a lock at mind" instead of "Take a look at mine" will pass the Spellcheck test but it shouldn't escape your eagle eye.

You may want to work with a template of your first message. This is a file that says all you want to say in your first message, and you can use this text over and over without having to retype it. You have the ability to add words or comments, delete something, or make changes. but you don't have to type the whole business over again. If you know your way around your email program, you can create an email template. If not, go to your email Help and search for "Templates." You will most likely receive instructions for creating one. Whether they are understandable is another story. Otherwise, do it the simple way: type your opening message in a word processing file, such as Microsoft Word or WordPerfect. Save this file as *Opener*.

You now have a form that can be sent to anyone. Each time you make a new contact, copy the language from *Opener* and paste it into your email. Personalize each message by making small changes like the ones I've suggested.

Unless the recipient's name appeared in the profile handle, I would use an initial for the salutation. Someone whose address came up as anon. Diane2@match.com would merit a "Hi Diane," and anon.gorgeousgal@ match.com would receive a "Hi G." Send your message out into the world and your aspirations are on their way.

Remember, you can respond by sending a message either through the site email, or from your own email address. Stop to think. Keep in mind the security measures we talked about in the last chapter. I won't repeat them here, but go back and read them again. Don't be too hasty in responding. You want your Internet experiences to be happy ones. *So be careful!*

NO RESPONSE TO YOUR EMAIL?

Let's go over your options when you get *no* reply.

Did You Get the Address Right?

Your email flies off; a couple of days later, still no response. Did the SMC receive your mail? You may have made a mistake in addressing the message; look closely. I frequently sent email addressed to "anon.handle@ hotmail.com" when I meant to send it to "anon.handle@match.com" A return email message would later tell me of my error. I then copied and pasted the message into a new email that was correctly addressed.

Alternatively, you may have missed or added something to the handle portion of the address. For instance, searching at one site you will find the following:

> CaliforniaGuy will net you a twenty-four-year-old male in San Francisco who bills himself as an "Ultra-hard-bodied stud for your pleasure," and is looking for a male partner.

> California_Guy turns up a forty-six-year-old male in Ukiah, California, looking for female companionship of Christian persuasion.

If your SMC of choice is CaliforniaGirl, you get a twenty-four-year-old in San Diego. CaliforniaGal connects you with a forty-year-old woman in Bakersfield. CaliforniaGel brings you a fifty-year old in Redding in the process of moving East.

Similarly, there are twenty-six varieties of "Eric" followed by numbers, letters, or a combination of both, not to mention fourteen variations on "Erik." There is also an Erk.

I once sent some emails to an SMC, but the address I typed was missing a single letter. Somebody else was receiving my efforts and ignoring them. The fact that the wrong person didn't reply saved me some great embarrassment, but the reverse could very well have been true, as I will explain later.

So address your messages correctly. Replying through a matchmaking site may help eliminate this potential faux pas. But as your chailing increases, at some point you will most likely swap personal mailboxes with your SMC. This raises the potential for misaddressing your messages.

When Your Email Arrives but a Response Doesn't

At times, a week or more may pass before you receive notice that you misaddressed your email. If you don't hear back, on some sites, you can take a peek at when the SMC last logged onto the site. If the last log on is after you sent your message, you probably aren't going to get a response; so it's on to the next SMC.

Let's say you have a pretty active chail going, and suddenly your SMC runs silent. You verify that you have addressed your latest missive correctly. Your SMC has been online since you sent your last email, and obviously he or she received it. What to do?

Nita, a strong-willed forty-two-year old, explains her approach:

> "Beggars bother me a lot: 'you haven't answered me,' 'what did I say wrong?' etc. Sometimes I don't get to my email for a few days and then I find these whines. If someone doesn't answer me after we have been corresponding a while, I send one last email asking if they wish to continue corresponding. I don't ask, 'what did I do wrong?' or 'what did I say wrong?' How demeaning!"

When I would run into this situation, after a few days or a week I would send a short message:

> "Are you still there?"

Occasionally my SMC would offer a valid reason for her tardiness. At other times, the SMC would respond by explaining why hers was intended to be the final message between us. No answer was handwriting on the wall: I moved on.

KEEPING IT ALL STRAIGHT

Over the course of the time that it will take to bola your soul mate, you may correspond with hundreds of SMCs. If you don't keep them straight from the start, you will end up confused about what you've said to whom—an ungodly mess. It's downright embarrassing to ask an SMC a question about her twenty-four-year marriage after she's already told you she has yet to wed. Or to inquire as to the continuing good health of her pet when she has none.

In addition, if you get to the point where you chat over the telephone or meet with an SMC, you want all your correspondence in one place for review. Avoid egg-on-the-face instances such as not being able to remember the name of an SMC's cat. Or whether the SMC works in computers or at KMart. Make consistent use of your checklist and organize your email as we discussed in Chapter Four.

You might occasionally deal with two SMCs with the same first name. To keep them straight, indicate their handle (or part of it) after their folder names. So if you have two Daves, one with the handle "Bushwhacker" and the other "WisconsinDreamer," name the folders something like, "Dave Bwkr" and "Dave Wisconsin."

MINIMIZING MESSAGE LOSS

Frustration can be defined neatly as preparing most of a long email message just before your computer locks up. When you reboot, or terminate the email program, your efforts have gone up in smoke. There are two ways to avoid this:

1. After you have written the first few words of your email message, save it. If you know how to save it as a draft, fine. If not, just save it as a file and remember (better, write it down) where you saved it. Keep saving the message each time you complete another paragraph or two. If your computer goes down, pull up the file you saved, and most of the message will be there.

2. Alternatively, type your message in a word processor like Microsoft Word. Similarly, after you have typed the first few words, save the document immediately and keep track of the directory you saved it to. I created a directory that I named "SMC letters." I would save as "Diane 12-10" a message prepared on December 10 to send to an SMC named Diane. Keep saving your message every few minutes as you prepare it. When you finish, save again. Then copy the text and paste it into your email as your message.

PLAY THE PERCENTAGES

Expect that when you send off email, your first attempts will garner nothing from fully half of the SMCs. Many will come back with the equivalent of "Thanks, but no thanks." Don't be discouraged; this is all part of the chase. A president elected by a 60 percent vote is considered to have won "by a landslide" even though 40 percent of the voters want nothing to do with him. At times when the reject streak seemed to be running particularly strong, I would assure myself that all those women were losing out on a good thing. My soul mate agrees; so will yours.

I found that of every ten emails I sent off, only three or four yielded reasonable prospects. If your average is higher, ask yourself if you are being selective enough in your search (accepting smokers when you really want a nonsmoker, for example). If your average is lower, you are probably searching in too wide an age range. A classic example of this would be the fifty-year-old woman looking for someone from thirty-five on up; raising the bar to forty-five may produce a greater percentage of higher-quality prospects.

HAVE AT IT PART-TIME

Treat your soul mate search as a part-time job, or better yet as a hobby. Set aside a portion of the day to search, compose email, and respond. Work at it regularly. For instance, you might spend two hours at night searching and sending emails, and half an hour in the morning reviewing the previous day's catch.

Be consistent. Do this five days a week, or four weekdays with a weekend stint. Don't expect results overnight. As you progress, you will quickly become much more savvy about searching. Identify with General H. Norman Schwarzkopf, who at a decisive moment said, "The truth of the matter is that you always know the right thing to do. The hard part is doing it." Finding your soul mate is too important to ever consider throwing in the towel; just keep at it.

In Summary

To win at the soul mate search business, be the shark rather than the anemone. That means actively trawling for your soul mate, rather than hoping that you will get swept up in an SMC's seine. By all means, make your profile as attractive a draw as possible; lightning may strike. But don't just sit around checking email three times a day, waiting for your soul mate to come over the horizon.

Read profiles carefully. If red flags unfurl, cast your net anew. Yellow flags will take some further investigation. The green flags are not always obvious at first, but when you stop to consider and suddenly think "Aha!" you know you're on the right track.

Keep your opening contact brief and right to the point. If you don't get an answer, make sure you sent your message to the right address. If after chailing for a while your SMC suddenly clams up, try one last time with "Anyone home?"

Organize your email by creating special folders for serious correspondents. Examine closely all the replies you come by. Pick out the nuggets that strike favorable chords that warrant continued contact. At the same time, look for inconsistencies that may signal that it is time to call it quits with a particular SMC.

Next let's take a look at what to do when your first e-ball comes bouncing back into your court.

Ask-and-Tell: Exploring Your Soul-Mate Candidate and Vice Versa

6

I am simple, complex, generous, selfish, unattractive, beautiful, lazy, and driven.

—Barbra Streisand

Seriously, I do not think I am fit for the presidency.

—Abraham Lincoln

The day after you send out your first Here-I-Am-You-Lucky-Fool emails, your computer boings—you have mail. Here come all those SMCs. Now how to separate the honey from the comb?

A lawyer taking the deposition of someone on the opposite side in the case wants the witness to give him as much information as possible. The more the witness talks, the greater the likelihood that the witness will end up with foot-in-the-mouthitis. And as I discovered when I was practicing law, the best way to make a witness ramble on was to zip it myself. After asking a short question, "Tell me more about that" might be the only other contribution I'd make to the conversation.

The principle is the same with questioning a soul-mate candidate (SMC), but with a twist: you have to pitch in some info about yourself at the same time. Let's assume that you make a promising contact with an SMC. You'll ask some stock questions. If the answers are in line with your expectations, you'll have to dig carefully for more information. It is tempting to cross-examine or ask too many questions at once, which might overwhelm the SMC. To offset such a tendency, give a bit of your own answer to the questions. I call this the Ask-and-Tell (A&T) technique (see Chapter Four).

Exploring Your SMC

Use open-ended questions that can't be answered with just yes or no. For example:

"Tell me more about…"

"Help me out a bit. Could you explain more about your thought that…?"

"I'm a little slow today. I don't quite understand what you mean by…Can you clarify it a bit for me?"

Avoid being confrontational when using this technique. The following two questions ask for the same information. Notice how the first is more abrasive and might cause the SMC to become defensive.

"What do you mean when you say, 'I'm much like a kid who wants it right now'?"

"In your profile you say, 'I'm much like a kid who wants it right now.' Tell me more about this."

See how the second question is milder and gives the impression that you are more interested?

"Why" and "What do you mean" questions often come across as too blunt. "Tell me a little more about…" is a gentler approach. Or "I'm curious about…"

In response to my question, "Are you wedded to the Dallas area?" an SMC responded indignantly, "What do you mean am I wedded to the Dallas area? Where do *you* live?" My question could have been better phrased, for instance, "Do you see yourself remaining in the Dallas area permanently?" On the other hand, "I'm curious why you ask if I am wedded to the Dallas area" would have been more gracious on her part. Each of us was unnecessarily short with the other.

Whenever you discuss what you are expecting to see in your SMC, say, "The person I'm looking for will be…," rather than "I want…" Better still, "You will…"

Don't talk about your "ideal man [woman]." This sounds like your SMC must clamber up on a pedestal to meet your requirements. "A compatible man [woman]" is a better phrase.

Be complimentary if the occasion arises. Perhaps you have been discussing the general topic of health, and the SMC comes back with something that particularly pleases you. Try:

> "To go from the hypothetical to the specific, I like the way...[and then detail what you find interesting about the SMC]."

At least early in your correspondence with a particular SMC, don't feel compelled to respond immediately. Let a day or two pass. Otherwise, you may get locked into daily responses, which take time, and may hinder further search.

If you are going to be off the Internet for a while for some reason, be courteous enough to let your SMCs know. Maybe you are traveling out of town to visit one of them. Or perhaps you are off to the wilderness for a few days of solitude. You might be moving to a new home. Anytime you plan to be gone for several days, clue in your SMCs as to when they can expect further chailing.

BASIC QUESTIONS TO ASK

All of your questions should be based on the A, B, and C lists that you composed in Chapter One to identify the characteristics that you do and don't want in your SMC. You will be asking pretty much the same questions of each SMC. As we'll discuss below, it will pay to do some preparation ahead of time. I'll begin by showing how I drafted questions based on my SMC criteria. A "must" for me was a fit and trim woman who could bicycle twenty-

five to thirty miles in one day without the need of medical assistance. If an SMC's profile indicated an interest in bicycling, one of my first-round questions would be:

"How far do you bike when you go?"

Another of my must-have yardsticks was someone who was in good physical condition. This meant a "slim or athletic" body type in most instances. Occasionally an SMC would make the first move and contact me. At times, her profile was hidden from view, or it would indicate a body type other than slim or athletic. I would generally respond with as much of the following as was appropriate under the circumstances:

"We do have many tastes in common, but I am pretty active physically. So fitness is of primary interest. What do you do to keep yourself in condition? Are you happy with your weight? Do you backpack? Jog? Bicycle? Tennis? Hike? I'm not looking for a world-class athlete, but I do need someone who can share some or all of these activities with me. I've included a bit more about myself. [I would attach the text I had composed as a supplement to my profile.] Take a look. If you think we are on the same wavelength, get back to me so that I can explore more about you."

By typing this text in advance, I saved having to generate over one hundred words each time I made contact with a new SMC. And I didn't have to re-invent the paragraph over and over.

As I mentioned in Chapter Four, I divided my basic questions into four sets. The first batch went out right after an SMC responded positively to my first email contact, or when the SMC pushed out the first pawn. The second and third sets would stream off in later connections, once I had received answers to the first set. If chailing continued beyond the third email, I would gradually introduce the topics in the fourth set of questions, one or two in consecutive emails. You'll notice that in each set, there is a lot of material from the Ask-and-Tell that I spoke of earlier. Besides asking a question, I would dish up a bit of my point of view. Thus the SMC would have an idea of my own thoughts on a particular subject.

Beginning with the second set of questions I would usually lead off with a sentence or two that applied directly to the SMC's response. Then I would attach the questions and off would go email 2 (or 3, 4, and so forth, as the case might be).

As you will see, I covered a lot of ground with each set of questions. Most often, an SMC and I didn't make it beyond the first set or two. In your own opening volley, cover the most important topics. No need to continue flapping if the essentials just aren't there. If the comebacks are ambiguous, hang in there; ask more questions on the same subject until you are satisfied that it is a "go" or a "gone." Remember, this isn't an application for bagging groceries; this is dead-bang-serious interviewing. Anytime the SMC doesn't measure up right across the board, head for the next SMC.

Naturally, I would modify some of the questions depending on what was in the SMC's profile, and eliminate others if the profile already supplied the information. It is an unflattering reflection on you to have an SMC point out that the answer to your brilliant question was smack in the middle of her profile. Also, asking an SMC who displays a profile advertising two children if she has ever been married does not endear you to her. I've been there, and more than once.

You might want to use some of the following questions just as they are. Others you will need to adapt to your own situation. You will also want to add your own, of course. Start by making up a file called *Ask* in your word processing program. Save all your stock questions in that file. Cut and paste them into your email as you work.

Set One

I would start off by stating the obvious reason I was making contact: "We appear to have some tastes in common. I'm pretty active physically, so fitness is of key interest to me."

From here I would ask about whichever of my major interests didn't show up in the SMC's profile: "Do you backpack? Bicycle? Hike? Jog? What else do you do to keep yourself in condition?"

If the SMC's weight were in question, I would cover that in this first round. I would also touch on religion to determine if our ships were sailing in the same latitude.

Reading is a big part of my life, so I would get into that as well. Then I would finish up by asking about kids (if any) and past relationships. Finally, I would elicit an opinion about a controversial personality. Rush Limbaugh was my favorite personality to toss into the mix.

Set Two

In many cases, I got answers to the entire opening salvo. If not, I'd ask again. "You probably overlooked my question about..." Anything that was not clear, or that raised a yellow or red flag, I would pursue in this second set of questions. In addition, I would move on to travel, work, TV, pets, and a typical weekend. I also wanted some details on health, which is a natural A&T subject:

> "How is your health overall? Any major operations? I'm in the best condition of my life outside of my last year in college. When I was a kid, I broke my arm a couple of times. [I would go on to explain about an appendix that bit the dust when I was twenty-seven and a couple of other minor items.]
>
> "Just recently I saw some news on TV. The reporter was jogging alongside his interviewee, and having trouble staying up. The latter was a man 104 years old who ran five miles every day. I truly expect to dog his steps."

If the SMC's profile came without a photo, I would throw in a request for a picture at the end of this set.

Set Three

I began the third round by following up on any unclear answers. For new material, I'd ask how a typical weekday went for the SMC. Beyond that, I would stir in a mixed bag of questions, some of which are listed at the end of this chapter. If I had not already beaten on it at length, I would also ask more about the SMC's line of daily labor.

Set Four

The SMC and I survived round three if the answers had gone well for both of us. By now I would start to get into the B-list types of questions, the frosting-on-the-cake items in a mate that would be nice to have but were not absolutely necessary. This was also a good place to sift in more of the mixed-bag questions.

Let me emphasize again: Most of the questions you compose should address a point on the A, B, and C lists you made up in Chapter One. Others, such as "Are you pro-choice or pro-life?" will furnish clues as to whether there may be fundamental areas of disagreement that might make partnership less likely.

FOLLOW-UP QUESTIONS

Let me repeat earlier advice. When you lob questions, pay close attention to the answers that come bouncing back to you. Chase down everything that does not come across clearly. Persist. Remember the formula:

"You said…Tell me more about that."

Occasionally a baseball umpire will ask the pitcher for the ball. After scrutiny, the umpire will often toss the ball out of the game because he didn't like something he saw. So look at all the seams on the ball the SMC is serving up to you. Better to do it now than after you've moved your furniture or taken in a new boarder.

As you continue to chail with one particular SMC, you will become more specific with questions in order to decipher information the SMC provides. These new queries you will, of course, improvise as you go. But be careful to work with your Ask list to cover the basic information you *must* have from every SMC.

Don't hesitate to give as much as you get. If an SMC asks you to answer the same questions you are dishing out, do so. Maybe the SMC wants you to go first; nothing wrong with that. Just keep in mind that with all the words flying back and forth across the net (Net?), you must get your own questions answered to your satisfaction.

Frequently a question one of you asks will bring your chailing with that SMC to an abrupt adios, amigo(a). To my inquiry about some long-distance biking, one SMC frankly admitted, "That's not my cup of tea. Ta ta, and good luck in your search."

Remember that most of the SMCs you chail with will fall by the wayside for one reason or another. Just keep on chugging ahead.

WHAT TO TELL ABOUT YOURSELF

You're starting to get some tugs on your line. At the same time, you are un-reeling questions to get a better look at who is on the other end. You have taken your time to prepare your questions carefully based on the lists you made up from Chapter One. No need to wing it or shoot from the hip. But now your SMCs are going to want to know more about the person on the other end of *their* line.

At an Irish banquet, the host introduced the guest speaker as "Sean Foley, who made a million dollars in real estate." Foley came to the podium and began:

> "First, let me set a couple of details straight. I didn't make a million dollars in real estate; it was in lumber. And it wasn't a million; it was only $400,000. Also, I didn't make it; I lost it. Moreover, it didn't happen to me; it was my brother-in-law."

Foley wanted to clarify the record. You also will want to be clear to your SMCs about yourself.

Over time, you are likely to chail with a great number of SMCs. If you are on the catching end of the inquiry, tell it like you really feel it. Don't pull any punches; don't try to guess what the SMC wants to hear. The soul mate for you will want to hear what comes directly from your heart without embellishment. Otherwise you have the wrong SMC.

Avoid stream-of-consciousness messages with lots of ellipses (...). This style confuses a reader and gives the impression that you are unable to complete your thoughts or that you are taking a stab at being mysterious. Your messages are sales tools. Use them wisely. Say what you will, but do it clearly and succinctly. You have only words to convey your personality; verve doesn't count until you both get together over bagels.

Some of your SMCs might not ask many questions of you. Regardless, you will want to tell them certain things about how you have been swimming along. You can save a great deal of wear and tear on your fingertips by preparing in advance short chunks of information about yourself, the inside scoop about the real You.

Save these literary gems in a file, ready and waiting. Entitle your file, *Tell,* and include the topics suggested below. At the right moment, copy the appropriate chunks and paste them into an email.

For instance, if you scout much beyond the city limits, inevitably SMCs will question why you are ranging so far afield. Lana, fifty-eight, asked after my first email, "Do you realize I'm in North Carolina?"

I wanted to get the message across that I was serious, and not on email just looking to fill in the time between soaps. My standard response to a question that implied a distance barrier was:

> "The distance from me to you depends much on the mode of travel. Donkey is more demanding than jet. I have a very good idea of a com-

patible woman. While it would be nice if she turned up in my neighborhood, realistically that probably won't happen. So I'm not limiting my search geographically. But neither am I looking for a pen pal."

Every time the question popped up, I just copied that paragraph out of my *Tell* file and sent it along with the rest of my deathless prose.

Meshing the Big Gears

Let's take a look at the major-league topics that you and your SMC both will want to backhoe. Some are areas of lesser importance, but all are in the relationship maker/breaker division.

WORK

If the profile gives no clue, ask:

"If you work, what field are you in?"

Otherwise ask for more detail:

"Tell me more about your work as a [whatever]."

If your SMC doesn't work, you'll want to know his or her means of support. Is the SMC getting welfare, unemployment, support from an ex-spouse? All of these sources of revenue can dry up abruptly, then what? One SMC, for example, was living on monthly alimony from an ex-husband who was sixty-two and in poor health.

If the SMC is not working, handle the matter delicately, saying something such as, "If your support ends, what have you planned for the future? Do you have some long-range goals?"

When I mentioned to one SMC that I owned a company, she asked: "Tell me more about the company you own. How many partners do you have, if any? What is your particular job specifically?"

If you appear to have a workaholic on your hands, and that isn't a card you want in your deck, you might say: "I'm curious about how you plan to work on reducing the long hours you work." Read the answer closely. One woman told me that she planned to hire an assistant and cut back on her hours. Three months later, the assistant had not materialized. Neither had the plan moved off dead center. Bear in mind that certain professionals, both male and female, tend to marry their work.

Prepare a short paragraph or two about what you do to keep the wolf from the door. If you do it well, don't hesitate to say so. But do it in an enthusiastic, rather than an arrogant, manner. If you like your job, let your SMC in on the secret. For instance, I wrote:

> "I didn't even think of becoming a lawyer until late in my thirties. I worked as an engineer days and went to law school nights. In all, I've had more than fifty jobs. Until I became a lawyer, I never stayed at one of them more than two years. My philosophy was…"

Melia, forty-seven, of Phoenix, said:

> "I've been an independent insurance agent for more than twenty years now. This was originally my uncle's business. I worked with him to learn the ropes for a few years. When he retired, it was a natural for me to keep it going. I love it."

From Indonesia, Jody, thirty-seven, expressed her enthusiasm for her job. She didn't go into a lot of yawny detail, but she got the message across in one short paragraph that she liked what she was doing:

> "I am a health teacher/counselor in an international school in Jakarta, where I teach the children of the American employees. I love it! Also, I don't mind getting a two-and-a-half-month summer vacation, a long winter vacation, and two weeks in the spring. I've been doing this for three years, but this is my last, as I long for home turf."

Randy, thirty-nine, in Los Angeles, shed more light on a job that he clearly enjoys:

"My background is in anthropology, with a major in archaeology. I work for a large environmental consulting firm as an SME, subject matter expert. The firm's major client is the Department of Defense. It is my job to…This means extensive travel all over the United States.…I've been with the company for eleven years.…[I] can't really see myself ever wanting to go elsewhere. The work is interesting, as is the fact that I always get to go first-class all the way."

Anita, fifty-seven, in Sacramento talks about a job that doesn't enthrall her, but she does so in a positive way. She tells us how she will use the job experience as a stepping stone to better things:

"I've been a successful real estate broker for many years, but I'm tiring of hauling customers around in my car—especially in the wintertime. I've been taking classes in escrow practices, which will lead me into this field. A good friend of mine owns an escrow company and has already offered me a nice position. My background will give me a better understanding of what has to be done when. If necessary, I can nudge the agents at the right time."

I wrote the following to an SMC who felt that her work schedule might conflict with my lighter one:

"I'm not looking for a woman who can start cruising around the world with me, or who is home all day long to keep me company. Happiness is someone who can go off after work for an hour or two of hiking or bike riding, and take an occasional three-day weekend to camp out."

RELIGIOUS VIEWS

Here is a definite A&T area. Cover this right up front to determine if there is a basic conflict. My religious inclinations are faint at best. I accept others' beliefs as long as they make no attempt to inflict those beliefs on me. If a potential SMC expressed firm convictions about any given religion, I proceeded to the next SMC. If there was little or no indication in the profile, I would ask. At the same time, I told.

"To what degree does your religious preference influence your life?...[I inserted a sentence about my present religious view.] I was raised a Catholic, but most memories revolve around the nuns rapping me on the knuckles when I could not remember the catechism. That, and the interminable time Christmas Mass used to take (we kids couldn't open our presents until afterwards)."

I was asking indirectly, "How religious are you?" By expressing my own feelings, with a bit of true humor, I was hoping to make my question more palatable to an SMC.

In the response, I looked for involvement with a church (or the equivalent). One woman wrote:

"I'm not very religious, more spiritual than anything else. I do like to sing in the church choir, however, and I help out at various functions. I have quite a few friends who go to the same church."

What I gathered from the description was that this woman had religious friends. The social atmosphere at times would probably become a trifle uncomfortable for the agnostic or atheist. Although the woman herself might refrain from influencing my thoughts and beliefs, there was no guarantee that her friends would be similarly restrained. This atmosphere could very well prove to be a barrier if your religious tendencies are tepid.

On the other hand, if you have an inclination toward a particular religion, you will want positive answers from the SMC. The following would be appropriate:

"I have a strong feeling for [whatever religion], and it is a daily part of my life. Tell me your thoughts on [the religion]. Are you involved in any way with [church or whatever] activities?"

Phyllis, fifty-six, beat me to the punch on this issue:

"How do you feel about religion? I am quite involved with the [name of church] and would be comfortable only with someone who has the same abiding love for the Lord that I do."

Julie, forty-one, in Boston, explained to me:

"I belong to the local Presbyterian church, though I rarely attend. Occasionally I help out with bake sales and things like that."

Petra, fifty-four, in Buffalo:

> "Not too long ago, I went to the local Catholic church with a friend. I hadn't been for over thirty years and was amazed at how the Mass has changed. I'm more spiritual than anything else, so it is apt to be another thirty years before I go again."

Albert, twenty-seven, in Scottsdale:

> "All my life I have been very active in church affairs. The woman I'm looking for must feel the same way and be willing to donate some time to do the same thing."

MARITAL STATUS

Don't assume that everyone trolling around on a matchmaking site is single. Many disclose the fact that they are married and are looking for additional tête-à-têtes. Clear up this issue quickly before you waste time: "Have you been married? If so, when did your marriage end?"

Once you have pinned down that your SMC is not married, follow up by finding out what happened: "What caused your [marriage or relationship] to end?"

Once again, read the answers closely. Does the SMC accept any of the blame? Does the story ring true? Is the SMC over the ordeal? Follow up with questions if anything is not clear.

Pam, fifty-four, came right to the point:

> "I've been married twice. Once for five years, the second time for ten years. I was divorced both times, the last two years ago. I'm still friends with both ex's."

RELATIONSHIPS

You want to know when an SMC came off a marriage, but you also need to know when the last relationship ended. Assure yourself that it has been long enough since that relationship that the last flame is not still aflicker in your SMC's mind. Anything less than a year could be a yellow flag. Perhaps the SMC is still hoping to resume the previous relationship? Is it finally over? Begin by asking, "How long ago did your last significant relationship end?"

I once dated a widow for a short period whose husband had died just one year previously. She felt she needed to date, but she admitted that she and her husband had been very close during their twenty-five-year marriage. He turned out to be competition I couldn't overcome.

Roger, a fifty-two-year-old widower, flew a yellow flag by asking in his profile:

> "Soooooo you ask why is this guy available?...[I'm a] widower [who] lost my lady twelve years ago after she/we fought leukemia for three years....We had a good relationship and I'm ready now to find someone who is looking for a heads-up guy."

Twelve years is a long stretch. If you were interested in Roger you might want to ask him early on: "Tell me about any meaningful relationships you've had since your wife passed away."

Occasionally you will run into an SMC who detests all past partners (including ex-spouses). That SMC may not like you any better. Find out what went wrong so you can avoid stepping into an emotional morass. Often a simple, "What happened?" brings a wealth of detail.

No breakup is all one-sided. Don't be reluctant to accept some of the responsibility. When I asked Lisa, thirty-nine, in Little Rock, what went wrong in her marriage, she explained:

> "We were way too young when we married. Neither of us had the tools to make a marriage work. Both of us were too embarrassed to seek help. We just gradually drifted apart without hardly knowing it. After a while, I don't think even professional help would have done us any good. After the kids were grown, we realized that we had nothing left in common."

Elizabeth, forty-one, in Trenton:

> "Dieter and I just sort of ran out of steam after seventeen years. He became absorbed in his work, and I in mine. He was also manic-depressive and would go through periods when if I did the slightest thing wrong, he would sulk for days. We never fought, but in the end we hardly spoke to one another. We became strangers."

Norma, forty-eight, in Honolulu:

"I met my first husband at the School of Nursing, where he taught Anatomy and Physiology. Even on our honeymoon, I was upset because I knew I had made a mistake. We couldn't communicate well from the start. He hated change and was obsessed with prevention. He kept trying to anticipate anything that could go wrong. I welcomed change and wanted adventure."

Wilma, sixty-two, in Philadelphia:

"During the divorce period, I met an attorney who seemed to offer me the security I craved, and we married. He had been abused as a child and wanted a wife he could possess, and who would mother him. He abused me in every way possible. He threatened me with guns, fire, and beatings. I found a counselor who helped me pull myself away from his control. We were divorced in 1995."

Jason, fifty, in Salt Lake City:

"When I was twenty-eight, the gal who was going to be my wife, I got her pregnant. I was at that stage of life where I had the urge to get married, so I figured why not? She was a good woman, and we stayed married for eighteen years, but once the kids were out of the house, we both got bored with each other. The divorce was pretty easy on both of us."

SEX AND RELATIONSHIPS

When chailing gets further along with a particular SMC, you'll want to exchange views on sex and thoughts about relationships. Leave surprises to teenagers.

If your whoopee interests are dissimilar, discuss your thoughts and feelings openly. Come to an understanding to eliminate "I have a headache" and "I'm really tired tonight" from your respective lexicons. Good literature on this topic has proliferated. Be aware of this issue; discuss it early on. Explore each other's enjoyment druthers.

Here's an easy way to bring up the subject: "Where and how do you feel sex fits into a relationship?"

Some nuggets:

Angelo, fifty-nine, in Providence:

> "Not that sex isn't an important part of a relationship for me; it's just down the list a bit in priority. A woman has to have sex appeal for me. So it *is* on the list of necessary items, just not at the top by any means. After all, you can only spend so much time in bed."

Harriet, thirty-nine, in Bowling Green:

> "I don't look to develop a friendship with a man and wait to see if it will go deeper. I would only start a relationship if I felt there was the potential for it to be an enduring one. I'm well past the stage of thinking, 'This is THE ONE.' But I have to feel this *could* be 'THE ONE,' and take it from there. Sex is definitely not at the top of the list."

Melissa, thirty-eight, in Jackson:

> "Fortunately, I'm not looking for nurturing, active or passive. Not that I'd refuse a pat on the cheek and a consoling, 'Don't worry, everything will work out' when days are longer than they should be. But that's in the nature of support and should be an integral part of a relationship. I anticipate an equal partner, neither a father nor a son. One of each is enough."

CHILDREN

If you plan on making children part of your mutual portfolio, check to ensure that you and your SMC are in accord. "Do you want [more] children? If so, how many?"

If one of you cannot have any children for some reason, that information should be brought to light early on. In such a case, you might inquire, "What are your thoughts about adoption?"

Also exchange ideas about raising children: "Tell me how you feel children should be raised."

If the SMC seems reluctant to volunteer the information, follow up with, "How would you discipline children? How were you disciplined as a kid?"

A related question in this area will give you an element for comparison: "Tell me about your childhood. What are your fondest memories?"

If there are or were siblings, you might ask, "How did you get along with your [sibling(s)]?"

As an example of a response to this question, Jeanine, fifty-three, of Rutland, admitted:

"In my early youth, I remember slinging an ax at my sister. More correctly, I slid it across the ice at her. She was seven years old and forty feet away, which afforded her the agility and plenty of time to dance out of the way. Other than that, she and my brother have been on my best friends list for many, many years."

If your SMC's answers seem to be at variance with his or her thoughts on raising and disciplining children, explore the disparities carefully.

"You mentioned that you would [whatever the SMC said about discipline]. It seems that your parents raised you quite differently. Most people tend to raise kids the way they were raised themselves. I'm curious as to why you are taking a different approach than your parents did."

If your SMC gets bristly about any of these questions, that in itself may very well be a red flag to look into: "You seem upset with my question about [whatever]. I don't know why. After all, I'm just trying to see if we are both tuned in to the same station."

Children from a previous marriage can be a joy, but they are also potential hurdles. Adult children can also be problematic. So find out if children beyond college age are living at home with your SMC. If so, why?

Adult children come in three flavors: those residing with your SMC, those living reasonably close by, and those at a distance. The first fall into three subheadings: students, those with jobs, and those without.

If the adult child is a resident of the SMC's household, investigate whether the stay is permanent or only temporary. "Is your daughter planning to move to a place of her own? Does she have a job nearby?"

Some older children may still be going to school. One SMC had a thirty-one-year-old son whom I met. He was working on a second doctorate and had been in college for over twelve years. There was no sign that he intended to vacate his childhood bedroom anytime in the near future.

Frieda, forty-eight, met a charming man with a twenty-four-year-old daughter living at home with a young child from a failed marriage. The relationship went well, but Frieda sensed that the daughter regarded her as an intruder and as competition for her father's affection. Frieda invited the daughter for coffee, and at the end of a long discussion she found that they had several interests in common. By the time Frieda moved in a few months later, the daughter had stopped seeing Frieda as a rival and welcomed her as a friend.

I spent a lot of years with a fine lady whose three children had a proclivity for calling her in the wee hours of the morning, asking her to post bail in varying amounts. She always got out of bed immediately and rushed to comply. This posed difficulties for me. Thus, indications of adult-child dependence waved a red flag for me. Though it may not necessarily be one for you, be aware of this potential relationship breaker.

Caroline, fifty-five, had a twenty-nine-year-old son living with her who had "scads of computer equipment just all over." The son had a girlfriend, but I gathered the girlfriend was not willing to support him. He paid no rent, as it turned out, although he did adjust and repair Mom's computer whenever necessary.

Christine, fifty-six, told me that her son Alan *and* his girlfriend lived with her. I asked quite straightforwardly, "Do they pay you rent? Is this sort of a permanent thing, or are they on their way to someplace else?"

Her tangential reply:

"Alan is having some difficulty finding himself. I feel that I can best give him support until he decides what he wants to do in life."

Hello, red flag. Most of us have to hustle up a job while we ponder this mystery of finding our way. Neither Alan nor his squeeze was visibly employed; how much time and effort Alan devoted to studying his compass for a direction was left up in the air.

If there are adult offspring close by, how often do they visit? If the off-spring, in turn, have progeny of their own, is the SMC pressed into service as a babysitter? If so, how often? If the adults are out of the area, how much telephone contact takes place? Who calls whom; what is the telephone bill apt to look like after a month's wear and tear? Finally, you should explore the parent-child bond if the children are not living at home. You might ask:

"How do you get along with your kids? How often do you see them?"

One SMC had a special bike trip planned for the weekend. When I later asked her how it went, she replied:

"The bike ride did not happen for me last weekend. I ended up spending the night in San Clemente with some friends, and then took dinner to my son and his wife who were packing up to move. Typically, my plans usually are tenuous, and subject to change, especially if I'm needed—old habit."

Anticipate that this woman may have a tendency to put herself last so she can be there for her son whenever she perceives the need to do so.

Regardless of where an adult child might live, consider the odds of that child's wanting to move back home. On occasion, a past love and I gave shelter and board to all three of her children at one time or another. Wives or girlfriends moved in as well, often for lengthy stays. Children of various ages came and went as part of the bundle.

Spend some time ferreting out your SMC's thoughts about kids. Children from a previous marriage, both yours and those of an SMC, can present some difficulties. We'll talk further about getting the whole tribe together later in the next chapter.

PETS

Pets can provide a fertile area of contention that could undermine an otherwise good relationship. Get the topic out in the open: "Do you have pets?"

And the follow-up questions for cats and dogs: "Where do they sleep?" Miss Boots or Fido may share your SMC's bedroll. Find out up front. If a cat or dog now sleeps in the same bed with your potential SMC, will this be acceptable to all when the bed has another occupant? Also, pets have fleas. And they have accidents on the floor occasionally. Whichever side of the picture you are on, check it out. At the same time, slip your own views into the picture: "I've always owned cats [dogs, lizards, tarantulas, boa constrictors, whatever]. What are your feelings about pets?" Or if pets are not your bag: "My lifestyle hasn't lent itself to having pets. What are your ideas about this?"

Sara, forty-one, of Portland goes one step further:

> "I always want to know where a man gets his dog. I pick up a stray from time to time, or cruise the pound when I need a dog. One man I corresponded with for a time sounded like it was beneath him to have less than a purebred. He had a Boxer and a Doberman, each complete with sliced ears and a cut-off tail. That's not me; I go for the mutts."

To many people, including me, pets are like children. At the time of this writing, my companions are Peanut, a five-year-old husky-lab mix (fifty-five pounds), and Annie, a sixteen-year-old Australian shepherd weighing in at forty-five pounds. An attractive SMC who shared many of my interests flew this red flag in her second email:

> "I don't want the responsibility of caring for a pet. The only living thing that occupies my home now (besides me) is a self-watering plant on the windowsill. If I want to go away on a trip, all I have to do is cover it with a plastic bag. You can't do that with a dog."

So true. But my joy was to her just a responsibility that she couldn't put a plastic bag over.

You or your SMC may have an older dog, and thus you both may be aware of the time and effort that one must devote to easing the later life of a pet: "How old is your [whatever]?" And if Rover has a few extra miles on the odometer: "Does he or she need special care?"

Suzanne, thirty-three, of Raleigh, told me:

> "I once had an old dog who had cataracts, and gradually went blind. My friends kept telling me I should put him to sleep. He was a lot of work, but didn't seem to mind that he was blind. In the car, he would stick his head out the window just like he knew what was passing by. I cried for days when he finally died. He had been my buddy from my teens."

A cat may not take to one of you. Or vice versa. Time may or may not overcome this aversion. Birds are messy, but to the aviarist, this is just part and parcel of such ownership.

Sean, thirty-three, in El Paso:

"A past girlfriend owned a green parrot named Houdini. He would bill and coo on her shoulder and take tidbits of food from her mouth. I got nothing but growls and a sharp beak. My girlfriend said this meant that a male at some time had abused Houdini. I could understand fully."

Someone must care for and clean up after all pets, from dogs to turtles. This can become a joint effort, or it can detract from your relationship. Does Bowser clean up dinner dishes? Does Bootsie the puddytat jump up on the table to reconnoiter? Does Houdini get to fly around the house, leaving evidence where he will? Find out:

"Does Bowser get to clean dishes for you?"

"Does Bootsie ever get up on the table to scout the territory?"

"Do you ever let Houdini out of his cage to fly around?"

What about the disciplining of pets? Development of character to one man is cruelty to another. To me, rubbing a pet's nose in its own excrement to "teach him a lesson" is an inane practice that says more about the rubber than the rubbee; others disagree. "Kicking the dog" is not just a figure of speech. A fleeting acquaintance of mine owned a German shepherd who had tangled with a porcupine for a second time. The man left the dog all afternoon with quills imbedded to teach him not to do that again. I'm certain the nexus between cause and effect was largely lost on the poor dog.

Know what sort of a pet situation you are getting into. Question whether the arrangement will present problems for you or your SMC. Can you both live with the status quo? If neither of you have pets, discuss acquiring them in the future, including what breed.

Sheila, thirty, of New York City, shared this adventure with me:

"I had met this guy Ed for coffee a couple of times, and then agreed to play some tennis with him. We went back to his house afterward, and what does he have for a pet but a boa constrictor. I almost died. Then he told me that on Sundays he would let the thing get in bed with him. I couldn't get out of there fast enough. That was the end of Ed and his playmate for me."

Corinne, thirty-six, of Detroit, wrote:

"I have a Chow, Shelly, who is a great protector, but sometimes she carries it too far. If I have someone for company who is afraid of dogs, Shelly will sense that. She will growl and snap, and do her best to intimidate."

Barbara, forty-eight, of St. Louis, wrote:

"I think dogs can teach us all about what unconditional love means. When you give them the care, attention, and affection they need, deserve, and demand, the rewards back from them are tenfold."

Jacqueline, fifty-five, in Dover, chimed in:

"I think dogs by nature are more loving than humans, and I know if I had one, my heart would be his. I don't have one because I worry about leaving him alone and confined all day simply because I want to work and have a pet too. The poor thing is at the mercy of his owner."

My response in this particular case was:

"I agree with you about leaving a dog alone. That's why for the last fifteen years I've always had *two* dogs, so that each would be company for the other. They travel with me also. I had the backseat taken out of my VW, and reconfigured it so that each has her own level. It's like a home away from home for them. In fact, if I stay at a motel, they refuse to come in; they prefer to sleep in the car."

Mike, forty-three, in Charleston, told of an enlightening experience:

"[An SMC] owned three greyhounds. We walked our respective pooches one afternoon. The neighbors must have thought the circus had come to town. We weren't even close on the care and feeding of five dogs, however, so that was that."

Judy, forty-four, in Kansas City, candidly admitted:

"I like dogs, but I'm not really into owning them. I look at them like grandchildren: great for a day, but also great that they go someplace else at night."

PHYSICAL FITNESS

Although an SMC might list activities such as bicycling and hiking, explore the extent of his or her engagement with that sport: you'll want to see if you both have the same viewpoints about what dosage is fun. Widely disparate abilities or inclinations can discourage both you and your SMC. Being unable to keep up or having to back off can be a drag.

> "Tell me more about your [activity—bicycling, for example]. How far do you go, and how often? Same for [hiking, backpacking, for example]. What else do you do to keep yourself fit?"

If you wish to convey the reverse sentiment, that no sports fanatics need apply, the following comment might be appropriate to add:

> "Although I enjoy these activities, they don't rule my life. I treat them as fun, rather than as tasks that must be performed with regularity."

Jennifer, thirty-three, in Detroit:

> "I used to bicycle until I fell during a triathlon. I gave my bike away. I have not backpacked in a long time. Enjoy tennis and jogging and hit a golf ball once in a while."

Jan, twenty-nine, a nurse in Hartford:

> "I get in plenty of walking at work, so at the end of the day I'm ready to sit down with a good book. I have a bicycle, but rarely use it, and then only around a couple of blocks at a time."

Jack, thirty-one, in Albany:

> "If I go more than two days without some sort of workout, I don't feel good about myself."

Sheila, thirty-four, in Duluth:

> "I'm sitting down at work most of the day, so I need my time in at the gym. I usually do about forty-five minutes and then wrap up with a shower. On the weekends, I sometimes go for a walk afterward, and then shower at home."

HEALTH

This is unquestionably an A&T area. Be certain that you are not inadvertently applying for a caretaker position.

> "How is your health overall? Any major operations? I...,"

And then go on to briefly tell what's been happening on your medical chart. Don't be dreary. If you had an operation of significance, no need to draw pictures. Say it and move on:

> "Ten years ago I had a hysterectomy. Haven't even had a cold since."

If there is an ongoing ailment that you must deal with, cough it up:

Sandy, forty, in Richmond:

> "I was in an auto accident some years ago and injured my spine. It is difficult for me to sit for extended periods."

Joe, forty-one, in Mobile:

> "A couple of years ago I was diagnosed with diabetes. I changed my diet at the doctor's suggestion and have it pretty well under control now."

Sharon, forty-two, in Australia:

"I was in a car accident three years ago and have not completely left my wheelchair behind. Probably because of the lack of exercise, my blood pressure has gone up. I used to play tennis, but arthritis in my fingers makes it difficult to hold the racquet anymore. I am working on all these things, however."

Mary Lou, fifty-four, in Colorado:

"I have some degenerating discs in my neck and also some bone spurs from an auto accident a couple of years ago. They are really giving me lots of problems right now, and I don't think that running, especially on the asphalt, is helping at all."

WEIGHT

Occasionally you will be clueless about your SMC's poundage, so ask:

"What does the scale say to you on a good day?"

"What is your normal weight? Are you in normal mode right now?"

One SMC wrote me back,

"My scale is not talking to me right now. Silence is golden."

I appreciated the candid humor, but it was a red flag for me that eliminated that candidate. Another woman admitted that she was five feet three and "135 pounds *or so.*" When I met her, she had interpreted *or so* quite casually.

If, on the other hand, *your* scale has taken the vow of silence, you might say:

"I'm not apt to blow away in a strong wind. How do you feel about [full-bodied women or hefty men]?"

CONTROVERSIAL TOPICS

Questions like the following will bring you interesting answers, some of which may constitute red or green flags for you:

"What are your feelings about homosexuality?"

"What are your thoughts about [any minority group—blacks, Asians, Mexicans, and so forth]?"

"What do you think of Dr. Kevorkian?"

"How do you feel about coming and going: abortion and the death penalty?"

"What are your thoughts on legalizing marijuana?"

If you get an answer that conflicts with your personal feelings, it doesn't necessarily mean you should automatically reach for the Delete button. For years I had a close friend whose views on the matter of homosexuality diametrically opposed mine. We agreed to avoid discussing this topic; it worked. So explore further when you clash on a controversial point.

Too many people parrot the opinions of others. I've found the quickest way to unearth this particular fault is to ask about a well-known controversial personality: "What is your opinion of Rush Limbaugh [Howard Stern, Gloria Steinem, and so forth]?"

Betsy fifty-four, in San Francisco, responded to my third degree by stating:

> "There is one little thing we had better find out first, before continuing what is appearing to be a promising correspondence, and that is the little matter of Rush Limbaugh. A more obnoxious and odious person has not been born, unless it is Jesse Helms. I was actually appalled once a number of years ago that I agreed with one thing he said. I do not recall what it was, but it was buried by the rest of his (here insert the expletives of your choice). Now you have an idea of where I stand on Rush. Where are you with this? Is it curtains for us?"

I respected that she evidently based her opinion on her own observations. In response I asked:

> "Let me ask you a different question. Would you truly forgo a relationship simply because a potential partner had a different viewpoint on

some aspect of politics? What else can rub you the wrong way besides La Limbaugh? Do you have a temper at times?"

Whenever I received a strong reply such as "He's a total jerk," I would come back with:

"I'm curious about your thoughts on Rush Limbaugh. Have you heard him on the radio or TV? Or have you read something he's written?"

Jane, thirty-two, in Omaha, gave me her candid reflections:

"Most people I know think he is either the new messiah or a poltroon. I've listened to Limbaugh three or four times and seen him on TV once or twice. I've also read a bit of his writing. Some of what he says makes sense; some seems to be much ado about nothing. Personally, I don't know what the fuss is all about one way or the other."

FAULTS

A bit of soul-searching is in order, because this is definitely an A&T area. Meaningful answers will follow if you give a little of yourself up front. Here was my approach:

"What would you say are your weaknesses? Not being a ten, I have a few. First, I have a tendency to be optimistic about how much I can cram into a day. The result at times is arriving someplace (often breathless) just at the last moment. Second…"

Noreen, forty-eight, in Denver:

"I have had a tendency to attach less importance to my partner's activities than to mine. I was riding with a friend not too long ago and we went past a section of a river where there are a lot of birds. My friend has always been fascinated by bird life. When she wanted to stop and use her binoculars to look over our feathered friends, I waited and was not ungracious about it, but I would rather have been riding along. Undoubtedly that urgency came across. Instead I could easily have passed maybe five more minutes discussing birds, and it would have added immensely to her enjoyment of the trip."

Dan, thirty-eight, in Houston:

"Sometimes I'm carelessly inconsiderate in small ways. For example, with my girlfriend I would come home and immediately turn down the TV. I should first have discussed the fact that I thought it was too loud. We did clear it up later, but I should have thought of the effect my action would have on her. So I don't do things like this deliberately or because I refuse to change; I just don't think at times."

This sort of an exchange would usually come along after chailing had progressed fairly well. Whatever your own frailties might be, tell them like they are. If you intend to change yourself, explain how. Otherwise your SMC must take you as you are, warts and all.

PET PEEVES

Everyone has them; trot them out on both sides. Find out right quick what your SMC *doesn't* like in a partner: "What irritates you in a [man or woman]?"

Pay attention to the answers, because small irritants can easily undermine even strong relationships. Are you guilty of doing what the SMC deplores? For example, I wear sunscreen every day. I once had a lady friend who had white bath towels. It was obvious when the sunscreen survived the shower. My forgetfulness caused an unnecessary annoyance. Enough of these small items, and your relationship will suffer the fate of a stone canoe.

TRAVEL

If travel is on your wish list, ask: "Where have you traveled?"

Seventy-five percent of all Americans are born and die in their hometown. I once worked in a small town forty-five miles away from Boston. One of the workers, Harry, enjoyed minor celebrity status for having visited Boston once (he didn't like it and never returned). Whenever a worker in the plant would refer to Harry, it would inevitably come out as, "Harry—you know, who's been to Boston."

Let's assume that you and your SMC are in accord over travel. In what fashion? Your SMC may look askance at your plan to tour the country in a motor home, or by bicycle, and may prefer taking Amtrak. A leisurely drive to Cabo San Lucas at the tip of Baja California is not in the same league as getting there on your friendly cruise ship. Or by walking the shoreline, pack on back. You might ask:

> "What forms of travel are your favorites? Have you ever considered [biking in Europe, hiking in the Himalayas, a walking tour of Ireland, whatever appeals to you]?"

How you get there is only part of the picture. The other is how you go about local discovery once you arrive. I prefer to make my own way and pick my own sights. Tour packages are not on my wish list. Neither are rental cars for the most part; my druthers lean toward train, bus, and two-wheeled locomotion. Ask: "How do you feel about going with tour groups?"

Another factor is the region you wish to grace with your presence. A lady friend of mine cared little for the bustling air of the local Costco. She would not do well in a bazaar in Calcutta, nor in downtown Mexico City. I for one would be hesitant to expose myself to encounters with the large crawly things (with and without legs) that inhabit portions of Africa. Find out your SMC's thoughts by asking:

> "How do you feel about travel in [Mexico, the Orient, the interior of Africa, or wherever]?"

A closely related issue is whether you and your SMC think alike about weather conditions. Linda regularly rides her bike in Oregon rain, and she would think nothing of such touring in Ireland. Ute became used to the eighty-degree weather that Oahu serves up. She was comfortable with nineties in Jordan but has had to adapt to the relatively chilliness of San Diego's sixties and seventies.

If you have travel plans, lay them out for reaction:

"I plan to do some bicycling in Europe this summer. A cruise to Alaska is in the works for next year. After that I would like to do some trekking in Nepal. Do any of these activities interest you?"

Louise, fifty, in Fort Lauderdale:

"I have absolutely no urge to go anyplace where I ever have to put on more than a light sweater. Places that advertise snow will miss the opportunity to advertise me even as a visitor."

That definitely eliminated the plateau of Tibet.

So although you may agree with an SMC that travel is in your future, make sure you are both reading from the same brochure.

A TYPICAL DAY

Generally, you and your SMC will want to know each other's daily agenda. You might ask a prospective SMC:

"How does a typical weekday go for you? What time do your feet generally hit the floor?"

Todd, forty-eight, in San Francisco gave his version:

"I'm usually up by six or six-thirty. I do half an hour of weight work and hit the road for work by 8:45. At noon, I usually brown-bag it in the park right across the street. I usually don't get home until about six, which is when I catch up on the news from the paper. Dinner anywhere from seven to nine. After supper I often piece a jigsaw puzzle, play my keyboard (strictly amateur), or maybe write a letter. Ideally, I'm in bed with a good book by ten-thirty or so."

A Typical Weekend

On the weekend, is your SMC off to the beach or the mountains, or is yard work the agenda? Does work intrude into a weekend that you see as a time for rest and relaxation? Find out: "How do you typically spend a weekend?"

An SMC who enjoys the weekend will generally supply details. Vagueness may indicate that the SMC hangs around with little to do or works too much. Craig, forty-nine, in Albany, gave a look:

> "This weekend I did a little work on our Web site and caught up on some computer courses I'm taking over the Internet. Went to the bagel shop and did the *NY Times* crossword puzzle (flailed away at it, that is), jogged a couple of miles over to get my mail. Took all the shelves out of the refrigerator and washed it (annual bath), did a little flower watering, and a few minor things around the house. Walked the dog, washed him and the car, tightened a couple of bolts on the latter, made dinner for the two of us, and retired with some books.

Mariella, forty-six, in San Diego:

> "On Saturday a friend and I packed a lunch and took off for a hike up San Clement Canyon. It was about ten miles round-trip. That evening we both went to a little Mexican restaurant in Coronado for dinner and took in a movie. On Sunday mornings I stay in bed with the paper for a few hours. After, I did hair stuff, and then went to the library. In the evening, there was a Japanese dance group performing, and it was free, so I figured why not? That was about it for the day."

FINANCES

Early in my marriage I boasted, "No wife of mine will ever have to work." Two children later, I recognized the hastiness of my bravado. When my former wife broached the idea of going back to work, I was enthusiastically supportive.

Financial questions come down the line a bit, generally after you have met your SMC face-to-face. If it seems to be a take to that point, talk about money. And you have to give when you are tiptoeing around in this pasture.

> "How much do you earn? Are you able to save? My salary is $————, and I have a little income (about $200 a month net) from a small rental house I own. Usually I put the rental income into savings."

> "Do you have a particular financial goal?"

Closely related is this question:

"How much do you owe? I have a MasterCard that I pay off each month, and a car payment of $300 a month. Beyond that all I have is my [rent, house payment] of $———— a month."

For sure, don't leave this next one up in the air, because there are many ways to deal with such a hot potato. This issue becomes particularly important if both partners plan to provide income one way or another.

"In a relationship, how do you think the money should be handled? You know, like paying the bills, buying things for the home, shelling out for travel and entertainment, and so forth?"

Continue on to discuss pension plans, life insurance, and other security blankets.

Another touchy one is arrangements for grown children. If things really work out for the best, do you become part of your soul mate's will? If this is of importance to you, ask.

"If we make a permanent thing of this, how would you suggest we handle our wills, given that [I, you, or we, depending on the circumstance] have children?"

POLITICS

Whatever the extent of your passion for politics, sound out your SMC—not that you are going to change someone's errant philosophy. But if your views are mismatched, at least you can assess whether the gulf is acceptable. I once telephoned an SMC and mentioned Bill Clinton. "That bum" was the beginning of a tedious harangue about Clinton's moral character. Although she was pretty much on course, I didn't have enough interest in Bill's after-hours recreational pursuits to get into a discussion. Unfortunately, the SMC then proceeded to dissect the Senate, giving her views on the licentiousness that prevailed in that august body. Again, maybe her comments were not far off the mark, but they were simply not of interest to me. That was our one and only conversation.

Here are a few questions that may elicit political emotions:

"How do you feel about our president?"

"How are you going to vote [in such and such an election or on such and such an issue]?"

"Who do think the first woman president will be?"

"Which party do you lean toward?"

DINING

Are we talking pizza and beer or tofu and salad on a regular basis? Check the refrigerator. I wanted a woman who could, and liked to, cook. A disinclination for kitchen duty was not an eliminator, but it was an easy topic for an SMC to address in the first round. I also wanted to let it be known that I didn't eat everything out of a can or the microwave. I wrote:

> "If you cook, what are some of your favorite dishes? If you don't cook, do you eat out or call Domino's frequently? I dine out rarely, as I prefer company when I do so. As I don't date for the sake of dating, most of my meals are at home. I make my own meatless spaghetti sauce, and do a lot of pasta, chicken, and fish. For the most part, I have quite a varied menu, and I enjoy the fruit of my limited talents. What do you like to eat if you are not doing the cooking?"

Danielle, forty-one, in Montreal:

> "My grandmother taught me how to cook, and she was a wonder. I'm not in her class, but I can still bake up a storm when the occasion calls for it. Or even when it doesn't. I enjoy being in the kitchen and having a man alongside, tasting as I work."

LEISURE TIME AND HOBBIES

In your profile, you will make reference to the activities you enjoy. Expand upon them in later chailing. Give examples of experiences you have had while pursuing such activities: "Do you have a particular hobby? How do you usually spend free time? What do you do when you're on vacation?"

Prepare some short paragraphs to include in your *Tell* file. After you inquire about leisure activities, your SMC will want the same info from you. Explain whatever hobbies absorb your spare hours:

John, thirty-six, in Redding:

> "A good friend once joined me for a backpacking trip along the Pacific Crest Trail, which is way, way, away from any civilization at all. It was his first such trip, and he was expecting stores along the way where he could pop in for a soda or a hot dog. After a tough eighteen-mile first day in heat, the best I could offer him was an isolated horse trough full of water. No questions asked, however. We were both happy to have it by that time."

Michael, forty-three, in Casper:

> "In 1995 I took a weeklong course in high-mountain climbing at Mt. Rainier in Washington. It was enjoyable and I learned a lot, but I also got that particular desire out of my system."

You can only devote so much in-bed time to athletic pursuits. I like to read in bed; a nonreader will want the lights out. This is not a big item, but it could be a potential source of aggravation that I wanted to avoid. So I would ask:

> "Do you read regularly? Who are some of your favorite authors? I just bought the latest edition of Bartlett's *Familiar Quotations*. It opens by quoting a study that shows that 60 percent of the American public have never read one book. The majority of the other 40 percent read one book a *year*! Do you read in bed?"

Closely related is whether a bedtime reader regularly falls asleep with the light on. Find out.

If you are a reader, someone will occasionally ask for *your* favorite authors. Make the list up ahead of time and save it as a file called Favorite Authors:

> "The favorite authors I think of first are [and then list your collection]."

Jenny, thirty-five:

> "I like most music except heavy metal, most opera, and hard rock. Much of the soft rock is nice. I prefer jazz. In the classical field, Mozart is way out ahead. All my family is musically inclined. I've played cello in a string quartet for years. For some reason, my notes come out a bit differently than when Pablo Casales plays. Recently I bought a new keyboard and gave my old one to one of my sons."

Paul, thirty-seven, in Manchester:

> "I took flying lessons for a while, but never got my license. I handled everything except about the last twenty feet. I couldn't seem to get the hang of where the ground was precisely. Just recently I flew an ultralight and am thinking of building one when I have the right partner to help me."

Edith, forty-nine, in Springfield:

> "I love to do jigsaw puzzles. The bigger the better. I'm working on one now that is the New York City skyline at night—7,500 pieces."

Lou, thirty-eight, in Columbus:

> "I have a collection of more than twelve hundred Hot Wheels. Most of them are in boxes and packed away."

HUMOR

Try to make light of some of the things you *don't* like to do, but avoid sarcasm and put-downs. Poking fun at yourself comes across much better. I would say this about my lack of joy in horseback riding:

> "I'm not inclined toward horses. One ride sufficed. The horse had the better of the encounter. Somewhere I picked up two tickets for a free polo lesson, but I haven't made any effort to capitalize on my good fortune. But at least I haven't thrown them away, either."

Dorothy, fifty-five, in Clarksburg:

> "While I would enjoy growing things in a garden, I'm not interested in cutting grass, weeding, trimming bushes, and the like. Last year I spent the better part of a day clearing out some brush in back of my house. I then put in a whole bunch of vegetables, along with mulch, fertilizer, gypsum, the whole nine yards. The next morning, everything was gone right down to the stems, compliments of the local rabbits. The following morning, even the stems disappeared."

Brandon, thirty-two, in St. Louis:

> "I've tried reading Shakespeare, but never got very far. I went to see *Hamlet* onstage some four or five years ago. The emoting was outstanding, but I didn't have the faintest idea what they were saying, though I was familiar with the story. My date fell asleep in the first act, and I did the same in the second, so we skipped the third. I haven't been as intrepid since."

THE MIXED BAG—GRAINS OF SAND

One bit of sand in your shoe is hardly noticed, but a few grains can bring the hike to a halt. A parcel of otherwise minor aggravations can make or break a relationship. Explore all the nitpicky areas you can think of, little by little. Here are some questions that I have been on both ends of:

"How long do you spend with your computer in the evening [weekends]?"

"How much time do you spend on the Internet?"

"Do you wear pajamas to bed?"

"How does rainy weather affect you?"

"Do you take vitamin supplements?"

"Do you usually shower in the morning or in the evening?"

"How are you as a housekeeper? On a scale of one to ten, outright slob to cleanliness fanatic, I'm about a six."

"Do you consider yourself pro-life or pro-choice?"

"Do you keep plants in the house?"

"Do you sleep with your window open at night?"

"Are you involved in any volunteer work?"

Various SMCs have posed questions to me to elicit information or views that are important to them. Most are open-ended questions requiring some discussion. But even those that can be answered with a "yes" or a "no" could be handily followed up on, as I suggest later. These questions were undoubtedly addressing items on the SMC's A, B, and C lists.

"What would be your ideal vacation if money wasn't a concern?"

"You wake up with a headache and feel lousy. What would you do first?"

"The last time you had a day where nothing went right, what happened? What did you do?"

"When you feel like having friends over for an evening, what do you like to do with them?"

"What does 'dressing up' mean to you?"

"What kind of events do you dress up for?"

"If you were about to sit down to dinner and your neighbor came over and asked for help fixing his car, what would you do?"

"What is your schedule for meals?"

"How much time does it take you to get ready to go to work in the morning?"

"Do you like to gamble?"

"What does 'romantic' mean to you?"

"Do you shave every day?"

"What makes you laugh?"

"How do you feel about guns?"

"What do you think about partners having their own circle of friends to do things with, but without the partner?"

"What does 'drinking socially' mean to you?"

"What do you do to get rid of stress?"

"Do you feel comfortable talking to a partner about your feelings and problems?"

"Do you think married couples [or couples living together] should have separate checking accounts?"

Incompatible habits will frustrate both partners. TV is often a bone of contention. Ask: "What do you generally watch on TV?" If you go light on TV, you may not be happy with an SMC who maintains a regular soap-opera schedule. Or who props up in bed for dawn-to-dusk talk shows and old movies. Conversely, an SMC who enjoys absorbing a variety of TV shows would not in that case be happy with you.

If you are into dancing, ask: "What kind of dancing do you like?" If you can float across the boards, you increase your eligibility. If, alternatively, you have two left feet, dance school is a quick cure. In San Diego, I became Mr. Twinkletoes (well, sort of) at age sixty by taking some ballroom lessons at a night group dance class for a few months. The lessons were $6 each. It was fun, and I was amazed at what I had been missing all my life.

Find out if your SMC is a day or night creature. I originally asked, "Are you a day or a night person?" until I got a precise answer: "Both." So I changed my question to read: "Do you function better in the morning or in the evening?"

If you jump out of bed at 5:30 to exercise before going to work, you won't be happy with an SMC who comes to life at midnight. I operate better in the morning, and I am usually under the covers with a book by ten. Thus the following response from Louise, fifty-nine, in Los Angeles, was an eliminator: "I'm a night owl. It takes a pot of coffee to get me going in the morning, but come evening, I'm ready to roll."

Trot out your skeletons as you become more comfortable chailing with each other; everyone has them. Avoid trying to be mysterious. If you make the cryptic remark, "I have skeletons in my closet," your SMC will suspect the worst. Without fail, let your SMC know about any potential relationship breakers before you ever arrange a meeting. If your SMC is going to be put off, best to find out before you make a heavy emotional investment in a relationship that may clank abruptly to a halt.

Josey, fifty-five, in Tulsa:

> "You should know that I use to be an alcoholic, but I have been sober for thirteen years."

Albert, thirty-nine, in Toronto:

> "Seventeen years ago, I spent six months in jail for a joy ride that came out to car theft. It certainly cured me. Though it's not the kind of thing that's apt to pop up every day, I want to be up front about it."

Shirley, forty-six, in Philadelphia:

> "When I was a teenager, I had a son who I gave up for adoption. His father and I were not married, nor would it have worked if we had been."

In Summary

Ask *and* tell. Go back to the lists that you prepared in Chapter One. Use them to build the questions that will help you identify the characteristics that you do and don't want in your SMC. Prepare short, interesting paragraphs about your life and viewpoints. Save them in your *Tell* file. Spellcheck them! Work on the wording carefully to convey your precise thoughts. If you are not that talented in such efforts, ask for help from a friend who is. Use the material in future contacts with different SMCs. By doing this, you can whip up an interesting and informative message about yourself with a minimum of effort. And remember: on the Internet, the ability to write decent emails equates to being drop-dead gorgeous.

Next we'll talk about boo-boos, avoiding them, and unwinding them.

Ask-and-Tell: The Advanced Course

Life is rather like a can of sardines; we're all of us looking for the key.
—ALAN BENNETT

The first sign of maturity is the discovery that the volume knob also turns to the left.
—CHICAGO TRIBUNE

By now you are in the thick of chailing back and forth. You may have half a dozen or more SMCs who look great, and/or think you're the cat's pajamas. Or maybe you've got a nice little association going with one SMC who with a bit of luck could very well be your ultimate soul mate. But don't get carried away just yet. This is both one of the most exciting and one of the most hazardous stages of Internet matchmaking.

Bloopers and Recovery

With countless emails flowing back and forth, inevitably you'll run into Murphy's First Law: Anything that can go wrong, will. So slow down. You don't want to blow it at this crucial time by making a dumb mistake that will leave your SMC wondering about your ability to dress yourself without help. By now you're probably pretty good at fielding the line drives that come your way. Now let's talk about how to handle the ones you drop. And you will boot them on occasion. When you do, remember Teddy Roosevelt's observation, "The man who makes no mistakes does not usually make anything."

When I turned thirteen, I no longer qualified for the children's admission price to the Rialto Theater in Lowell, Massachusetts. The ten-cent increase

threatened to chew up my allowance for snacks in the course of thrilling to an afternoon of vaudeville, movies, cartoons, serials, and Movietown News. Being small for my age, I made an attempt to extend my preteen advantage. Right after my birthday, I bought the kid's ticket. The usher looked at the ticket and then gazed long at me.

"How old are you?" he demanded to know.

"Twelve," I shot right back.

"What year were you born in?" he persisted.

I thought I was up to the mental gymnastics. I was alleging to be a year younger, so I subtracted a year from the year of my birth, 1934. Right?

"Nineteen thirty-three," I replied with confidence.

The usher was a bit slower at math than I was, but eventually he gleefully announced, "That makes you fourteen!"

I do not recall where the interview went from there, or whether I had to pay the additional tariff. It was one of the more embarrassing scenes of my younger days, but I learned my lesson. Later in my youth, I carefully worked out such numbers before ordering beer.

In the course of corresponding with numerous SMCs, I've certainly made my share of goofs and then some. In the following pages I will share my dunderhead moves, as well as those of other people, and what we have learned from them. There are suggestions for recovering from mistakes as well as pointers for avoiding a repeat of the same blunder.

You can sidestep many of these simply by checking your message carefully before you send it. You don't have to read it over word for word, but make sure that you are addressing the right person, that the email address is correct, and that nothing is left out or repeated from an earlier email. And make the most of your education—run Spellcheck.

COPYING AND PASTING TWICE

Blooper A

I advocate carefully preparing ahead of time paragraphs of information that you routinely ask or tell. But be careful you don't copy and paste the same information twice in the same message. This not only looks dumb, but it's a dead giveaway that your message is not original.

RECOVERY:

If you are fortunate, you will notice this mistake after you've sent the message but before the SMC calls your attention to it. Send another email:

> **"I don't know how I managed to duplicate that paragraph. Just trying to make the email longer, I guess."**

If the SMC calls your attention to the goof before you notice, respond similarly.

AVOIDANCE:

Read your email before you send it.

Blooper B

A closely related error is when you send a well-crafted paragraph in one email, and a couple of emails later you manage to send along the same paragraph again—word for word.

RECOVERY:

As I've been culpable of this several times, I either ignore an SMC's comment or make light of it, saying something along the lines of this:

> **"You know, I liked that paragraph so much I just had to send it again."**

AVOIDANCE:

Keep your charts current for each SMC. After each email, look at your chart and check off those items you just covered. When you are getting ready to send off a new email, study your chart to decide what new questions or information you want to include.

WRONG SALUTATION

Blooper

You make up a message, copy it and paste it into your email, and send it to Dan. Then you use the same letter, make a few changes, and email it to Steve. Too late, you discover that you forgot to change the salutation, so both emails start with, "Hi Dan." At the very least, Steve is going to be perplexed.

A woman in Des Moines spent five hours on a first meeting with an SMC. Her name was Betsy. The following day she received a chatty little email from the same SMC, going over some of the topics they had discussed. The salutation read, "Hi Darlene."

RECOVERY:

There are two possible responses. I've used a short no-big-deal statement in such instances:

"That was a mistake."

Another person suggested saying,

"So sorry I goofed and sent the last message with the wrong name. I really don't want my lapse to be a turnoff to our communication. I really do want to have an opportunity to know who *you* are."

AVOIDANCE:

Let's assume you are going to use text from one email in another message, rather than retyping the same news twice (or more). Before you make changes in the second letter, get in the habit of changing the salutation first. Then, before you send the letter off, make a final scan of your work of art. Scroll right back up to the top of your email to ensure that you have the names straight.

MISTAKEN ADDRESSEE

Blooper

I was chailing with a woman with two email addresses. Our correspondence was somewhat advanced, so in one particular message I asked some rather personal questions. I sent the email to both of her addresses, or so I thought.

Her name was Maria. When I clicked on what I thought were her two addresses, I actually got one of hers and that of Mary Ellen, the next entry in my address book. That was not good. In fact, doubly not good. Maria wanted to know why I was sending copies of our email to some other woman. Mary Ellen came back with a frosty, "You sent this to me by mistake."

RECOVERY:
I explained the error to Maria as just a mistake. I said to Mary Ellen:

"Sorry about that. There is competition."

AVOIDANCE:
In your address book, if you have adjacent addresses for two different SMCs, insert a false address between the two. This will minimize the chances of clicking on the wrong one. After the Maria/Mary Ellen debacle, I inserted "Marlene" as a new address with "spacer" instead of an email address. Thus the chronology of names ran,

Maria	maria@isp.com
Marlene	spacer
Mary Ellen	marye@otherisp.com

WRONG ADDRESSEE

Blooper

I was in contact with two women, one in Denver and one in Tacoma. I had asked each to send me a picture. Neither had been in any hurry to respond. One day a group photo showed up in my mailbox. The SMC had enclosed a note saying, "Can you tell which one is me? Guess before you turn it over." I guessed correctly, as I found when I turned it over. There was no name, but the letter came from Denver.

That night I wrote to Denver explaining my clever detective work in determining which was she. I complimented her on her attractiveness. The following day I received an email from Tacoma saying, "Did you get my picture? I mailed it last week while I was in Denver."

On another occasion, a woman accidentally sent me an email that should have gone to the next person on her address list, a close friend. In the message were some distinctly unflattering comments about me. I didn't know if that was a hint, but I took it as such anyway.

RECOVERY:

I never heard from Denver again, and I was too embarrassed to try to remedy the situation. In retrospect I could have tried telling Denver:

> "Sorry about that. I had asked another woman to send me a picture, and she did so while vacationing in Denver. As I had also asked you for a picture, I naturally assumed it was yours. Our correspondence has shown me that we have a great number of common interests. I would hope that the fact that there is competition doesn't put you off completely."

AVOIDANCE:

If you are not sure whom correspondence or a picture is from, wait until someone asks if you got it.

WRONG INFORMATION IN THE MESSAGE

Blooper

I was once planning to spend a few days with two different SMCs. The planned meetings were a week apart, and we had tentatively set dates. Houston was to be November 12, and Phoenix was penciled in for November 19. Houston then wrote that a conflict had come up, and could we possibly move the date up a week to the nineteenth. While I was pondering my response, Phoenix asked if we could possibly move things *back* a week. So far, so good.

I made plane reservations through the Internet for both trips. In my email to Phoenix, I typed in the information I had received on flight numbers, times, arrival and departure, and so forth. When I wrote to Houston, I got lazy. Rather than type all the information, I simply copied the flight information from the email confirmation I had received from the travel agency. Then I pasted it directly into Houston's email and sent it winging on its way.

The following day, to my horror, I discovered that the information I had sent to Houston was from the *Phoenix* confirmation. The times were the same: arriving on Thursday afternoon, leaving on Monday morning, but with a different date and a different city. Silence from Houston. In a low-key attempt to rectify the error, I simply sent another message to Houston with the correct information with the note, "I misinformed you. Here are the correct flight times, as I doubt that you are interested in picking me up in Phoenix a week early."

More silence from Houston. A couple of days later I sent another chatty message about how I was looking forward to visiting Houston once again at a nice time of year, and so on.

More silence.

A week after the erroneous message went out, I sent another such amiable bit, though I was becoming a trifle desperate by now. Nothing. I had just about decided to cancel my flight when a message arrived from Houston:

> **"Are you still coming? I haven't heard from you for over a week."**

I looked closely. At the time, I had just learned how to work with the email Address Book. I had entered Houston's address as *beverly@friendly-ISP.com*. Wrong! Houston's address was *beverlyb@friendlyISP.com*. Houston had never received the email containing the wrong flight information. One mistake had canceled out the other.

Fortunately, there was a *beverly@friendlyISP.com* out there somewhere who had been receiving, and ignoring, these messages. Otherwise, the email would have come back to me, I would have corrected the email address (but not the flight info), and put myself in the soup.

RECOVERY:

This was a near disaster of the first magnitude. Houston had written excitedly to me, "I think this is so neat what we are doing!" If she'd received my Phoenix itinerary, it would have been obvious that I was doing this neat thing the weekend before also. If you face a problem of this size, emphasize the good and minimize the bad; don't spend a lot of time apologizing:

> **"I mistakenly sent you some reservations elsewhere I have for the previous week. I'm really looking forward to our meeting. I wouldn't be investing the time, effort, and expense if I weren't excited about our prospects. Let's hope the weather is good so that we can [go on to talk about whatever it is you might have planned to do]."**

AVOIDANCE:

Confirm that you are sending along the right transportation information, to avoid a capital gaffe like the one I almost made. If the SMC is going to pick you up, you also increase the likelihood that you will both be in the right place at the right time.

COPYING THE WRONG MESSAGE, OR ONLY PART OF IT

Blooper

You prepare a message and block it out to copy, but you forget to hit the Copy button. You then go to your email message and click on Paste. Instead of pasting your message, you paste whatever text you had copied or cut previously.

RECOVERY:

The ramifications of sending this botched message will depend on whether what you actually send is harmless. If so, just send another email with the full and correct message. If you sent something you wish you hadn't, often a quick explanation does the trick:

> "Sorry. I made up the message I wanted to send in my word processor, but I somehow copied the wrong text."

AVOIDANCE:

Give your email one last careful look before sending it.

USING ANOTHER SMC'S COMPUTER

Blooper

You are visiting one SMC and using that SMC's computer to contact a different SMC. Your host SMC discovers this fact.

RECOVERY:

None that I can think of. Moreover, if you are in this situation, you apparently have nothing going with the host SMC to make recovery worthwhile or you won't after he or she discovers what you've been up to.

AVOIDANCE:

If you feel compelled to do this, your best bet is to use your own laptop that you bring along. If you use your SMC's computer, get rid of all the evidence.

REMOVING EMAIL TRACES

To cover your tracks if you are composing in a word processor, delete all messages from that program after you have sent them. Remember that if you are using Windows 95 or above, deleting files or messages only sends the messages to the Recycle Bin. So you must also go in and delete the messages from the Recycle Bin. Double-click on the Recycle Bin. When the window comes up, click on File at the top left. When the drop-down box appears, click on "Empty Recycle Bin," and then select Yes when prompted.

Next, delete any messages you receive from the distant SMC. Also click on the Sent folder of your email program and delete the email messages you sent to the other SMC. These two steps only remove the messages from the folder and send them to the Trash folder in your email. To complete the operation, go into the Trash folder and delete everything you sent and received from *that* folder.

Finally, if you are not intimately familiar with the procedures I've described, go to a local copy shop if you must cheat. Use a computer there. And remember Sir Walter Scott's warning,

> Oh, what a tangled web we weave,
> When first we practice to deceive!

ASKING A QUESTION THAT HAS ALREADY BEEN ANSWERED

Blooper

This predicament can arise in two ways. You ask your SMC if she ever goes to the ballpark to watch your favorite baseball team. She says tailgate partying is one of her favorite weekend activities. A week later you ask the same question. She responds with a frosty, "You already asked me that. Are you having trouble keeping everyone straight?"

Or you ask your SMC the age of her children. She explains patiently (or perhaps less tolerantly) that if you read her profile again, you will find that she has no children.

RECOVERY:

Don't take offense, no matter what the measure of sarcasm might be; you're the one who screwed up. Make light of it. And add a little oil to the troubled waters:

> "Sorry about that. Obviously I have trouble just keeping *myself* straight. And I certainly am interested in keeping *you* straight because…"

AVOIDANCE:

Work with your checklist. Each time you get an email response, add the appropriate information to the list. Review the information you have before you send your next email.

Most people don't like to admit to mistakes. But everyone flubs from time to time. Oscar Wilde remarked, "Life without mistakes would be dull."

Games People Play—Detecting Frauds

Now that you have more of an idea of the potential bombs you can set off, it's time to take a close look at what might be coming from the other end.

Once you've invested a lot of time and effort with a particular SMC, it can be easy to lose perspective. While you're still in the email stage, take the time to study your lists for any evidence that you're corresponding with predators—the con and scam artists and the thieves. There are certain indicators that should clue you in:

• *The person sounds too good to be true.* Anything too good to be true generally is. Pin your SMC down on small details. If the SMC doesn't respond, or is evasive, it's probably time to move on.

• *Something doesn't make sense.* If your SMC offers a quick and overly-simple explanation for something, do a reality check. Does what the SMC is saying make sense? Run the scenario past a friend if you are in doubt.

• *"I love you."* If an SMC professes love without ever meeting you, chances are you are facing (1) an extremely lonely person, (2) immaturity, or (3) a scam artist. "Love at first sight" is for teenagers and other souls who are not yet worldly wise. You should be chilled, rather than thrilled, to see this come across your screen before you've even met the other person.

If there's any doubt in your mind about whether someone might be a fraud, you can run a background check. At agencies such as *www.infotel.com* you can scope out your SMC. For fees ranging from $39 to $99, Infotel will give you a great deal of information about anyone. For an additional fee, the company will run a criminal check for you.

Occasionally you will encounter someone who professes to be earnest about finding companionship but is in essence just flirting, afraid to take a step into the real world, or just plain nuts. Not everyone is determined to find a mate, even though some will claim that they are.

I carried on a correspondence for a short time with an SMC in Pennsylvania. She seemed in line with what I wanted. After several weeks of chailing, she sent a photo. I then offered to visit for a weekend. If things went well, I suggested she might consider a return visit to California. That was the last communion; she never responded again.

In another instance an SMC delayed sending her picture, telling me that she wanted it to be just right. It finally arrived. I should have been more specific; it was a picture of her two dogs. She didn't respond after that.

An unusual profile caught my eye once. The woman (?) wrote sensually but not in an offensive manner. She disclosed nothing about herself, other than that she had a way with romantic words. When I sent my usual first-round email message, she came back with another sexy message that ended with, "and so, with a trembling heart, I waft you a kiss on the winds." Looking over my basic email message, I found little to make hearts tremble. Nor was I looking for wafted affection at that stage. Nevertheless, I responded by saying:

> "While I am not adverse to plucking kisses out of the ether, I much prefer close-range osculation. On a more pragmatic note, tell me what you do to stay in condition. What does the scale say to you on a good day? Do you backpack? Jog? Bicycle? Tennis? Hike?"

Evidently my concerns were too earthbound; nothing else came wafting my way.

Getting Down to Brass Tacks

You've found an SMC who has forgiven your email gaffes. All systems are "go"; he or she seems to be the real thing. But don't cancel your matchmaking site membership just yet. You have only scratched the surface; time to get out the shovel and dig for the real gold. Let's step up to the tough issues, the advanced course of sounding out your SMC. You may want to chaw over some of the following issues face-to-face.

THE CHILDREN, PART TWO

Before you clinch a deal for soul-mateness, if either of you has children, test the waters. Ed with the snake might have been persuaded to farm his scaled pal out to the Los Angeles Zoo, but that isn't an option with children. Existing children may be coffee-shop-conference material. On the other hand, some discussions may work better by email—whatever you are more comfortable with.

Although I will touch on some major considerations in the following paragraphs, you might want to explore some expert advice. There are some excellent books on the various points. For general parenting, try *Ten-Minute Life Lessons for Kids* by Jamie Miller (Harper Trade, 1998). To get some down-to-earth thinking on merging families, take a look at *Merging Families* by Bobbie Reed (Concordia Publishing House, 1992). When you are steeped in knowledge, sit down and have a heart-to-heart with your SMC.

Living with Stepchildren

Your SMC has two young children. All you have to do is move in, give them love and affection, and everyone will live happily ever after, right? A yes answer betrays the fact that someone still walks you to the school bus stop. Whatever the age of the child(ren), you'll want to arrange a trial get-together to do a group introduction. This may be a backyard barbecue or a day at the beach. With younger kids, a few hours at a playground may suffice. Note the interaction and reaction of the kids as well as that of your SMC.

Georgina, thirty, in Richmond, related this experience:

"When I was going with Doug, his boys seemed a little wild [ages six and eight]. I felt this was because they didn't have a mother to take care of them. When I moved in, I assumed that my being around would cure the problem. Foolish me! I had never been married, and here I was stuck with two kids who got even more out of hand.

"Whenever I tried to set limits, they would appeal to Doug, and he would overrule me. I just couldn't cope with it. It ultimately became a major hassle that killed my relationship with Doug. When I left, I felt like someone must when they get out of prison. My dad had warned me that I should start my own family, and I hadn't listened."

Jody, forty-three, in Tampa, shared with me an awakening from her younger days:

"My second marriage lasted only four years…[S]hortly after we got married, we went camping for a weekend. Randy went off in a boat to fish all day every day. He wouldn't take my kids because he felt they would scare the fish. A bee stung Lois, who was only six at the time. Randy's only comment was, 'Doesn't she know that bees do that? She's old enough to be careful.' It was this way for the rest of our marriage. Randy really wanted nothing to do with them, and they knew that. They were both adorable, and I assumed that Randy would grow to love them as much as I did. It just didn't happen."

If your SMC is supplying the young one(s), you come in as a stepparent. Often children's initial reception to you will range from less than enthusiastic to downright hostile. Whether the feeling is openly expressed or not, children do not give up easily on the idea of divorced parents reuniting. The age of the children when the family separated will have a big effect on whether their treatment of you is warm or frigid.

Janet, forty-one, in Oakland, had such an experience:

"Ray had twin girls aged twelve. At first they would have little to do with me, no matter how I extended myself. Each kept making comments that began with 'When Jody [their mother] comes back…' What finally turned the tide was Ray's patience. He kept telling them that their Mom was happier where she was now, and that she would come back, but only to visit.

"He never got mad, and neither did I. It took almost a year, but they finally came around. All on their own, they bought me a beautiful present for my fortieth birthday. One of them even called me 'Mom' by accident, and we all laughed. I think it was at that moment that we became a family, and not separate war groups."

If young children are part of *your* package, the problems are the same. Insisting that the children call the substitute parent "Dad" or "Mom" generally fosters resentment.

If both of you bring children to the new party, the potential for conflict is threefold. Each adult has to get along with the other's children, and the children have to get along amongst themselves. As the number of children increases, so does the coefficient of potential friction. There is always the possibility that one SMC will feel the other is favoring his or her own children to the detriment of the other partner's.

Very young ones still in the diapering stage require a lot of hands-on care. It takes time to strap Junior into a car seat and disengage him at the end of the journey. "No, no. Don't do that" or "No, no. Don't touch that" come easily and often to your lips at this stage. Feeding, bathing, toilet training, and tucking into bed are included. Bedtime storytelling becomes habitual. Are each of you ready and willing to share in these treats?

Children in the early grades have ball games, dance and music recitals, and school functions. All demand parental attendance. Periods of time spent with children on a park playground need to be given reasonable priority.

Teenagers

Adolescence carries along problems even for biological parents. Anticipate "You're not my Dad." "My *real* mom would let me do that" is also a favorite. An affinity for music that bears no audible resemblance to anything played on your favorite radio station will assail your ears, even through closed bedroom doors. Your telephone wires will heat up from extended usage. Items of clothing of odd appearance will become wardrobe musts. A teenager shows his or her individuality by very carefully dressing exactly like his or her peers. Hair of colors unfound even in rainbows, and styles from other planets are often de rigueur. This is a turbulent time of life. Are you and your SMC both prepared to turb along?

Part-time Custody

Even if your SMC's children are living with the other parent, the world turns on occasion. Discuss with your SMC the possibility of one or more of the children returning to your nest. A past love had three teenage children living with her ex. The thirteen-year-old daughter felt living conditions would be more bearable with Mom. The three of us discussed the matter and laid out a few rules. When we mentioned a curfew of no later than midnight on the weekend, the daughter's eagerness evaporated. Discipline with Dad offered more freedom.

Loving an SMC's children doesn't happen overnight. Give yourself time to adjust. Look at them objectively. Don't take resentment personally; it is directed at the divorce situation rather than at you.

FINANCES

Each of us has an idea of how much financial risk we are willing to tolerate. You and your SMC must talk about this crucial subject. Going broke at age thirty, as I did, allows for considerable time to make up lost ground. If you are a risktaker, there is a sufficient span to recover from going broke again (and yes, it happened to me a second time). At any age, however, most of us will minimize risk in order to preserve what we have.

An SMC told me that a previous aspirant for her affections had suggested that they sell her $800,000 home (no mortgage), buy a smaller place, and put the difference into "some sort of business." She had wisely declined the proposal. At fifty-five she had no inclination toward making any investment not backed 100 percent by Uncle Sam.

Once you reach a comfortable spot with your SMC, sit down and talk a bit on this topic. Speak frankly about your respective positions and outlooks. Who has how much, and in what form? What changes do either of you visualize if you combine your efforts at pulling the wagon? If you have the urge to make economic suggestions to your SMC, back them up with fact and sound reason. This topic doesn't lend itself to easy conversation. But as author Rita Davenport was quoted as saying, "Money isn't everything,...but it ranks right up there with oxygen."

Someone who has been his or her own breadwinner for a lengthy time may not be used to being treated. Even simple gestures like picking up a dinner tab or sharing the cost of groceries may sit uneasily. Sometimes going Dutch treat can ease discomfort.

Each of you must feel comfortable with the other's potential fiscal plans. To invest in $500 worth of software to get into a phase of the computer business is one thing. Laying out $20,000 on hardware for a venture is another. Shifting funds from one mutual fund to another may increase or lessen your risk slightly. On the other hand, going from the NYSE to NASDAQ may stretch your comfort level.

Real estate is a long-term investment. Sometimes *very* long term. I bought a home in 1989. Nine years later I sold it for $65,000 less than I paid. When your SMC proposes any venture involving risk to your capital, ask yourself whether you have the time to recoup if the market goes against you. When my soul mate Ute opted to relocate to San Diego with me, our plan included the sale of her condominium. Her comment:

> "Instead of selling my condo home, I decided to rent it. This helped tremendously. As the current housing market was depressed, I would have lost a considerable amount of money. Also, psychologically, I still had a home to return to. It gave me the feeling of remaining independent and somewhat in control of my choice. My love was supportive all the way, and helped with the decision."

You can handle the touchy topic of finances in person, by email, or perhaps in both ways. It's your call. Just don't ignore this key issue.

STRETCHING SINGLES INTO DOUBLES

One or both of you may have become accustomed to living alone. The longer the solo period, the more work will be required to mesh (rather than mash) your respective lives. This is where the little items begin to count: bedroom window open or closed at night? Pajamas or skin? Toilet paper unwinding from the top or the bottom? Kitchen trash can in the open or under the sink? Walk or drive to do groceries? Dogs inside the house or out? My car or yours? Beyond that, who will run the dishwasher, run the vacuum, select the radio station, or pick the CDs to play? And on and on.

Once you think you might both fit aboard the same dogsled, take time to go over these small points. Consider different options; allow ideas to flourish. What is important to each of you? Thrash these topics out via chailing on the Internet or in person, depending on which mode of communication is more comfortable for you both.

PHYSICAL LIMITATIONS

You or your SMC may have physical problems that prevent you from enjoying an activity. One of you may have hearing, vision, or movement limitations, or other sensitivities or phobias. And no matter how fit you may be, what foods you ingest, or how healthy a lifestyle you pursue, once you're out of your twenties, things ain't gonna work as well as when you were a kid. One of you may be in the first flush of youth but have a disability that confines you to a wheelchair. A congenital condition may have required a person to take a different approach to life. The question is whether you and your SMC are at the same "don't-work-as-well" level. If not, does this present a problem for one of you?

PARENTAL CARE

The parents of SMCs of any age may have health problems. The parents of SMCs in their fifties and upward are most likely over seventy. Many, regardless of age, cannot take care of themselves; others will reach that stage. Prudence dictates an exchange of viewpoints if you or your SMC has parents who presently are in this category or might be in the foreseeable future. That encompasses virtually all parents. Disablement can occur at any age, regardless of the health history of the parent. A fall, a stroke, a sudden lump; all can bring about a calamitous change in lifestyle for an elder. What responsibility, if any, will you and your SMC consider bearing? Neither underestimate nor overlook this critical question: "Do you anticipate having to care for one or both of your parents when they get older?"

One of your SMC's siblings may provide care, or all may be expected to contribute to assisted-living expenses.

THE CARE OF OTHERS

I once met an SMC at her twenty-six-year-old son's home. He had severed his spinal cord in a diving accident some years earlier. A positive-thinking young man, he had moved out on his own for the past few months. A loving girlfriend was helping him with the transition. Had my SMC and I been match material, we would have needed to examine the care options quite early in our chailing. What if her son were to lose heart or his girlfriend were to lose interest, for instance?

Another SMC had been caring for crack babies—those born to addicted mothers—for several years. A childhood affliction left her unable to bear children, and an ex-husband had been unwilling to adopt. At all times she had two or three of these unfortunates in her loving care. Her soul mate would have had to be similarly disposed.

Another SMC was caring for her ten-year-old granddaughter while the mother was receiving free room and board at the state's expense over a misunderstanding involving cocaine. The granddaughter was in a wheelchair with a recently broken leg. The leg was healing rapidly, but her mom was grounded for another two years, even on the condition of exemplary deportment.

BALANCING FREE TIME

Your work schedules may differ, giving one of you more free time than the other. Anticipate that one of you might thus be dealing with a partnerless schedule more often than not. Is this acceptable to both of you?

David, a good friend of mine, sold his company and became a part-time consultant to the new management. His fairly new bride had seven more years to work until she would retire from her firm. David used the free time to learn some aspects of computers; he now has a second part-time business in that field. When his wife retires, she intends to help David in his computer venture.

If you work and your SMC does not, how does your SMC fill up his or her time? Does your SMC have hobbies that can be performed solo, such as reading, writing, woodworking, gardening, crossword puzzles, and the like? Or does your SMC have only interests and inclinations that require other people: tennis, dancing, chess (although this can be done with a computer as opponent), partying, and so forth? If the latter, bring up this point. Also, if you're the kind of person who doesn't want a bunch of people in the house all the time—lots of noise and activity and comings and goings—will you be able to live with someone who is so social? What will the SMC do while you are working? And more important, what will it be like when you come home bushed after a tough day?

If, on the other hand, you will get first shot at more free time, ask yourself the same questions. Will a relationship founder because the time you can spend together is not as extensive as you might wish? Your vacation plans may be limited by the weeks of vacation your SMC draws each year. In most cases, the weekend will define your togetherness activities, assuming that your SMC does not have to work on the weekends.

You and your SMC can spend only so much time playing bridge, kayaking, walking moonlit beaches, and dining in exotic restaurants together. Compare notes on activities that will bring both of you closer. Volunteer work attracts some people. If your SMC is not similarly inclined, make certain that he or she will not mind the hours that you invest in such efforts.

Consider taking courses together. Perhaps you can study a foreign language together, or get schooling in computers. You might even consider taking different classes, but ones that take place at the same location on the same nights.

These are all-important considerations. And as you age, the importance of fostering affable companionship in an SMC grows apace. Each of you should ask yourselves, and each other, whether the amount of togetherness time you might presently enjoy will suffice to sustain a lasting relationship.

The flip side of the coin is when both of you have time on your hands to spare. Can each of you stand up to marching together full-time? Two months after my sweetheart moved here from Hawaii, we took a car trip. In three and a half weeks, we covered 9,300 miles cooped up in a 1989 Toyota lacking air-conditioning and loaded with clothing, camping gear, two computers, two bikes, and a sixty-pound dog. From Northern Michigan to Boston to Atlanta to Yuma, temperatures ranged from 40 degrees to 110, the terrain from below sea level to 10,000-foot passes. We slept wherever, including once or twice in a motel. We dined on Dunkin' Donuts and McDonald's "senior citizen" coffee. And we returned home loving and liking one another more than ever. All three of us.

Now you needn't go to this extreme, but at the very least, plan some practice time together.

ISSUES IN THE LATER YEARS

When I turned forty, I said to myself, "Where did my thirties go?" I asked the same question about my forties when I passed the half-century mark; the forties didn't look so bad in retrospect. But when I turned sixty, my viewpoint changed for the better. Instead of bewailing the brisk passage of another ten years, I congratulated myself on having ten years of sixties ahead of me to enjoy. And another ten years of seventies before I would even have to consider slowing down.

Middle age brings different insights and attitudes. Certain areas require exploration with your SMC. It's best that you are both poring over the same chart.

Attitudes toward Retirement

Somewhere in the fifties your thoughts may turn from career advancement to termination. The idea of finally stopping to smell the roses gathers appeal. Priorities shift. Motor home ads seem to multiply; the Travel section of the newspaper attracts you. The end of the rat race, retirement, is finally within grasp. To help with retirement planning, Social Security now sends everyone an estimate of how much they can expect to collect each month when they retire. Expect this around your birthday. Be sitting down when it arrives.

You may opt instead for an alternative. The Social Security office report may chill the idea of full retirement; part-time work may be necessary. Or you may decide to keep your hand in the business world in some other fashion, such as in the network marketing field (Herbalife, for example), or real estate sales.

If you are searching for a soul mate aged fifty or older, your SMC's thoughts may parallel yours. But don't take that for granted.

For instance, Sheila, an Internet start-up executive at age fifty-two, wrote:

> "From your remarks, Eric, it looks as though you want a travel partner. I just started this position, and I'm determined to be successful at it. Theoretically, I have two weeks of vacation a year. If I'm able to take more than a few days of that at a time, I'll be lucky."

Sheila was on the career track; I had stepped off. We discovered that this was a mismatch while "hello" was yet reverberating.

I don't mean that you and your soul mate necessarily have to be at the same place—either working or retired. I top my soul mate by seven years. Part of our feeling-out process involved discussing our attitude toward the immediate years ahead. She was ready to put her academic career behind her to consult part-time.

On a larger note, will your careers be affected by togetherness? Ute had taught for fourteen years. Her dream had always been to build a "Healing Garden." Several attempts had failed. We agreed that she would step out of the economic race for six months or so to indulge this fancy. She had to adjust to a day without schedules imposed by the workplace. We also explored developing a small business in which our respective talents would complement each other's interests while reaping some economic benefits.

The bigger the age difference, the more important it is that you compare viewpoints. When and to what extent will you start reversing the work process?

Sex for the Mature

Only in your youth do you go to bed first and then worry about topics of conversation in the morning. Sex over fifty is certainly important, but it rates below other considerations.

When I asked Sylvia, fifty-four, in Fremont, her expectations about meeting potential soul mates, she replied:

> "A red light for me is someone who wants to hop right into bed without getting to know the other person. I want someone who doesn't push on this and respects my way of doing things. I have decided that this time around I want to get to know someone first."

The fifties can begin a sexual epiphany for women. The fear of pregnancy is past, as is the concern over what children might see or hear. It's time to cut loose. On the other hand, the sexual urge is beginning to diminish for most men at this age. As George Burns once noted in his seventies, "My get-up-and-go got up and went." The frequency of lovemaking will tend to turn on the slower partner's inclinations.

Author Walter Kemp observed that the best thing about growing old was that it took so long. Disadvantages can be rife, however. Talk at length about each other's thoughts and feelings about sex.

In Summary

When you blow it, bite the bullet and admit your gaffe. It isn't the end of the world. In the vast marketplace for affection, most SMCs understand that you will be chailing with multiple SMCs. Establishing a relationship is akin to selling a house; until both parties agree, all shoppers are welcome. When you make a mistake, admit and correct it. Learn. Do something to prevent it from happening again. If you must, make a different mistake instead next time.

Cover with your SMC all the areas suggested in this chapter as applicable, before jumping full bore into a relationship. Each subject can be a thorny path to follow. Avoid the nettles by having in-depth discussions with your SMC. What we have covered in this chapter just barely scrapes the top layer. Books on the more complex subjects are plentiful.

Next we'll talk about stepping away from the computer to do the real-world thing.

8 Stepping into the Real World

Spectacular achievement is always preceded by spectacular preparation.

—ROBERT H. SCHULLER

You win some, you lose some, and some get rained out, but you gotta suit up for them all.

—CASEY STENGEL

In the fifth grade, I had a crush on a classmate, Janet. To further a romance, I devised a foolproof method for conveying my feelings. I sneaked a small rubber eraser with her name on it from her desk. I planned to go to her house with the eraser and hold it out to her when she answered the door. Then I would accidentally drop it at her feet and upon picking it up, quickly grab and kiss her. That was the plan. Simple, just a little derring-do on my part required.

The first part of my plan went well. Janet came to the door. I explained that I had found her eraser, held it out to her, and "accidentally" let it fall at her feet. Well, actually, I gave it a little toss to get it closer to her. To my horror, the eraser took on a life of its own. It hit the doorstep, bounced back against my knee, hit another step, and disappeared into the bushes by the side of the house. By the time I found it, Janet had closed the door. I left it on her doorstep. So much for that romantic endeavor.

The First Telephone Contact

As best you can, remove chancy elements from your first phone conversation by doing better planning than I exhibited with Janet. You've chailed to the point where the next logical step is some chat on the telephone. This step

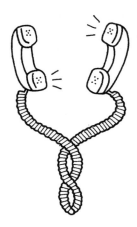

will help you decide whether to arrange a face-to-face meeting. Well, what do you talk about? What are you looking to find out from the SMC that you can't get from email? How long should you talk? How do you end the conversation?

Let's talk about striking a balance between ringing up before you are ready, and waiting overly long to make telephone contact. Don't rush the first telephone connection. Phone calls lead to meetings. If you meet too soon, before you scratch around in some of the dustier corners of your SMC's tent, you might find that chemistry will overpower good sense. An SMC's charm might short-circuit your intended course of questioning, to the detriment of one or both of you at a later time.

On the other hand, let's assume that each of you has a good feel for the likes and dislikes of the other. It's a good idea to meet before you invest too much time and emotion. It is easy, particularly if you are lonely, to look forward to receiving email from a person who has taken such an apparent liking to you. If you carry on an extended correspondence, there is a tendency to feel that you have banked something of yourself. You then expect a return on your investment when you meet. You will have the urge to jam the square peg into the round hole, to make your meeting work.

You don't want to do that. Ideally you should be at a point with your SMC where you can handle an unsuccessful meeting with a shrug. If a meeting turns out well, it will be a pleasant surprise. I had nineteen unsuccessful meetings of varying durations before I found my soul mate.

And remember: there is an inexhaustible supply of SMCs on the Internet. Make certain you are zeroing in on one who fits your explicit sweep before you reach for the phone.

PREPARING FOR THE CALL

An experienced attorney goes to trial knowing precisely what information he or she wants from each witness, both the attorney's witnesses and the witnesses for the opposing side. The attorney prepares in advance of trial *every question* he or she is going to ask of *every witness*. Without such an effort, the attorney stands a good chance of losing, no matter how strong his or her case might seem.

Approach your first telephone conversation in the same manner. Determine what you want from the conversation, and write out your questions in advance. Where appropriate, make reference to previous answers the SMC has given you. This is a healthy step toward determining whether you want to invest additional time getting to know this SMC. Don't just pick up the phone and go for it; have your blueprint handy.

Go back over all the emails you have sent to each other. Make up questions in three areas: fun topics, current events, and touchy stuff. Start with fun topics your SMC will enjoy discussing. Move to a question or two about current events. Then if everything has gone well up to that point get into some of the touchy stuff.

Fun topics might include questions such as:

"How did you do in your tennis match the other night?"

"How was your trip to Hawaii?"

"In your travels, what country did you like the most?"

"What's happening in your favorite sitcom?"

"How did your weekend visit with your kids go?"

"Tell me more about your kids."

Also use this first conversation as a time to get some answers to tougher questions about current events or other issues that are important to you. Through this exchange you will be able to gauge the quality of an answer when it must come right off the top of the SMC's head:

"What do you think of what's happening [whatever the latest national or international news might be]?"

"How do you feel about [a current issue such as a political candidate's stand or a network's decision to cancel a certain TV program]?"

Once you get past these areas, if you are feeling comfortable with the SMC, bring up the touchy stuff:

"What led up to your divorce?"

"I'm curious as to why you never married [or remarried]."

"Did you ever regret not having kids?"

"Which of your four spouses was most compatible with you?"

This is also the time to revisit previous email questions that the SMC answered vaguely, or perhaps even avoided:

"You mentioned in our email that...Tell me more about that."

"I don't remember what you said when I asked you..." [What you remember is that the SMC ducked the question.]

As you ask a question and get a satisfactory answer, check the question off on your A&T chart. If the SMC avoids a question or only partially answers it, come back to the same question again later:

"I wasn't quite clear what you meant when I asked you..."

There may be something that you want the SMC to know about yourself. But keep it brief, and phrase your sentence(s) to get a reaction from the SMC. For instance,

"I don't know if I told you that my dog sleeps on my bed at night. Have you ever had an animal who did that?"

"I keep my house clean, but I don't always rush to get things picked up. How about you?"

At the same time, remember that you can't learn anything while you are doing the talking. So don't get carried away telling about yourself. You can always do that at a later time. Use your telephone time to determine whether there *will* be a later time with this SMC. You're not trying to convince the SMC to get to know you better; you expect the *SMC* to convince *you.*

TELEPHONE COURTESY

Time your call appropriately. Give the SMC an idea of when you will call, and get his or her approval. I once planned to enjoy a particular documentary about some episodes in the life of one of my heroes, Sir Winston Churchill. Fifteen minutes after the program had begun, an SMC called me out of the blue. We chatted for fifteen or twenty minutes, although reluctantly on my part.

Your SMC may have to put kids to bed at a certain time, want to watch a special basketball game, call a client, or have a bucket of other things that may have to take priority over your call.

In email, I generally say:

> **"I thought of giving you a call this weekend, possibly early Sunday afternoon. Is that a good time for you?"**

When you call, identify yourself sufficiently. Don't assume that yours is the only call the SMC is expecting, or that you are the only person of that name with whom the SMC is chailing. When the SMC answers the phone, say:

> **"Hi, this is [your name] in [your hometown] from [Match.com or whatever site brought you together]."**

Confirm that the SMC can talk at that moment. Don't just call up and start rattling off your set of interrogatories. After you identify yourself, ask, "Is this a good time to talk?" I've blundered directly into conversations without first inquiring about convenience, only to find that the other party (a) has a call on another line, (b) just got out of the shower, (c) has just taken dinner out of the oven, (d) is in the midst of one of life's ever-present minor emergencies, and so on. If this should be the case, offer to call back later.

LISTENING

Keep several factors in mind as you talk. Does the SMC make grammatical mistakes? Misuse words? Does the SMC have a pleasant voice or one that is grating? Is this a voice you could potentially listen to day after day for the rest of your life? What about the *tone* of voice? Can you detect a note of petulance or annoyance when the SMC touches on certain topics? Any bitterness or whining? Pay close attention to ferreting out such subtleties. This may be one of the few chances you have to check out your SMC when his or her guard is down.

You will be talking mostly about the SMC, and the SMC's likes, dislikes, and opinions. How does the SMC come across? Intelligent? Sarcastic?

Radical? Wimpy? Indecisive? Vague? Is the SMC considerate enough to want to learn something about you, or is he or she content to let the conversation orbit around him- or herself?

When you are not chatting face-to-face, you will be more sensitive to clues such as articulation and tone. How do you feel overall about the conversation? Is this a person with whom you will be at ease? Is there anything about the responses to your questions that leaves you dissatisfied? Are you both hearing the same note from the tuning fork? Trust your instincts here. If it doesn't seem right for any reason, consider calling it quits.

MURPHY'S LAW

You may have a plan for the order of questions, but be ready for the bounce of the eraser, Murphy's Law. Even though you have a specific list of questions to go through, take the opportunity to explore other areas of interest to your SMC as the topics present themselves. If the SMC raises a topic you want to explore further, "Tell me more about that" is a safe bet.

Don't feel compelled to ask your question 6 immediately after you get an answer to question 5. Go with the flow of the conversation. But keep asking the questions on your list, no matter what the sequence, for as long as you want to keep the conversation going. If you start getting answers you don't like, end the conversation as suggested in the following section.

FINISH ON A POSITIVE NOTE

Bring the conversation to a definite end when you run out of questions. Leave the SMC wishing that you had talked more, not less. I find an easy way to do this, rather than mentioning that I have to knock it off, is to say:

> "I'd better let you go. I really appreciate your taking time to talk with me."

Be positive, no matter which way you plan to head from here. At this point, you will have decided either that you would *like* to meet with the SMC, that you *don't* want to meet, or that you are undecided.

If you would like to meet with an SMC who is local, don't beat around the bush. Ask:

> "How about if we get together for coffee sometime soon and chat some more?"

If meeting the SMC requires travel, it depends on who might visit whom.

"I'm going to be in your neighborhood next month for [whatever]. If you are going to be in town, I'd like to meet with you."

"I'd enjoy it if you could spend a couple of days in my neighborhood. Is there a particular weekend next month when this might work out for you?"

In the next chapter, we'll discuss an out-of-town meeting in more detail.

But maybe during the conversation, you have decided that you don't want to explore this SMC any further. There isn't any way that you can avoid hurting the SMC's feelings, but you can minimize the effect. If you truly want this SMC out of your life, don't offer words of encouragement.

Don't drop the grenade right up front. First, to salvage the SMC's ego, say something nice before passing along the bad news:

"I really have enjoyed talking with you, but I don't think we'd be a good match."

"I've really enjoyed our talk, but I don't think our chemistry is quite right. You should do well in your search."

If you have a problem being that direct, be neutral:

"I'm glad we had a chance to talk. Now I have a lot to think about [smile—it will come across, even on the phone]. I'll get back to you shortly."

And do get back as promised; you've set up the expectation. Be considerate enough to send your exit by email.

The SMC may want a clue as to why you have no interest in pursuing further sets of verbal tennis. If there is a specific reason that the SMC cannot cure, say so:

"You want to live in Maine; I'm a Southern California person through and through."

"You're still married."

Otherwise, to avoid any argument, present the unassailable:

"I can't really put my finger on it, but I just have this sense that we wouldn't fit. But I know you won't have any problem finding the right person for you. I'm just not that person. I have to run. Thanks for chatting."

If the SMC attempts to convince you otherwise, hear the argument out. Then repeat your refusal. If the SMC becomes overly insistent, recite your refusal more firmly. You don't have to explain *anything*; the word *no* says it all. If you think you might have trouble being firm, practice in front of a mirror.

If you feel you can't be that direct, try this:

> "You've given me a lot to think about, so I'll go do just that. I have to run, and I don't want to keep you any longer. I'm glad we had a chance to talk. I'll get back to you [and you will, in an email, to say that it won't work out]."

Don't make the mistake of telling the SMC that you will call back at another time, and don't suggest that you remain "just friends." Don't beat about the bush; be clear and unequivocal either right then or in a later email. Let the SMC move on to someone else. Otherwise it may become tougher to get this person out of your life.

If there's a possibility that you might want to meet but some cloud of doubt sits in your mind over a specific point, discuss that point a bit more right then. If further discussion doesn't resolve your conflict and you are still in doubt, use a slight variation of the advice I've already given:

> "You've given me a lot to think about, and I'll go do just that. I have to run. I'm glad we had a chance to talk. I'll get back to you via email in a couple of days [this week, and so forth]."

You may decide after reflection that another conversation by email or telephone is in order so that you might clarify something. After you collect your final thoughts, email your decision. If it's curtains for the SMC, take the sting out of the bad news by saying something like this:

> "I really enjoyed talking with you. For some reason, however, there is not the spark that I am looking for; our chemistry isn't quite right [or express whatever reason cannot logically be countered]. You impressed me as a very nice person, and I know that you will have no trouble finding the right person. Unfortunately, it isn't me. Good luck in your search."

The First Face-off

You've connected with an SMC and decided to take your mission into the real world. How do you go about setting up a meeting? What should you be careful about? Where and when should you meet? What should you talk about? What if the chemistry just isn't there? How do you leave smoothly?

Right after receiving my commission as an ensign in the U.S. Navy, a friend arranged a blind date for me. Seeking to impress, I casually suggested that we patronize the officer's club at a local base. It was to be my first visit to such an establishment. I dressed in my new white uniform, expecting to dazzle the young lady, Claudette.

As it turned out, I was the only person in uniform. A small combo played dance music. My dancing skills were on a level with my aptitude for underwater welding. Claudette should have worn steel-tipped boots instead of the open-toed pumps that invited misery. I spilled beer down the front of my uniform at the earliest possible opportunity. I was interested in sports; Claudette went for the latest feminine fashions including bridalware. Parting that evening brought relief to both of us.

Meeting with an SMC furthers the process of elimination, as much as that of selection. When you go to buy a car, you have a pretty good idea of what will fit the bill. Perhaps you have make, color, and age pretty firmly in mind. Once at the dealer, you will kick the tires on a few models and then take one for a test ride. If you like the feel, you will discuss price and terms. Everything has to fit, or you are on to the next dealer.

The process of finding a soul mate is similar, though without the thought that you will be trading up within five years. Your initial face-to-face meeting equates with the kick-the-tires stage.

When you meet with an SMC for the first time, be prepared to see something different from what you got in the picture. You may like the real thing better; you may not. But chances are your SMC will not be exactly the person in the photo. Nor will your SMC come across in person as he or she did through your chailing or on the phone. Make allowances. You are not coming together to fall in love, but to see if there's any reason to try for second base. In person your SMC may be boorish, charming, self-absorbed, humorous, gentle, sloppy, or even sialoquent ("spraying saliva while talking"). Your purpose is merely to find out if there seems to be enough going to warrant having another kick or two at the tires, or maybe even taking a test drive.

THE RELUCTANT TÊTE-À-TÊTER

Let's say that you find an SMC who has interests similar to yours, and who says the things you want to hear. You suggest a meeting. Your SMC procrastinates or comes up with excuses for not meeting face-to-face. Almost without exception, his or her hesitancy stems from one of the following two situations:

1. The SMC has misrepresented an aspect of his or her appearance in some manner. Assuming you have exchanged pictures in some fashion, the SMC's photo may not be current. Perhaps the SMC is desperately trying to lose weight before meeting with you.

RESOLUTION:
Back off on your email. Keep your next message very brief:

> **"I have a lot I'd like to discuss with you in person. Let me know when you can meet with me."**

If you hear nothing back from the SMC within the next few days, go back with "Are you still interested in meeting?" If you get the same runaround, look for another SMC; drop this one.

2. The SMC is married, has a live-in, or is still in a relationship. It may be that the SMC is in the process of divorce or is severing a present relationship. That is all well and good, but the SMC should be honest enough to disclose this detail up front. Moreover, a spouse or significant other can

put a real damper on a rendezvous by appearing suddenly with demands for explanations from the both of you.

RESOLUTION:

Get a home phone number if you don't already have one. Call at an unexpected time. If you don't get the warm reception you anticipate, you are probably chasing the wrong SMC. Call again unexpectedly a week or so later. If you get the same result, you may want to lose that SMC and find another.

My friend Mona had an SMC candidly admit to her that he was in a relationship. To test their own relationship, he and his girlfriend had agreed to try other partners. Declining to become part of the research effort, Mona decided to look elsewhere.

SAFETY FIRST

Let's talk first about meeting locally, which includes anyplace within driving distance. We'll cover out-of-town rendezvous later.

Big Rule Number One: *Keep your own safety foremost in mind.*
Always tell a friend or relative where you are meeting the SMC and what time to expect you back. Ask that person to write the information down and to call you at a certain time. Give instructions to call the police if you are not home within, say, thirty minutes or an hour of that time.

In addition, there is a service that you may want to look at, *www.smartdate.com*. For $1 a month you can register with this outfit every time you go someplace. If you don't return, the company will pass that revelation along to the police, along with whatever information you provided.

Be back in time! Make allowances for traffic. If you don't return, you place your monitor in an awkward situation, particularly if he or she calls the police needlessly. If you know you're going to be out later than anticipated, pull over and call. Don't be the modern-day counterpart of The Boy Who Cried Wolf.

Try to select a casual location that doesn't serve alcohol, so you can remove that temptation; for example, choose a coffee shop, a bakery with a sitting area, an ice cream shop, and so forth. Look for a place with a good bit of foot traffic. Set a limit for your stay, and tell your SMC the time frame.

If you meet after work, choose similar places. Don't extend the tête-à-tête or accept an offer to have dinner. After a full working day, it is too easy to give in to a drink or two to relieve stress. You might relax too much; even Miller

Light may cloud good judgment. Before you know it, you could find yourself talking too much and giving excessive personal information. If your SMC has treated you to dinner, it may be harder to leave.

Big Rule Number Two: *Never meet after dark.*

When the days grow short, meet on the weekend, or at noon. Always find a public place—inside. Don't get together in the parking lot, either coming or leaving. You have no protection and can be overpowered. Even in broad daylight, nobody may notice. Those who might come to your rescue may be disinclined to intervene in what could appear to be a marital spat. And a large portion of our population is simply unwilling to become involved in any matter not directly affecting their own well-being. If the proposed location has inconvenient or unsafe parking, spend a few dollars on valet service, or park elsewhere.

Even if you end up at any sort of liquor-licensed location, stick to something nonalcoholic. If the SMC has an alcoholic drink despite your nonindulgence, consider that a yellow flag flapping in the breeze. The same goes if the SMC throws down more than one drink without food.

Big Rule Number Three: *Guard against spiked drinks.*

If you leave the table, say to go to the rest room, either take your drink with you or when you come back, ask for a new one. Don't take the chance that the SMC might spike your drink. Tell the waiter you need a fresh cup of coffee, or dump the contents and get a refill if it is self-service. Also trade for a new cup.

Don't let the SMC's looks cause you to disregard common sense. He or she may look safe enough, but only time will tell. Don't make assumptions based on initial appearance.

Women: Never leave your purse unattended. Your SMC may browse through it while you are gone. If the SMC lifts your credit card, you may not notice until later.

Dress comfortably. If you are coming from work, you don't have much choice, though you can dress up just a tad for that day. Otherwise, dress as you would if you were meeting a friend. If this SMC turns out to be your soul mate, friendship will be part and parcel of the package. Let the SMC see the true You in relaxed form. The everyday You is what your SMC is going to see for the most part if you ultimately click. Don't deliberately go out of your way to make a statement; be yourself.

Big Rule Number Four: *Never let an SMC pick you up for the first meeting.*

To begin with, you don't want to give a stranger your address at work or at home. Second, you need to maintain control. Take your own car, a cab, use public transportation, or get a ride from a friend. One SMC bicycled five or six miles to our appointment. Consider the feeling you would have if upon entering the SMC's car you find that there is no handle to open either the door or the window on your side.

Judy, thirty-nine, in Boston had an enlightening experience:

"I hadn't dated since I was a teenager. Through a dating service I met a businessman. We talked on the phone a couple of times, and he was mature and articulate. He offered to pick me up for a 5 P.M. beer. His car was flashy and expensive.

"We had a beer and got into a heated discussion about religion and missionaries. Each of us was pushing the other's buttons. He ordered a second round, and after finishing his, he drank the rest of mine. We left, and neither of us had eaten anything since lunch.

"In my parking lot, where you hardly ever see anyone, he asked if he could use the rest room. There is no public restroom, but I realized he had drunk a lot of beer. The thought passed through my head that he should have gone at the restaurant. Despite my misgivings, I brought him to my apartment on the ninth floor.

"My place was a mess. I had dressed and left in a hurry, and there were clothes and papers all over. The bathroom was also a shambles. I apologized, but then became very uneasy. I was also pretty embarrassed.

"I'm sure he sensed my discomfort, and was a perfect gentleman about leaving, though it was awkward for both of us. I never heard from him again. If he had been a pushy person, I could have found myself in a very, very serious situation."

This advice holds true for men as well as for women. You don't want to give away your haunt or habitat prematurely. If the SMC's elevator proves to stop short of the top floor, you could just be inviting problems. During my term in the U.S. Navy I roomed for some time with a fellow bachelor in an apartment. He once made the acquaintance of a woman who ultimately refused to take no for an answer. More than once she planted herself in front of our locked door and announced her feelings long and loudly to the world at large. Simultaneously, she would assault the door with some sort of blunt weapon. Another time he came down in the morning after one of her nocturnal visits to find that all four of his tires had been slashed.

BE AT THE RIGHT PLACE AT THE RIGHT TIME

Pin down where you are going to meet and at what time. I once agreed to meet an SMC at Starbucks on 5th Avenue in San Diego, in the Hillcrest area. Simple enough? I arrived a trifle early and waited twenty minutes or so. No show. Back home, I sent an email asking what had happened. Her response was that *she* had come on time and had waited twenty minutes. Starbucks, 5th Avenue in Hillcrest. San Diego. California. USA. No way! While I was there, the only patrons were decidedly male. The only woman in sight was behind the counter.

A phone conversation solved the dilemma. Starbucks, without even asking me, had seen fit to open two shops on 5th Avenue in Hillcrest. One was on the corner of Robinson, where I had waited with bated (later abated) breath. The other was on the corner of Washington, a mere two blocks down. The moral to the story is to get the when and where straight without any doubt.

If you have set the occasion over the phone, send an email confirming the date. A trace of enthusiasm can help to make the SMC upbeat about the upcoming encounter:

> "It was nice to talk to you, Sheri. I'll see you at Coco's tomorrow at 1:30, the one at Broadway and F. I'm looking forward to meeting you."

Show up on time; better still, a little ahead of time. Being late is rude; don't get off on the wrong foot. An excuse, even the greatest one, is just that—an excuse.

Phil, forty-six, of Chattanooga, explains the result of taking the wrong turn on the way to meeting a potential SMC:

> "A great woman agreed to meet where it was more convenient for me. I allowed just enough time to get there, but because I wasn't paying attention, I took a wrong fork. That made me circle a mountain to get back. I ended up being almost half an hour late. She was still there, but by then she was in frost mode. She had to leave about ten minutes later, so we got no place. That was kind of the end of it. In one last email, she said she had a thing for being on time. An old boyfriend constantly used to make her wait."

WHAT DO YOU TALK ABOUT?

A *don't* is first in order: *don't talk about your problems!* Everyone has them. This is not a visit to your psychiatrist. You want the SMC to perceive you as an enjoyable person to be with. Having to absorb a litany of woes is not fun; the SMC has his or her own problems. I once met with an SMC who was going through a divorce. For a solid hour she recited book, chapter, and verse what she was suffering at the hands of her ex-to-be and his unprincipled lawyer. She held only slightly less contempt for her own lawyer. My contributions to the dialogue were limited to a series of comments such as "How terrible," "Really?" and the like. It was a real stem-winder. Put yourself in your SMC's place. Who wants to receive someone's long tale of anguish? If you succumb to the temptation to trot out all your woes, your SMC will soon be looking for the nearest exit.

Before you jump into religion and politics, be confident that you already have a good handle on your SMC's persuasions. And do so cautiously in any event. Otherwise you risk enmeshing yourself in a discourse that could turn acrimonious. The resultant heated discussion on say, religion or politics, may sink your hopes for future encounters with this SMC. You can always put on the gloves at a later point. If you do wander into these morasses, however, and your SMC begins spouting what to you are inanities, keep your cool. Murmur nonpartisan sounds. Afterward, you can reflect on your SMC's remarks and whether he or she can be allowed to roam about without a leash.

I always like to open the conversation with a genuine compliment such as

"I like your hairstyle."

"I like your earrings."

"You certainly are trim."

"You are better-looking than your picture."

If such utterances do not come easy to you, begin practicing with strangers you encounter in any public place, as I have done in the past. In a supermarket, I once complimented a woman on her multihued coat. She was delighted that I noticed, since she had made it herself of mohair. Another time I commented favorably on a tie a man was wearing. He beamed and said, "When I tell my wife, it will really make her day. She picked it."

Center your conversation on the SMC as much as possible; it will make you seem a great conversationalist. But remember that your objective is not to make the SMC like you. Accept as a given that the SMC will be delighted with you. The purpose of the meeting is to find out whether you are equally enthralled with the SMC. You can always fill in details about yourself at a later date if you so wish. So waste very little time talking about your likes and dislikes. Note whether the SMC is interested in finding out more about you, certainly. Chime in with a comment here and there, but keep the focus on your SMC. The more the conversation revolves around the SMC, the better you look. And remember, you can't learn anything while you are flapping your lips.

Try openers that are easy to answer.

"How long have you lived in Pittsburgh?"

"Where did you grow up?"

"How did you happen to come to Minnesota?"

"Do you have brothers and sisters?"

An easy follow-up is "Tell me more about [your growing up in Utah, your siblings, your job, and so forth].

SUREFIRE TOPICS

Many people approach small talk with an attitude normally reserved for tarantulas and rattlesnakes. If getting beyond the basics with a virtual stranger presents a potential problem, there are four surefire topic sources at your disposal:

1. *The current news.* Open up the newspaper and take a look at the headlines. Jot down four or five of the present national or international quandaries. There's never a shortage. If someone isn't blowing up the Middle East, the Russians and the IRA are perpetually active to some degree. Crime statistics proliferate. Movie stars are always up to something. Ask your SMC to comment:

   "What do you think about [whatever the news item might be]?"

   Keep your own observations to a minimum, especially if you are not in accord. Remember that you can't learn anything about the SMC while you are rattling your own cage.

2. *Past correspondence.* Now is the time to pull up whatever email messages you have sent back and forth with this SMC. Print them out and review them—both sides, yours as well as those of the SMC. I'm assuming you've told it like it is in every respect. Read over what the SMC has written to you to refresh your memory. Ask the SMC to expand on different subjects:

   "You said that your son is a traffic engineer in Hawaii. Tell me more about that. How did he happen to become an engineer? Where did he go to school?" [And so on.]"

3. *Your SMC's profile.* Maybe there are tidbits in the SMC's profile that you have not yet talked about. Now is the hour. You can never go wrong asking SMCs to talk about themselves. The favorite topic of conversation of *most* people, young or old, is themselves. I don't consider myself an exception.

4. *Your A, B, and C lists.* Consider bringing up some of the items on the three lists that you prepared in Chapter One, particularly those items that you have yellow- or red-flagged. You have the added advantage of seeing the SMC's reaction. When you ask for an opinion about our president, does the SMC laugh, become apoplectic, or stare at you blankly?

If you are not blessed with a good memory, there is nothing wrong with making up a list of items on, say, a 3-by-5 card and referring to it as you talk. Just say, "There are a lot of things I wanted to talk with you about, so I made some notes so that I wouldn't forget any of them." You needn't apologize. And then fire away. How many people do you know who can go shopping for more than three items without a list of some sort?

But keep the notepad small. If you haul a yellow-lined legal pad out of your briefcase, you risk creating the impression that you are conducting a job interview. In a roundabout way, you truly are, but let's not be so obvious.

I possess the memory of a cement block. Mere concern for my survival causes me to constantly resort to notetaking. I pulled out such a small list of questions once at an early meeting with an SMC. She asked, "Is this a test?" I said, "Of course." Which naturally, it was. We both laughed, and then went forward without incident.

Whether or not you work from notes, pay rapt attention to the SMC's answers. Exhaust a topic before you go on to the next. First, you can only weigh your SMC's answers if you are listening. And this is a golden opportunity to match your SMC's words with his or her gestures, facial expressions, and body language. Second, don't give the impression that you are in a hurry to get to the next topic. If you do, it may appear that you find the remarks your SMC is presently making unimportant.

All of us have had the unnerving experience of talking with someone who is obviously waiting for us to stop talking so that *he* or *she* can talk. If you don't give someone your full attention, you will come across in a like manner. I once had a meeting with a woman who had a list of topics. She would ask a question and then cut me off a few seconds later to ask the next question. I finally ventured that perhaps it would work out better if she let me have her pad to write out my answers. We differed in our assessment of the humor of the remark; that meeting was our last.

Make and keep eye contact. First, if you maintain eye contact, you'll be less likely to be apprehended assessing the bodily charms of the SMC. It is distracting to hold a conversation with someone who is constantly looking over your shoulder, down at your feet, and everyplace but in your eyes. And don't be checking out all the talent as it strolls by. Pay attention to your SMC.

Remember that you don't have to cover everything in this one session. You may even decide after a few minutes that your time would have been better spent finishing up the crossword puzzle. You just need to spend enough time with an SMC to see whether you want to go for a test drive, or even whether you want to keep on kicking the tires. That's your objective in this first meeting.

LISTENING

You can't learn anything about the SMC if you are banging your gums. Yes, I know I repeat myself, but this is ultra-important. Spend more time asking about the SMC's interests than you do talking about yours. Listen for hints of an abusive personality. Lest you think this advice applies only to women getting to know men, there are many women who think nothing of flinging weighty objects and fists at the men with whom they are involved. Women, like men, can be masters at emotional and verbal abuse. The instigation of arguments and fights is often an art form, non-gender-specific.

Does the SMC talk about previous relationships, or those of friends, where someone got "smacked around"? It makes no difference whether the SMC is the smacker or the smackee. Does the SMC talk about physical violence in a matter-of-fact way? This isn't passion; it is evidence of sickness. An SMC who is indifferent about cruelty toward animals may be an abuser.

ENDING THE SESSION

Your best bet is to set up your exit on the phone beforehand, or as soon as you arrive. Mention that you have some other commitment that requires you to keep the meeting short, let's say twenty or thirty minutes. Make it an event that you can't possibly skip; be a little late for, perhaps, but avoid—never. In this category would be a dentist appointment, a meeting with your son's teacher, or a date with your friendly IRS agent. This way your SMC won't be disappointed or upset if he or she had anticipated a longer rap session.

I was once hoist by my own creative petard. An SMC and I set an after-work tryst for a local restaurant. Not wanting to have to pop for a meal if the chemistry wasn't there, upon meeting I immediately arranged my getaway. I opened the conversation by mentioning that I was having dinner with my son and his family, which necessitated my departure in thirty minutes. This was a complete fabrication, of course. The lady was absolutely charming; the half hour flew by. I was toying with the idea of actually treating her to dinner when she reminded me that my son would be waiting. The more I wanted to stay, the more she insisted that I leave. So quite reluctantly, I did. To make matters worse, she had asked where my son lived. To make an apparent show of fidelity, I was forced to drive off in the opposite direction from the path home.

All in all, however, you are better off having a prearranged out. You won't have to sit there mentally biting your fingernails, reckoning how to withdraw from an ill-starred encounter.

If at any time you feel uncomfortable, forget about excuses and just bail. Bring the meeting to an immediate end politely:

> **"Bob, I have a feeling we aren't a match made in heaven. I really appreciate your taking the time to meet with me, but I'm going to run."**

Leave money for half the bill and a tip, smile, and go. If Bob wants to argue, tell him, "I'll get back to you." Smile again and take off.

If you find yourself in what you feel to be a potentially dangerous situation, head for the hills. Excuse yourself to go to your car to get some notes, or to the telephone to make the call your promised your aunt, or whatever. And keep going. If your SMC insists on accompanying you, don't argue. Later, excuse yourself to go to the rest room (where your SMC can't accompany you). Then split. If necessary, ask the manager of the establishment if he will walk you to your car. Explain why you need his company. He may decide to ask a burly waiter along as well. Don't worry about feeling foolish; *that* you will get over. If later on you have second thoughts about your speedy departure, you can always claim to have been overcome by some sort of sickness. In an extreme case, don't hesitate to ask the manager to call the police.

By the way, a cellular phone is a helpful tool to have if you should think that you might be followed.

WHAT NEXT?

You may be of two minds about meeting again, especially if you haven't gotten a good read on your SMC. Or you may be unsure as to whether you want the ball game to go into another inning. As you did after you called the SMC for the first time on the telephone, you will find yourself having one of three inclinations:

1. You want to continue to explore the relationship.

2. You have no further interest in the SMC.

3. You aren't sure.

Be mindful that your SMC is in exactly the same spot, although he or she may have a different selection in mind. Each of you may be naturally reluctant to tip your hand, for fear of receiving an unpleasant response, such as rejection. If your suggestion to meet again is met with derisive laughter, you might be off your feed for days. Certainly there will be times when it will be apparent that both of you are of the same mind, whatever that might be. So let's examine some gracious closings for the ambiguous occasion. Let's also assume that you have average sensitivity to brusque comments such as "You must be kidding!"

You Want to Continue to Explore the Relationship

Be positive and indicate your interest in moving the ball forward:

> "I really enjoyed meeting you. I'll get back to you if that's OK by you."

> "I wish I had a little more time to spend with you today."

> "Next time it'll be my treat."

All of these hints are comfortable for both parties, even if your SMC is in an opposite frame of mind. It makes it easy for the SMC to be pleasantly noncommittal. Alternatively, it opens the door for one of you to offer an encore.

You Have No Further Interest

I've found it easiest to be straightforward, but in a gentle way. I would first compliment the SMC before dropping the grenade:

> "I enjoyed your company today. I admire [the way you overcame so many hurdles in raising your kids, your business acumen, your refreshing viewpoint on life, your devotion to helping others less fortunate than you, and so forth]. But I don't think we have enough in common to make it worth our while trying to fashion a relationship. You have a lot of qualities that will appeal to the right man. I'm just not the right guy."

Smile, shake hands, and leave. Don't stick around for a discussion. You are doing the SMC a favor by closing the door and letting him or her get on to the next potential mate.

If you aren't up to biting the bullet in this fashion, be neutral:

> "I enjoyed your company. Let me get back to you."

You can then handle the "I'm just not the right person for you" via email. Don't leave room for argument. If the SMC doesn't accept your decision, ignore further emails and just delete them unread.

You Aren't Sure

For a variety of reasons, you may want to sort out your perceptions of the meeting before reacting one way or the other. You want to avoid either encouraging or discouraging the SMC:

> "I'm glad we had a chance to meet. There's quite a bit more to you than I expected. I'll definitely get back to you."

In all three of the situations just outlined you've avoided saying something that would provoke an argument or signal rejection. If for some reason you later change your mind, your options are still open. Make your leave-taking short, and in most cases somewhat ambiguous.

If the SMC expresses a wish to kick more tires with you, and this conflicts with your present thoughts, simply say, "Let me think about it and get back to you." If the SMC wants to argue, repeat what you just said.

> "I've got a lot on my mind today. Let me think over our meeting and get back to you. What's the best time to catch you?"

End of discussion.

The Next Step

If the meeting goes well, resist the urge to invite your SMC back to your home for coffee or whatever immediately after. The prearranged exit plan will help you to overcome this proclivity should it arise. Twice I was offered such invitations. I accepted both times, once reluctantly. The first time, I was stunned that the SMC would take such a chance—serial killers are not always wild-eyed—and didn't know how to say no. On the second occasion I knew the woman's adult son was at home.

Resist the urge to go when you are the one invited. Both times that I accepted such an invitation I should have reminded myself that unhappy endings in such situations are not limited to scenarios in which women enter male stomping grounds.

If you intend to meet someone again, I wish you the best of luck. Seek guidance, if you feel you might benefit from it. There are innumerable books on building relationships and developing a romance. This one is only designed to get you out to the track with a partner; you have to figure out how to run your own race.

In Summary

Plan carefully for the first telephone contact. Write out the questions you want to ask, but don't turn the conversation into an inquisition. Decide what information you want to disclose, but let the SMC do most of the talking. Observe telephone courtesy. Listen carefully to the answers to get a better idea of the SMC's personality. Finish up positively one way or another.

A face-to-face meeting gives you an opportunity to better appraise your SMC. The whole purpose of the meeting is to determine whether there will be future ones. Most of the time you will have nothing to worry about. When you meet, do so in the daytime in a well-lit public place. Set a time limit. Be on time, and watch whatever you drink. Be prepared with topics of conversation. Use your common sense and trust your instincts. If you think you may be steaming into harm's way, flee the scene immediately without tipping off your SMC; worry about excuses later.

Now on to the SMC who plays in an out-of-town ballpark.

9

Long-Distance Connections

In true love, the smallest distance is too great, and the greatest distance can be bridged.

—HANS NOUWENS

At the last dance of my junior year in college, I met and fell instantly in love with a bewitching young lady named Maureen. She professed reciprocal feelings, at least to some degree. A week hence I was scheduled to travel from my hometown outside of Boston to the wilds of Idaho. There I was to spend the summer in a tent, working in the forests for the U.S. government. My immediate concern was that during my absence Maureen would succumb to the wiles of some callous adventurer.

My budget did not allow for long-distance calls. Moreover, the nearest outpost was more than forty miles away from my tent. How would I keep Maureen's memory of me fresh? I went to the post office and bought a three-month supply of postcards. On the train out to Idaho, I spent countless hours addressing the cards to Maureen. I also added, "Dear Maureen" at the top, and "Yours, Eric" at the bottom. The middle I left blank for reporting future events.

When I got off the train, I sent the first card. Each day I completed another and mailed it. We exchanged some letters, but I shot off a card every day. Our relationship not only survived the summer, but Maureen and I were like old flames when I strolled back home.

Even if you are not beating the bushes beyond the local neighborhoods, a long-distance SMC could eventually single you out for contact. And sooner or later, if the ducks seem to be lining up pretty well in a row, one of you is going to land on the other's doorstep. To make a long-distance connection work takes some planning on both sides.

Your own safety becomes more of a factor in planning when you will be with an SMC for a longer period. Don't be too quick to lift off into, or accept a visitor from, the friendly skies. Before one of you starts packing, spend more time swapping convictions than you would with a local prospect. Typically I would chail for three months or more before deciding to call United. And make sure you've exchanged pictures! We'll cover long-distance connections from both perspectives: being the guest and hosting the visitor. But first let's talk about the one-day rendezvous.

One-Day Outings

Business trips, vacations, and visits to family and friends afford opportunities to meet with faraway SMCs. Make the best of such openings. For instance, during my search period I had to make several court appearances in San Jose. Each time I arranged to meet with an SMC in the area. I would have a few hours during the day after court to make acquaintance before catching my flight back.

If your meeting is for part of a day, plan an activity. Trying to wing it for a whole afternoon with someone on a different wavelength can be trying. Safety is paramount, because you are going to spend more time with your SMC than just a visit to the local coffee klatch entails.

When I made a trip to San Francisco, for example, an SMC and I spent a couple of hours walking though Golden Gate Park, which is a large, open, and busy location. Another time an SMC and I strolled through the Chinatown District to browse shops and sample pastries. Visits to a busy beach, a museum, or a noted shopping center are all safe and fun activities. In San Diego, for example, Balboa Park offers numerous museums; Horton Plaza is a four-story mall that is sheer delight to browse.

Avoid places that are isolated, or where foot traffic seems sparse. If the suggested agenda seems a bit scary or remote, do not be reluctant to voice your hesitation:

> **"Why don't we go to a place where there are more people? I love to watch crowds go by."**

If you are unfamiliar with an area and would like more control over the location of a meeting, take a look at a map. The Automobile Club of America (AAA) will furnish maps to its members covering anywhere in the country. You can find extensive maps on the Internet that you can print out. These range from state maps to detailed street maps of cities. Get one for the area you are about to descend upon. See what looks interesting. A rental car freebie map of Boston shows the site of the Boston Tea Party, several major colleges, Boston's Museum of Art, Boston Common, and the Public Gardens for starters.

Visiting Further Afield

You may have family or friends who live near an SMC. Before you shell out for airline tickets, you might want to arrange a meeting between your family member or friend and an SMC in order to get feedback. A friend of mine flies frequently to Hawaii on business. Twice I asked him to meet with SMCs to get an impression.

At such meetings information will flow both ways. You will get another's opinion about your SMC. At the same time, your friend can validate what you have been telling the SMC via email or phone conversations. Your friend can also verify that you really do drive motorcycles off ramps and over parked cars.

Overall, each of you may feel more comfortable with one another when you finally meet if someone else has laid the groundwork. Alternatively, your friend's report may cause you to stop wasting time and move on.

Take all such evaluations with a grain of salt, naturally. Your friend might dismiss out of hand an SMC who would knock your socks off. Or the flip side: your friend may slaver over an SMC. Upon meeting the same SMC, however, you may be scanning your watch every five minutes, hoping you don't have to stay much longer.

But sooner or later, you may find that you and a long-distance SMC both dance to many of the same activity tunes. First let's assume that you will be the traveler. If you are further than a few hours away by car, you will most likely want to fly. Since it doesn't make much sense to fly anyplace for just one day, try to arrange to spend a weekend with your SMC.

If you have laid the proper groundwork by chailing and putting in phone time, each of you may feel comfortable about staying at the other's home. This is a delicate subject, however. There are two good reasons and one poor one for staying with an SMC. First, this SMC has at least made the first cut. You are considering on some level the possibility of integrating this particular SMC into your life. Waking up and going to sleep in the same house, even if in different bedrooms, will give each of you more insight into whether living together is a practicality. Second, the less money you have to hand over to Tom Bodett at Motel 6, the more you have for entertainment.

The poor reason to stay with an SMC is to make sex convenient.

By the same token, there are two good reasons for *not* staying together. First, you may have difficulty establishing boundaries for your conduct that will not intrude on those of your SMC. There can be unforeseen consequences. Let Rosie, forty-nine, of the Big Apple, provide an example:

"I pride myself on cooking and keep a spotless kitchen. A guy I met, Saul, came to spend a weekend. I cooked spaghetti for dinner. Saul grabbed an apron and insisted on helping. I wasn't too keen on this, but I gave him the salad to do, which he did, part in the bowl, and part on the floor. When I went to dump the pasta into a colander, Saul snatched the pot out of my hands to teach me the Italian way in which you pour off most of the water but leave a little in the pot with the pasta. I already knew that.

"Saul started pouring, lost it, and managed to dump most of the spaghetti into the sink. Half of it went down the drain. So we ate a lot of salad. But the next morning, before I even got up, Saul was out in the kitchen making pancakes. It was a mess. He had flour all over the place, and a bunch of things he never even volunteered to wash afterward. This got to me, and we had a few words. He stayed out of my kitchen after that, but the rest of the weekend was kind of strained."

The second reason for not staying together centers on the possibility that things may not work out. You should have an alternative plan, as we'll discuss below. That plan will be easier to implement if one of you is overnighting somewhere else. It is easier to say, "Gee, this isn't working out," and leave if you don't have to tote your bags simultaneously.

If for one reason or another you are not going to stay together, don't book a fancy room just to impress your SMC. Since my only reason for getting a motel room was to sleep, I always opted for Motel 6 or the equivalent. I didn't want the SMC to get a wrong impression about how she might travel with me.

You can search by city on the Internet and come up with most of the commercial establishments in the area, including motels and hotels. But before you make reservations, ask your SMC about the area. He or she may recommend some other place; heed such advice. If you are on a budget, and most of us are, don't hesitate to say,

"I'm only going to sleep there, so the least expensive is fine. I'd rather spend the money doing fun things with you than give it to the local innkeeper."

PICKUP AND DELIVERY

Whenever I flew to visit an SMC, she met me at the airport. No need for a rental car or a cab. You may wish to err on the side of caution. Sit down with your SMC and have a cup of coffee inside the airport to get some vibes before you pack off into the unknown. Your bags will still be there, assuming they arrived with you in the first place. If you have any misgivings at all, head back to the ticket counter with your credit card. If you've carried on a lot of back and forth with your SMC beforehand, you probably have come to the conclusion that you will be able to safely endure one another's company for a few days; otherwise you wouldn't be standing around in an out-of-town airport.

Be crystal clear in communicating your arrival date, time, airline, and flight number if you are meeting at the airport. If your rendezvous is to take place elsewhere, make sure you have the right directions. Send the information off by email so that each of you is certain of touchdown time and place. The day before you leave, confirm the details again in a separate email. Describe what you will be wearing. Find out what your SMC will be wearing, driving, or both.

Don't expect instant recognition on either of your parts based on exchanging one or two pictures. Three-dimensional life forms are different. When arriving in an airport for the first meeting with an SMC, I looked for a woman with narrowed eyes and a facial expression that read, "I wonder if that's him." Most likely I wore the counterpart expression.

Get phone numbers to call if something goes wrong. If you carry a cell phone, give that phone number to the SMC. I once sat in an airport for two hours, staring at my cell phone. The SMC hadn't shown up. The idea of having a contingency plan flitted through my mind for the first time. It turned out that I had mistyped the flight time in my only email to her about the trip. It was a Thursday afternoon; I had her home number, but not her number at work. Thus I couldn't reach her to see what was keeping her. The passage of time (as so often happens) ultimately resolved the problem.

Be ready to pick up airport parking fees. Also it doesn't hurt to spring for a tank of gas even if you don't do a lot of tooling around while you're there. Don't make a big deal of it; just do it. But pay the cashier rather than handing the money over to the SMC.

EXPECTATIONS

Don't get your hopes up prematurely. I once wrote ahead of a visit, "I am coming with medium expectations." My SMC's response was "I have zero expectations." In other words, treat the trip as just long-distance coffee and bagels drawn out over a weekend. The mere fact that an SMC agrees to put up with you for a few days does not mean that the SMC is about to take you to his or her bosom permanently. Put yourself in a frame of mind to have a good time with the SMC, regardless of whether or not future romance is a possibility.

Don't expect sex as part of the package—sometimes it is; sometimes it isn't. I once spent a weekend with a delightful woman in the Bay Area. She stayed in her bedroom, and I slept in the guest room. She closed the door and probably locked it too. But we had an extremely enjoyable weekend. If you want to discuss sex ahead of the trip, fine. But it isn't really necessary at this point. The purpose of the trip is to see how well you get along standing up.

FIRST SIGHTING

When you first meet, do you shake hands, bear hug, or what? Here comes this SMC to meet you who, outside of some chailing and maybe a phone call or two, is a perfect stranger. Each of you is cautiously probing to see if the other is destined to be the Delight of Your Life. Be ready to follow the SMC's lead. When I got off the plane in Maine, Cecile came up and gave me a kiss. So did Susan in Fremont. I got a hug from Mary Ellen in Seattle, as well as from Linda in Portland, Oregon. Meeting Liliana in Oahu started with a handshake. If there seemed to be any uncertainty, I opted for the hug, light on the bear part.

As I suggested earlier, begin with a compliment, as when you meet any SMC for the first time. Just as with a coffee-shop meeting, start by centering the conversation on your SMC, rather than launching into the details of the rough flight you had:

> "Any trouble getting here? How is traffic this time of day? You must be tired after [a long day, a long drive, umpiring the Little League game, whatever]."

When the conversation turns to you, as it will eventually, avoid being boring. Keep your stories succinct. Bear in mind the advice of some unknown sage:

> Those with great minds talk about ideas. People with average minds talk about things. Those with little minds talk about people.

When you get to the car, if you are a male door-opener, do so. If you are not, don't start now.

CHECKING IN

Arrange to check in with a family member or friend at least once a day. This advice applies whether you are the host or the guest. You might choose to call a neighbor, friend, relative, or even a coworker. When you make the first call, you can make a trivial excuse if necessary: "It's a special birthday. I told my friend I'd call." "I'm expecting a letter [package, check, and so forth] and want to see if it came." Tell your friend that the mere fact that you call means you are OK. If you really want to cloak-and-dagger it, arrange in advance some secret phrase to mean that you are in trouble. "Tell George I'll call him next week," for instance, might mean, "Call the cops immediately." If you are the guest, tell your contact ahead of time where you expect to be with your SMC. If the gendarmes must make a house call, best they have the correct address.

Let your SMC know that you have this safety net in place:

> "My friend [mother, cousin, whatever] made me promise I would check in with her/him each day."

If you are the visitor, use your telephone card, call from a public phone, or call collect. Insist.

You should be ready with a contingency plan in case things don't work out for some reason. Let's talk about that right here.

In advance of her first trip, my soul-mate-to-be wrote:

> "If we get bored with one another, don't worry about it. I have a brother in Orange County who would love to put me up for a few days."

That was Ute's alternative plan if we didn't see eye to eye; her brother would receive a weekend visitor.

Even if you are going to quarter at your SMC's house temporarily, line up a local hotel/motel ahead of time. This will be your fallback if necessary. Carry your American Express card. Let's assume that you and the SMC just don't hit it off right from the get-go. You don't necessarily have to scurry home immediately. For one, your return fare will increase. You may instead decide to stick around and take in the local sights on your own. Pack up and head for the motel you lined up. Don't accept the SMC's gracious offer to drop you off; take a cab to ease your mind.

DON'T WEAR OUT YOUR WELCOME

Respect Benjamin Franklin's inelegant but germane perception, "Fish and visitors stink in three days." Make the stay for a definite period of time. I would usually try to arrive Thursday evening and leave Sunday evening or Monday morning.

One SMC who was to make the first long-distance move emailed me ahead of time that she was leaving the return date open. Uh-uh. That is a recipe for disaster. Suppose the SMC decided she liked my guest bedroom and wanted to stick around for an indefinite period of time? My enthusiasm about a prolonged stay might fall far short of hers.

While I was puzzling over how to persuade her to make a U-turn on a specific date, she phoned. In the midst of our discussion, I mentioned something about my dogs being considerate enough to drop their calling cards in one certain corner of the backyard. She was appalled that I let them do their thing in the home ballpark. I gathered that she preferred that I take them for a walk to leave donations on neighbors' lawns or wherever else. A couple of other comments led me to believe that we diverged on the care and feeding of canines. After the conversation, I thought for a while, and then I withdrew my invitation to Southern California. That solved the dilemma of the open-ended stay.

THE VACATION SYNDROME

Be aware that when you meet for a few days like this, you drift into a vacation atmosphere. To fill up the short time you have, your days are planned for fun activities. You're away from the job and local responsibilities; someone else is caring for your kids or your pets. Maybe both. You are looking forward to drawing a new person into your life perhaps. This carnival-like ambience can be misleading. The few days pass in a whirl. For a change, you have someone with whom you can do things. One of you goes home after a fun-filled time, perhaps even with some sex thrown in; one or both of you are aglow.

But hold on here. You can have fun at Disneyland with *anyone,* even your ex-mother-in-law. Especially if it is the first time, and without kids. What you've just had with this SMC is a long date. Who doesn't put his or her best foot forward on a date, particularly the first one? Your quick weekend stint doesn't address some basic questions. One of you probably took a day off to entertain through a long weekend. Yet to be resolved is how you will function on days when one (or both) of you has to get up and take the bus to work.

Undoubtedly the house got cleaned and picked up before the event. Is it like this always? Can either of you live with housekeeping that is otherwise? How will it work if one of you gets sick? Who handles the aftermath of poochie committing a social blunder on the living room carpet? And this is just the tip of the iceberg. My point is that a good weekend signals the need for further exploration rather than immediate full commitment.

It is difficult to assess what the relationship would be like on a regular or daily basis. I spent a weekend with a charming woman in Tacoma. We went skiing, snowshoeing, played tennis, dined out once, witnessed some Christmas pageantry, and saw two plays. In between we toddled her aged dog daily and did a five-mile walk around a local lake. All in the space of three and a half days. There was no question that we enjoyed similar fun things in life. How we would have fared with the mundane was something we hadn't had time to evaluate.

Playing Host(ess) Further Afield

To offer hospitality to the SMC in your own habitat, you must have an extra bedroom. You thus avoid giving the wrong impression that one mattress will suffice for the weekend. One of the reasons my soul mate first came to visit me instead of vice versa was that her condo came equipped with only one bedroom.

As a precaution, if you are the female host and are somewhat uneasy about the SMC visitor, ask help from a friend. Perhaps have the friend stay with you the first night, or at least pop in from time to time as if he or she were your roommate.

Another alternative is to leave the question open. When the subject of accommodations arises, you can weigh in with something neutral:

"There are plenty of places around. We can decide when you get here."

Spend the first few hours in your SMC's company before committing. If you have the slightest doubt, drop the SMC at Motel 6's front desk.

Carla, forty-three, in Chicago talks of a unique event:

"I had met Steve through the Internet, and invited him to dinner on a Friday night. We both agreed that this was a good start before committing to the rest of the weekend. I was a little uneasy about the situation, because he had become fairly aggressive in his email once I agreed to meet with him. I asked a friend, Nicole, to join us for dinner so that I could get her impressions.

"When Steve showed up, he was visibly upset to find Nicole there, but he calmed down. During the evening, Nicole told me that her feeling was that I shouldn't stay alone with this guy. That sort of confirmed something that I couldn't quite put my finger on. The dinner was a success, but I decided to pass on the rest of the weekend with Steve. When I told him that, he seemed OK with it, but I never heard from him again."

When you are on the receiving end, you have the burden of making the trip work. You are familiar with what your area has to offer; your SMC is not. This doesn't mean that you must spend a lot of money. A beach picnic, a bicycle ride, a downtown walking tour—all of these can be relished with minimum expenditure. And if your comfort level is high enough, plan events like a hike along a mountain ridge.

Don't put on the dog when you pick up your SMC at the airport. I drive a '73 VW that comes furnished with my two pooches. When I first went to pick up my soul mate at the airport, a friend was horrified to learn that I was going to do so in the VW. "Rent a car," he urged. Why? The rental car wasn't me; the VW complete with fragrant mutts was. That was part of the package.

Try not to eat out every meal. Prepare at least one meal at home together. You have the opportunity to learn a lot about each other's likes and dislikes when it comes to food and preparation. You each can get a feel for how comfortable you are in the kitchen environment. For instance, I love to sample dishes as a meal is in process. My love could have felt that I was in the way, which I truly am most of the time. Instead she delights in the exchange of little pats and hugs that such proximity brings (I do this on purpose to retain nibbling privileges).

Before You Part

If after a weekend spent together more of the same appeals to you, talk about it. One of you should not go down the ramp without some discussion of tomorrow. If your SMC does not broach the subject, the best time to do it is at the airport (or if one of you is leaving by car, just before you put the bags in the trunk). Factor in maybe fifteen minutes for this last-minute dialogue. This way, if you find that your SMC is tuned in to a different station, at least someone takes off one way or another in short order, putting an end to embarrassment.

Don't just let the matter slide and don't assume that the SMC is a mind reader. This falls in the same category with "I don't have to tell him I love him. He knows." I once had a great time with a woman in Oregon. At the airport, there was an air of discomfort that I couldn't put my finger on. We parted, and I presumed that we would pick up where we left off at the earliest opportunity. I neglected email over the next couple of days while catching up. Two days later she wrote:

> "I feel like I just rushed into trying to have a relationship with you. That's not like me at all, and I'm sorry I did."

We eventually repaired the breach and visited again. She felt that because I made no mention of my intentions upon leaving, I had no further interest in pursuing a relationship. She read my reticence as Big-Time Rejection. The damage could have been avoided had we merely aired our thoughts just before my flight left.

You may be comfortable with being direct:

"I'd like to see you again."

If testing the water is more in order, try saying:

"I really enjoyed being here [having you come]. I hope you'll stay in touch."

Unless you have a complete dunce on your hands, the SMC should pick up the hint and go from there.

On the other hand, if you aren't looking for an encore, avoid argument and recrimination. Be nice but noncommittal:

"I enjoyed your company [whether you did or not—what does it hurt to say so?]. I'll be in touch."

Then do your sayonara by email.

Round Two

If all systems are "go," reverse the visiting order. Let's assume your SMC made the first move and visited you (you may have split the cost of travel). Now it's your turn. Go see your SMC's surroundings, friends, and haunts. Your SMC has some sort of a feel for life around your digs; you need to gather the same impressions. Go to your SMC's place of toil and meet some coworkers. Perhaps you can arrange to go spend a week with your SMC. This will give you both a chance to experience more of the ordinary events you will encounter together. All the better if your SMC *doesn't* take vacation time but stays on the job. After a week, you will be better able to gauge whether spending the rest of your life with this SMC is in the cards. It would be better that one or both of you pull back at this stage than after you've taken the step of moving in together permanently.

Keep an eye on the compass; don't forget which way is north. Tattoo on your forearm, if necessary: "NO COMPROMISES." When the Oregon trip worked out, I found that subconsciously I was ready to compromise. In retrospect, the items I was ready to sweep under the rug for the sake of finality would have come back to haunt me. I was fortunate that the SMC had more sense than I did, and was not reluctant to put on the brakes.

After a week, sort out your experiences. Get a friend in to discuss where you think you want to go. Listen carefully to your friend's advice, as it will tend to be more objective than your own thoughts at this point.

Staying in Touch

Let's assume things still look rosy. Which maxim applies: "Absence makes the heart grow fonder" or "Out of sight, out of mind"? Act as if the latter were law. Your SMC's membership at the matchmaking site that brought you together is probably still valid. New members, potential competitors, stream in every day. If you want to continue this fledgling relationship you've established, strengthen it.

The wizardry of today's electronic communication makes continual contact easy and inexpensive. Beyond email, you have voice mail and web telephones. The technology for the latter is still much in its infancy, but it works on occasion, and it is free. This isn't a computer book, so I'll explain in a nutshell. You and your recipient each install a generally free web telephone program in your respective computers. When you are both on the Internet, you can call each other through this program. You use a microphone attached to the computer to communicate, rather than the real telephone. Any electronics store will sell you one for $10 to $15. The cost for your conversations: $0—no matter where you call or how long you talk.

The same program will also allow you to send a voice mail just as you would an email. You first record a message, using the same microphone. Enter your recipient's email address, click on send, and your dulcet tones are on the airwaves. Your recipient will get an email with a link to click. Upon doing so, your words of wisdom will flow through flawlessly (most of the time).

My soul mate and I had good luck most of the time with voice mail using MediaRing and Firetalk. See *www.mediaring.com* and *www.firetalk.com*. You can also search for "web telephone" (include the quotation marks in your search to find more listings).

MediaRing lets you record a message of up to fifteen minutes. The drawback is that when it doesn't work, you've just spent a quarter of an hour talking to Jupiter; what you've said is gone, and you can't get it back. Firetalk limits you to one-minute messages, so your loss is limited when the system fails. Firetalk also forces you to get right to the point.

These web telephone systems also have a chat feature. Set a time to ring one another up, and you can chat by interactive email. Telephone chats can be relatively inexpensive if you have the right service and schedule your calls accordingly. For instance, Sprint allows me to dial anyplace in the United States for 5 cents a minute as long as I call between 5 P.M. and 7 A.M. Thus I could spend 30 minutes catching up on gossip with my soul mate for only $1.50.

Also, there are various 10-10 plans where you dial, say, 10-10-345 (California) or 10-10-811 for low-cost 24-hour long-distance. You'll get these in the mail from time to time.

I once mentioned to Ute that the way the math worked out, I had talked with her one month for a total of 55 minutes at 5 cents a minute, but because there was a $5.95 monthly fee, it really came out to almost 15 cents a minute. She pointed out that I just wasn't calling her enough; if I called more often, the cost per minute would go down. She's right, but there was something peculiar about that logic I just couldn't put my finger on.

Don't overlook the opportunity to send greeting cards of all types. I particularly like Webmania, found at *http://freewebcard.com*. You can pick from zillions of cards, animated or not, and then rummage around and add poems, as well as music. Do an internet search for "greeting cards" and you will turn up hundreds of such sites.

You can order flowers from asters to zinnias at *www.proflowers.com*, or any of scores of other companies. Search by typing in "flower delivery" and you will find florists around the world.

Ute and I sent each other an average of three voice mails daily to bring the day's events up to date. We also sent a few short emails, and an occasional electronic greeting card. A couple of times a week we would chat on the phone for 10 to 20 minutes when the rate was 5 cents a minute. At times I would run a magazine article through the scanner and attach it to an email.

Extras

When an SMC was going to give me room and board over the weekend, I immediately expressed my appreciation with flowers. I would order a dozen flowers through *www.proflowers.com* for about $25 and ask to have them delivered the afternoon I was to arrive. When she and I came back to her home from the airport pickup, the flowers would be waiting on the doorstep in a sturdy cardboard box. And Proflowers always did a first-class job. Inside, each flower's stem was contained in a separate waterproof plastic vial to retain freshness. I would profess ignorance about the contents until my SMC read the card. The inscription would read, "Thanks in advance for your hospitality." Men appreciate getting flowers too, by the way.

A nice gesture is to send flowers *after* a successful encounter, whether you were the visitor or the host(ess).

Getting Serious

You've spent a weekend with your SMC. Both of you hit it off well. It dawns on you that this person might truly be The One. But your potential love lives a hundred miles, three states, or perhaps half a world away from where you hang your hat. Before you bare your breast to Cupid's full quiver, let's consider what is involved if one of you moves to the other's neck of the woods.

I once thought it would be invigorating to live in the Tehachapi Mountains of Southern California. Having driven through the area, I knew that smog was nonexistent; the air was bracing. The town of Tehachapi itself, at an altitude of 4,000 feet, is a blend of Old West and New Age. The wind-powered generators dotting the hillsides added picturesque charm. So I took up residence in Tehachapi for four months after selling a home in San Diego. That turned out to be roughly three and a half months too long.

The generators were in place for good reason. The wind blew hard, cold, and constantly. I once reached a speed of 38 miles per hour on my bicycle on a level stretch of back road. With only moderate effort. The return leg clocked in at 6 miles per hour. With hellacious effort. When a gust of wind blew the back legs out from under my dog Peanut one afternoon on a mountain trail, my love affair with scenic Tehachapi evaporated.

There is a reasonable likelihood that your soul mate will end up being more than a horseback ride away. Let's assume that for one reason or another, he or she is not in a position to move to your locale. You must then consider moving to your soul mate's playing field. There are up to four

factors to consider: weather, lifestyle, job opportunities, and closing out your present position. Love conquers all only in novels without sequels, or those that begin "Once upon a time."

WEATHER

When I jog, I do so with minimal attire. Part of my enjoyment comes from being able to float along unhindered by excess clothing. Winter jogging in Tehachapi necessitated full polar rig. I would not be a candidate to relocate to Seattle where outdoor activities mandate rain gear a good portion of the year. My brother Donald, on the other hand, braves the elements in Boston, often an exercise in sheer survival. To him, San Diego is only a nice place to *visit*.

An SMC, Cecile, delights in lakefront living in Maine, but for a significant portion of the year, the lake becomes a fairly solid part of the landscape. Mary Ellen in Seattle is accustomed to biking in the rain and doing the treadmill in lieu of running in galoshes. Before you commit to new scenery with your soul mate, look into the atmospheric conditions that you can anticipate. Parts of Florida feature benevolent weather year-round. Large sections feature live alligators, mosquitoes, and mushy underfooting—also year-round. Sell your mink coat before moving to New Mexico; buy it back if you settle in Bangor.

Weigh your activity list against the weather conditions you will encounter in your new setting. Hand-in-hand walks on the beach in Chicago are definitely seasonal affairs. Much of the biking you will do in New England will be in the cellar. Unless you have a well-heated garage, don't plan on doing much under the hood of your car most of the year in Wisconsin, other than bringing your battery inside at night.

One of the simplest ways to get a read on weather is to ask your SMC to give you a rundown. He or she will know how much of your tennis must be indoors and how many miles you can expect to put on your bikini annually.

LIFESTYLE

Whether your new life will be rural, urban, or suburban, set some time aside to picture yourself in the surroundings of what may prove to be your new home. Small town is not for everyone. Neither is big city. In San Diego, you can lease a loft over the Horton Plaza shopping center. This puts the majority of cultural activities within walking distance. The Gaslamp Quarter, a revitalized section of downtown, is literally at your doorstep, but your pets will be those of the cage variety. Elmhurst is eighteen miles from The Loop in Chicago; but if the Eisenhower Freeway can't accommodate you, frequent commuter trains will. Gardener types flourish in suburban Atlanta, but they will find it tough to shepherd watermelons through the short season in Boston. Forget about following the latest fashion trends in Nebraska or picking wildflowers in most of New York City.

When I moved to Tehachapi, the only local bookshop had closed some months earlier. The local library was one-twelfth the size of that in downtown San Diego. The only donut shop displayed more hole than donut, and at astounding prices.

Take a good look at the place you may call home. Can you picture yourself being comfortable with the ambience that you will find in such an environment? Ask yourself whether your lifestyle will match up with your new area. If not precisely, can you accept the changes that will be necessary to adapt to your new environment?

While you are at it, factor in that you may be moving far away from friends, family, and acquaintances. When I moved out of Chula Vista after nine years, besides friends, I missed chatting with the bagel shop owners and different clerks in stores I had patronized.

In a new city or town you may find a difference in the cost of living. Pin down the price of gasoline and groceries. Ute and I went shopping during the first trip I made to visit her in Hawaii. I was appalled to find that red grapes (for which I had anted up 39 cents a pound a few days before in San Diego) going for $2.99 a pound! On sale yet. This was not an aberration; all Oahu food prices were breathtaking, sale items notwithstanding.

JOB OPPORTUNITIES

Ute, on her quandary:

"At the University of Hawaii, I was soon up for tenure and promotion from assistant to associate professor. As benefits, I had a pension plan and generous health insurance. My job was comfortable, relatively secure, and came with a nice office I could come and go to at any time. Most of all, I was very at ease in my position and had an ample stable income that allowed me to afford some extra 'kudos.' I had reached a high level of competence and specialty in my life. I had worked very hard to achieve such independence and was in the best situation I have ever been in my life. Was I ready to give that up?"

If work is a necessity, as with most of us, investigate the local possibilities. Being a master mechanic won't help much if the only garage in town is family-owned and -operated. The Internet has opened up amazing possibilities, however. For instance, at *www.jobs.com*, you can search a huge database for jobs all over the country. For those with computer skills, *www.ants.com* posts job opening in various fields and affords you the chance to bid on projects.

PLAN WELL AHEAD

Get your act in order early on. Begin making a list of all the chores that have to be taken care of to relocate. Ask others for their ideas of what you might have forgotten.

Ute's schedule:

"I made up a TO DO list, and, of course, I kept adding tasks to it. But I just took things a little at a time. Gradually, I crossed off items faster than I could add new ones. But even though I had three months to take care of everything, at the last moment I had to fall back on friends."

PACKING UP AND LEAVING YOUR HOME

There is much more to a move of this sort than getting cardboard boxes at the supermarket and having your utilities turned off. You may have a job to leave, friends and possibly family to bid good-bye, as well as a myriad of practical details to address.

Ute wrestled with this:

"I had developed unique friendships, women with whom I feel a special kinship. I had become very involved in the Oahu community through my work and had developed special programs in various organizations, for example, prison, halfway house, community health, and others. I was very active in our Home Owners' Association and ultimately served as its president. I was also active in other professional and private organizations. In other words, I became and felt part of the community and had built a network. I knew where, how, and what to get and reach out to from car mechanics to hairdressers to grocery and specialty stores. Moving meant starting over again completely."

To make it all work, you must be in the right frame of mind. Set the move date down the road a piece. This will let the doubts percolate and rise to the top. Deal with them one way or another. As they come to the surface, talk them out with your SMC, a friend, a family member, or all of the above.

Ute on working through this wave:

> "As doubts came up, I would discuss them with my friends. If their advice didn't resolve the conflict, I would talk with Eric. He was very supportive. I particularly appreciated the fact that at times he would play the devil's advocate for me.
>
> "Every item I crossed off my list meant I was closer to San Diego and my sweetheart. I don't feel as though I have moved far away. I told my friends that the technology available today would let me stay in close contact with them. I live in a global village; I just moved to another street."

In Summary

Do a goodly amount of chailing before traveling to meet an SMC, or inviting one to deplane in your vicinity. Determine to have a good time, even if the SMC does not excite you romantically. Be absolutely clear about flight times, and arrange a means of contacting one another if necessary. Have a contingency plan in place in case things flop right off the bat. Always keep your own safety in mind!

The first time around, a two- or three-day weekend is plenty. You can plan for longer visits later. Just before one of you leaves to return home, discuss future plans. If the visit turns out well, stay in contact daily.

Look well before you leap. If you are considering relocating to be with your soul mate, don't ignore weather; it is part of the equation. Take the time to learn exactly what you are getting into. Removing yourself from quicksand is much more difficult than avoiding it in the first place. Similarly, assure yourself that you will be comfortable with your new milieu, and that it will afford you the opportunity to continue to pursue the type of activities that make up your cultural and work inclinations.

10

When the Trolley Goes Off the Track

You may not realize it when it happens, but a kick in the teeth may be the best thing in the world for you.

—Walt Disney

You don't drown by falling in the water; you drown by staying there.

—Edwin Louis Cole

In the ninth grade, a redheaded slip of a girl named Shirley blazed into my life. I was certain that our destinies would merge. Well, at least for more than four months, which is how long it took Shirley to find my replacement. I found out the hard way. For her birthday, I bought a portable record player, complete with her initials, SNU. As an added element of surprise, I refrained from telling her that I was going to show up at her house, gift in hand. She was somewhat distant toward me in class that day. I assumed that it was because I not had alluded to her birthday at all; I merely made mention that I would see her that evening. My presumption was three feet off base.

That evening I walked two miles to her house and rang the bell. Her grandmother answered the door with a message from Shirley. The gist was that Shirley presently had other romantic interests, it had been nice, and I should take care that the door did not strike my posterior as I left. The grandmother was unwilling to accept the record player. As I trudged home broken-heartedly, my anguish was alleviated by the realization that at least I now owned a nice record player. The SNU initials on the lid would peel right off.

The time may come when you will want to end your association with an SMC. Assuming that your social skills have progressed beyond a ninth-grade level, you'll want to take your leave gracefully. How you will manage this feat depends on how far you have progressed in your relationship.

Leaving the Scene Early

A simple way to end a brief SMC contact:

> "When I look over our emails, I really don't think we are in tune on enough things. Thanks for taking the time to write, and good luck in your search."

I felt comfortable with one woman's parting words to me:

> "There are, however, several obstacles which I feel would make ours a poor match. I am looking for someone local and settled. Realistically, I think your attachment to your lovely dogs would place me third in line. I am looking for a number one spot. It has been fun corresponding. All the best. I hope and expect you will find someone just right for you."

This was right to the point. But don't talk about being a "poor" match. That's a negative adjective, and no one likes to feel that he or she is supplying the "poor" part of the equation. This smacks of rejection. Instead, you might lighten up by saying something like "Ours is not a match made in Heaven" or "I don't think this match would work for either of us." Maybe emphasize your incompatibility by noting, "Our major interests are quite different."

Here's another gracious turndown I received:

> "Your active lifestyle and interests are very intriguing,…but I have just experienced an incredible weekend, with another skier, runner, pilot, writer who escorted me to a Harvard prom thirty-seven years ago. He just found me on the Internet."

And another:

> "I have just started seeing a fellow with whom I feel a lot of affinity. It would not be fair to you or him if I continue to correspond with you."

I hadn't heard from a particular SMC for some time, so I sent out an "Are you still there?" message. She replied:

> "I'm still here, but I am dating someone now I really care for, and I am hoping that we will work out long-term. So needless to say I am putting all my effort into that right now. I hope I won't need to get back to Match.com, but you never know. Good luck."

Be gentle in your reaction if you are the one getting the axe. Sarcasm and anger serve no purpose. I sent a message to a woman with whom I had just begun chailing. I mentioned my dad, who had died eighteen years before. I also included an Irish toast, which I have always liked:

> May the roads rise with you,
> May the wind be always at your back.
> May you be in Heaven a half-hour
> Before the Devil knows you are dead.

Her huffy response:

> "...and I did not at all appreciate your 'devil' reference, nor that to a father that has been dead for eighteen years. Find someone else to talk to, Eric."

Wham! My first thought was to reach for my copy of Calvin & Hobbes to see how to spell sticking out your tongue. Instead, I wrote back and apologized for having inadvertently offended her. I wished her luck in her search and said that she had a host of qualities that would appeal to the right man.

When for one reason or another, an SMC doesn't thrill you, bow out nicely. Let's say that you receive a picture that shows the SMC is not for you. Consider the one-message approach versus the two-message approach.

THE ONE-MESSAGE ESCAPE

First say:

> "You certainly are an attractive woman [or a good-looking man]."

Who is going to argue with a statement like that? When women occasionally compliment me on my looks, I might believe that they need some sort of vision correction, but I still feel good. When one woman said, "You have nice legs," I accepted the compliment gladly. You are on safe ground when you tell an SMC what he or she likes to hear.

Next, find a quality of incompatibility that the SMC cannot possibly change. If you are shutting off correspondence with an SMC whose height you know, that is a natural. You say:

> "Charlie [Linda], I think you would be a lot of fun, and you certainly are a good-looking guy [woman]. But we are not a match height-wise."

Finish with one of two endings:

- *If your SMC is about your height:*

Woman: "I recently spent some time at a party with a good friend who was the same height as you. Because I was wearing heels and had styled my hair up, I was actually taller than he was. I felt quite awkward and realize that I need to be with a man who is at least five feet eleven."

Man: "I recently spent some time at a party with a good friend who was the same height as you. Because she was wearing heels and had styled her hair up, she was actually taller than I was. I felt quite awkward and realize that I need to be with a woman who is no taller than five feet six."

- *If there is more than a four-inch difference in your heights:*

Woman: "I just had a date with a fellow who was the same height as you. I felt like he was towering over me. I've always dated men closer to my own height and realize that I feel more comfortable with someone shorter."

Man: "I just had a date with a woman who was the same height as you. I felt like I was towering over her. I've always dated women closer to my own height, and realize that I feel more comfortable with someone taller."

Then finish up with:

> "You have a lot of qualities that will please the right woman [man]. I just don't happen to be the one. Good luck in your search."

THE TWO-MESSAGE APPROACH

Another gentle technique is to give an actual scenario of a day's event. An example:

> "It was a gorgeous day here after a sullen Saturday. I hopped on my bike and rode down to the waterfront. It is a fourteen-mile ride that takes me about an hour. Then I ride seven miles.... Overall, I rode forty-three miles with only one sort of monotonous four-mile stretch each way, and one fairly steep two-mile hill near the end. I'm curious. Would something like this have appealed to you? Do you do enough biking to have ridden that distance? Would a three-and-a-half-hour ride be enjoyable to you?"

The response to this scenario let me know quite clearly if an SMC was a dedicated bicyclist. If I got other than an enthusiastic "You bet I would" response, my second email would read along these lines:

> "Biking is a large part of my life, and I really want to be with someone who enjoys these experiences fairly often. The tunes we are humming don't seem to harmonize. You have a lot of good qualities, [and so forth]."

Use the same approach to highlight other areas where you suspect you and your SMC are not stepping to the same drummer. In such a case, I would send back a message that includes "You certainly are a good-looking man [attractive woman]." Then I would use one of the following:

"Tell me more about

    a.   your involvement with your church."

    b.   your experience backpacking."

    c.   your workload."

    d.   your television habits."

The next message (according to which question I've asked):

"I'm really looking for someone

    a.   who is not so involved with the church. Even though you yourself are not that religiously inclined, you will have a lot of friends who are. I would feel uncomfortable."

b. who has done some long-distance backpacking. I go for extended periods, and it is strenuous and sometimes risky for a novice to travel where I like to head."

c. who has quite a bit more leisure time on her hands. I understand that you are working hard to get ahead, but I need someone who is ready to take life easier and smell the daisies along the way with me."

d. who spends very little time watching television. I enjoy the serenity that its absence brings, so mine is not yet unpacked from my last move. An earlier girlfriend and I were at odds over television, and I just don't want to go through all that again."

Getting Out After a Weekend

You've spent a weekend together. If you don't wish to continue the relationship, let the SMC know why, but gently. I once traveled to Maine to visit a woman, Cecile, who had two teenage boys living at home. Cecile was a lovely person, and I had a fun time, but the combination of the rural setting, the climate, and the two sons made it an improbable match. When I returned home, I wrote:

> "I had an enjoyable time with you. The weather brought home to me the fact that I am really a Southern California person. I couldn't picture trying to run or bike in the weather you have coming up. As this is a large part of my life, I had best limit my search for a soul mate to my immediate area. You need someone more inured to Maine weather than I am. I've had fun corresponding with you. You are an attractive woman with varied and eclectic interests, and you should have no problem finding a man who appreciates what you have to offer. Good luck in your search."

If the weekend doesn't work for *any* reason, you can always fall back on one of the email cancellation messages previously suggested. Perhaps the SMC is inattentive to personal hygiene or has table manners straight from the Middle Ages. Nevertheless, when you give your reasons for bringing things to an end, focus on the *relationship,* not personal foibles. Whether by email or in person, don't point out frank reasons for calling it quits, such as, "Your house is a mess. I could never live that way." Or, "Your driving is too reckless for me." The SMC isn't going to change; such bluntness will engender only

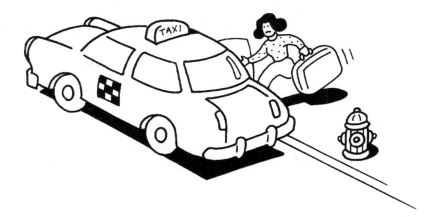

hurt feelings and resentment. Someone will come along for that SMC who feels comfortable in a cluttered house, or whose idol is Mario Andretti (or his sister).

Mary Ellen brushed me off so deftly that I hardly knew it had happened. After a fun-filled weekend, she was somewhat evasive about our next moves. Finally she asked my help in evaluating another SMC, Silver Fox, who had gotten in touch with her. She got the help; I got the message.

If you've had successful sex during the weekend but you don't see this SMC as The One, you could say:

> "I really enjoyed meeting and talking with you. Our time in bed was very satisfying. You were very easy to be with. For some reason, however, there is not the spark that I am looking for; our chemistry isn't quite right. You impressed me as a very nice person, and I'm sure you will have no trouble finding the right person. Unfortunately, I'm not that person. Good luck in your search."

If the sex was obviously not good (and it won't change, no matter what suggestions you make), you might want to modify what you say:

> "I really enjoyed meeting and talking with you. While our time in bed was not what either of us hoped for, this was undoubtedly a function of nervousness and the newness of our relationship. You were very easy to be with [and made me feel quite comfortable—add this only if it is true]. For some reason, however, there is not the spark that I am looking for; our chemistry isn't quite right. You impressed me as a very nice person [and so forth]."

AVOID DEBATES

After you lower the boom, the SMC may come back and ask you to reconsider. Don't reply. Your lack of response will be the answer; no need to repeat what you have already had to screw up your courage to say. Ignore later emails. Go on with your life. If the SMC has your phone number and calls, just say something like this:

> "I know this is hard, but I've thought this over carefully and have decided it was the right thing for both of us. I respect you and will continue to respect you. You will have no trouble finding someone else. I really have to go. Please don't call again."

If the SMC persists, just disconnect a couple of times as soon as you hear the SMC's voice. If the SMC still tries to hang in there, change your phone number.

Don't suggest that you remain friends. It won't work. A woman once terminated a two-year relationship with me. Six months later I called and took her to lunch. When she turned down my offer to renew the relationship, I suggested that we could just remain friends. She looked me right in the eye and asked if I could truly do that. I knew I couldn't and had to admit it. Charles Caleb Colton was right on when he said, "Friendship often ends in love; but love in friendship, never."

Let the SMC's hopes die a natural death. Don't prolong the agony by continuing to send long email messages or doing anything inconsistent with your announcement that you have no further interest in helping to paddle the same kayak together.

THE RULES GO BOTH WAYS

If you are on the receiving end of the brush-off, the same rules apply. Keep your dignity. It's over. Begging and pleading and whining won't bring him or her back. Accept the fact and move on with your life. Find your *real* soul mate. Acknowledge what has happened:

> "I'm disappointed and hurt, but I realize that both partners must want the relationship to work. I appreciate your being honest enough to address the fact that it won't work for you, because that means it won't work for either of us. Good luck in your search [*or* with your new love, as the case may be]."

If the SMC asks to remains friends, it's best that you remain noncommittal:

"That's nice of you, and it may be possible someday."

Accept the fact that the SMC is suggesting friendship as a way of softening the blow, rather than truly looking for comradeship.

Learn from your mistakes. Be honest with yourself. Was there something you did or didn't do that might have influenced the SMC's cancellation in some way? If there is, make a note for future reference. In the vast majority of cases, however, there will just be some missing element that the SMC feels is crucial to a relationship. You haven't done anything wrong; that element just isn't there.

Jump back on the Internet right away. Get some new contacts going. Don't sit around and feel sorry for yourself. Life is too short for that. Wasting time feeling miserable detracts from the time you could be spending looking for a more compatible SMC. Moreover, think back to the loves that have derailed along the course of your life. You've survived them all. Some you will even have forgotten about, although at the time it may have seemed as if your world was about to end. It never does.

When You Find the Needle in the Haystack

Sooner or later your soul mate will show up. If you still have open doings with other SMCs when you finally find your match, let the others know:

> **"I spent some time this weekend in the company of a woman [man] with whom I have been corresponding. We found a flow of interesting and exciting chemistry, and have decided to pursue it further. While I've enjoyed corresponding with you, I don't feel it would be fair to anyone to continue in light of my present situation. In any event, you are an attractive woman [man] of many and varied eclectic interests who will certainly appeal to the right man [woman] when he [she] comes along. Good luck in your search."**

If you haven't yet seen the SMC's picture, leave out that particular piece of information, of course. And cancel your subscription to your matchmaking service, if you are really going for it. You can always go back and renew if things don't work out the way you expect. At the same time, expect that your SMC will do the same without (but *with,* as needed) prompting.

In most instances, you will receive a farewell response, such as this one from a woman in Oakland,

"Thanks, Eric, for sharing with me your good fortune, and the kind words. I sincerely wish you the best for you and your newfound love."

If you get a different response, and an SMC wants an explanation or wants to "give it another try," ignore the request and any future emails.

When Your Blossom Turns to Seed

Let's assume that you have actually gotten into a real-world relationship with your SMC and put everyone else on hold. The time may come when you clearly realize that your SMC relationship is not going in the right direction. Here are examples of circumstances that may call for the time-to-end message:

1. You have the feeling that the SMC is trying to move things along faster than you want them to go.

2. *You* want to move things along faster, but your SMC is increasingly reluctant to discuss the issue.

3. The SMC ignores reasonable requests that you make, such as for a real home phone number.

4. A red flag pops up. When you ask more about it, your SMC doesn't explain, or the explanation defies logic.

5. You come across a lie. One lie is all you need to get the message that this is a person you do not trust. One lie leads to another.

6. The SMC talks vaguely of complications with an ex-spouse or ex-significant other. In most cases, the spouse or other is still very much on the scene.

7. You run a background check that doesn't paint a lovely picture.

8. The SMC asks you for money in any form. Besides the obvious, that can include asking you to send an airline ticket, to put something on your credit card, or to accept collect phone calls.

9. The SMC fails to show up at a meeting for the second time, or cancels at the last minute, no matter what the excuse. The "awfully busy" excuse is either a lie, or it tells you that the SMC had higher priorities than your meeting. Find another SMC.

10. The SMC is "getting a divorce" but can't give you a date when it will be final. Don't hold your breath; move on to a greener pasture.

11. The SMC claims to be behind paying the bills, is having a run of bad luck, or suddenly becomes unemployed with no job prospects. Such a person can't contribute a fair share financially in the relationship. Caveat: you may have a con artist on your hands.

12. You find yourself compromising. Maybe your SMC has not told it like it is regarding drinking, for example. You find you are telling yourself that your SMC's having a few extra belts doesn't really matter, when it does.

13. The SMC makes what you consider to be unreasonable demands.

14. When you talk to your real-world friends or relatives about your SMC, they suggest that you abandon ship. They may be taking a more objective look and see that you are on a wrong tack. Listen to them carefully.

If you arrive at this point, you may want to go back to Chapter One to review the lists you made when you first started searching. Were you overly eager to find your soul mate, and thus compromised or overlooked a key issue?

WARTS AND ALL

Should you try to change your SMC? Dream on; it isn't going to happen. The man who likes his beer and Sunday football is not apt to trade these pleasures for Perrier and an afternoon in the museum. The woman who is casual about picking up clothes around the house is not going to put away her romance novels and turn into the White Tornado at your request.

Let me stress that you have to take an SMC pretty much "as is." Wishing he or she would change is like wishing it would rain next Tuesday. Wishing doesn't produce results. The question is not whether your SMC will change, but rather whether he or she will try new things and learn with you. But if you don't like the warts, pick a different frog.

Don't make the mistake of pointing out something you don't like, only to be told that the SMC will change:

"You smoke." (I'll stop.)

"You're always late." (I'll try harder.)

"You're a Republican." (I was just about to switch parties.)

"You're a workaholic." (I was going to reform, cut back, hire an assistant, all of the above, or whatever.)

At times I cut off contact because a definite must-have was missing. To my question, "Do you function better in the morning or in the evening?" one woman replied:

> "Morning or night energy? Definitely night! I am very sluggish in the morning, use it to drink coffee, take care of office business, talk on the phone, and walk my dog. Afternoon, soooo, guess I'd better get to work. Evening, I'm alive! I used to regularly go to bed around 2 A.M. (all that theatre training creates night owls). I don't need much sleep. A lot depends on whether I'm with someone or not. How about you?"

I like seven or eight hours of sleep, and much prefer to rise early to get trucking. There was no match here. I said so and wished her luck.

Another SMC mentioned, "I am a sun and sand lover." I'm not. So I replied, "We aren't reading from the same blueprint. You have a lot of good qualities, [and so forth]."

When you give a respectful termination, plan that to be the end for you. If for any reason the SMC persists, ignore his or her messages. Don't respond one way or another.

To metaphrase Yogi Berra, "When it's over, it's over." Make a clean break one way or another. Cancel in a positive tone by focusing on the issue, rather than the person. Do it; don't just creep away in silence. Nobody likes to be left hanging, wondering what went wrong; provide closure. Be courteous whether you are on the pitching or catching end of the finale. Put it behind you and look for the next SMC.

When You Get Discouraged

When a potential match comes apart at the seams, don't follow suit. Look for the silver lining instead of the hailstones. Dwell on positives rather than negatives. You will encounter frequent disappointment in your quest. At times you will wonder if there truly is a soul mate for you. You will experience setbacks, get angry, and become disillusioned at times. This is all part of the process. Learn to live with, and through, it.

Shelly, forty-one, in Bennington, came upon a likely SMC her first day on Match.com. Both she and the SMC were psychologists, active politically, and strumming the same tunes in general. Her story:

> "Jerry and I sent emails back and forth for a solid month. All of a sudden, nothing. A week later he sent me a brief message saying that he hated the Internet and that I should look for someone else. That floored me. I never heard from him again. It took me three months before I felt like going back on the Internet to look for someone."

You may have a crackling correspondence going with an SMC, only to get a bolt out of the blue that someone else has stepped into the SMC's life, and "It's been fun, but...." Or you may meet someone face-to-face for the first time, seem to hit it off, and then never hear back again. Assuming that you bathe and brush your teeth with a modicum of regularity, consider these as minor speed bumps on the road of life.

"Easy for you to say" is a natural reaction. After all, you are the one sitting with your head in your hands in the midst of your electronic ruins. Well, I've been there.

At one point, after five months of chailing with more than a hundred women, an SMC in Oregon and I hit it off pretty well. I spent a weekend there; she came down to Tehachapi for a few days. I was scheduled for a return trip to Oregon for ten days. We talked in generalities about buying a house and doing some traveling together. Before I could get packed, my SMC called it off. So I was right back to square one again, after six months.

After crying in my beer for a day or so, I decided to look on the bright side. The only real negative was that I had to start again. There were many positives. First, if it wasn't going to work for her, it was better that we find that out now than to have misgivings after we had both committed. Second, there was no shortage of SMC candidates. Most important, I had seen that the system *would work for me*—the possibilities were awesome. Also I had gained a deeper insight into exactly what I could expect in a relationship. In essence, it was a crucial part of the learning experience. Rather than sit around pitying myself, I dusted off my mouse and went back to the fray.

Doris, forty-two, of Pocatello, is into metaphysics:

> "One of my first contacts was Dan, a university professor *teaching* metaphysics of all things. We immediately connected. I had been doubtful of ever finding a soul mate who shared my interest and knowledge in this field. We exchanged private email addresses right away and talked back and forth for two months. Right after Christmas, Dan just went dark. There was no discussion of backing off or terminating our relationship. I sent him a half-dozen emails but just never heard from him again."

Doris was crestfallen and upset with the Internet matching process. Instead of taking it in stride and searching anew, she threw in the towel and canceled her matchmaking membership.

Cindy, twenty-nine, in Raleigh, chailed at length and finally agreed to spend a weekend with an SMC:

> "This was our first meeting. To my dismay, Stan came up short in the bathing department. Not once during the weekend did he take a shower, only sponge baths. I could tell the difference, but I didn't know how to tell him. Also he spent an entire afternoon in the resort bar, shouting out advice to the coaches of a televised Big-Ten football game. By suppertime he was smashed and could barely make it to the dining room with me. It was embarrassing."

Although he didn't repeat his drinking feat, the overall performance disenchanted Cindy. Unlike Doris, Cindy immediately jumped back on the matchmaking horse, and within weeks she had connected with a more promising SMC.

DUMP YOUR NEGATIVES

There will come moments of despair as you search and don't find. You may say to yourself, "I'll never find what I'm looking for." You may begin to doubt whether you really have what it takes to attract and keep a soul mate. Don't! A previous mate may have taken pains to point out all your shortcomings, and you are reflecting on those. Maybe you want sympathy. Put such silly stuff out of your mind! Everyone has faults. Everyone! What you are looking for is the soul mate to whom your imagined shortcomings are of no consequence. Someone who doesn't care that you are bald, fat, have a big nose, walk with a limp, or whatever.

There is an Asian saying, "I was unhappy because I had no shoes until I met a man who had no feet." Years ago, I read *Your Erroneous Zones* by Dr. Wayne Dyer (Funk and Wagnalls, 1976). Twice. The second time I realized that everything he said pertained to me. It is a book about eliminating the negatives in your life: fear, anger, worry, guilt, and so on. So I put into action everything he advocated. It all worked for me.

I used to keep track of the miles I jogged and the beers I drank. A mile burns off the calories in approximately one beer. At the time, I was scoring four hundred to five hundred a year in each category.

In December 1984 I read Dr. Dyer's book. Since January 1985 I haven't had a drink. A sip now and then. But I found that I was able to take all the stress and all the negatives out of my life. And with the departure of these went the need for a beer or two or three at the end of the day in order to unwind.

You may want to pick up Dr. Dyer's book in paperback, or check it out at the library. So when things go wrong (or just don't go *anyplace*) instead of feeling sorry for yourself, sit back and take stock. Are you loving? Fun to be with for the right person? Loyal? Decent? Funny when the occasion demands? Of course you are. Aren't there things that some SMC will enjoy doing with you? Certainly, even if it is only holding hands and eating popcorn while watching TV. If you haven't already done so, when you slip into a gloomy mood, sit down and write all the *positive* things about you. Put any supposed negatives out of your mind. If you eat crackers in bed and leave crumbs, the positive is that you sweep the crumbs out. If you don't sweep the crumbs out, the positive is that you don't waste your time on trivial pursuits. You will be amazed at all the positive aspects there are about you that will thrill the SMC you are about to find.

COMPOSE A LETTER TO YOUR SOUL MATE

Prepare a letter to the soul mate you are about to find. When the blues strike, read the letter over. Bear in mind that at some point in the future you will be sending this to your soul mate. I assure you this will happen. Mine was as follows, and I dragged it out more than once:

A LETTER TO MY FUTURE LOVE

I want chemistry that springs up immediately. For me, a pleasant, loving relationship isn't enough. I want to be wildly in love, with all the hope and confidence and brightness and crispness of life that such kind of love can bring. I want a love that floods into my mind the first thing in the morning and is the last thought in my mind as I drift into sleep. Whether I'm with you or not. Love should be learning and sharing together, because there is so much of both to make a relationship soar. The balloons going up and up and up together so that a relationship only gets better, more exciting, and remains an ever-changing feast for the senses. Most couples don't have that. Maybe they just don't think of it, or it is too much work, or the football game intervenes. But I am positively going to have it…and *keep* it! Promise!

I see ahead of me, with you, more classes in computers, learning about physics, poetry, economics, languages, geography, history, philosophy, cosmology, politics, painting, playing the piano and clarinet and saxophone (being able to play a duet together), dancing, designing and building a home together, working with children and battered women, teaching, writing, traveling, lecturing, and expanding far beyond the activities I have now. I have to live life to the fullest with you; it's as much a part of my makeup as the mating urge.

It takes a special woman to do this with me. You are that unique person, you are going to have an interesting life with me—that I can promise. Too exciting for most, but never dull.

To you, my faithful readers, I extend a wish:

I WISH FOR YOU...

I wish for you...
Comfort on difficult days,
Smiles when sadness intrudes,
Rainbows to follow the clouds,
Laughter to kiss your lips,
Sunsets to warm your heart,
Gentle hugs when spirits sag,
Friendships to brighten your being,
Beauty for your eyes to see,
Confidence for when you doubt,
Faith so that you can believe,
Courage to know yourself,
Patience to accept the truth,
And love to complete your life.

—*author unknown*

DON'T GIVE UP

Setbacks are inevitable. Thomas Edison didn't invent the light bulb on his first try; persistence kicked in, or "The Old Lamplighter" might yet be a trade instead of just a nostalgic tune. Take another page from Sir Winston Churchill's book. In the early days of World War II, when prospects for England looked bleak, he told a graduating class at Harrow: "Never give in, never give in, never, never, never, never..."

In Summary

When you lose some yardage, look on the bright side; find the positives, even if it's just that you have eliminated one more candidate on your way to success. Once you have your ego pumped back up, go at it again. Don't you dare quit! Get back out on the Internet and find the soul mate who is desperately looking for someone *just like you*. Don't be selfish; don't let your soul mate down by failing to show up!

I wish you the best of luck. May the roads rise with you....

Epilogue

It's a funny thing about life; if you refuse to accept anything but the very best, you very often get it.

—W. SOMERSET MAUGHAM

To find my soul mate, I scanned more than a thousand profiles over ten months and emailed more than four hundred women. About two hundred responded. Of those, I met briefly with fourteen, and for an afternoon or longer with eleven others.

What happened to the eleven close encounters? I asked each woman to give me an update. The names and location have been changed, of course, but the words are their own:

Mary Ellen, in Seattle:

> "Yes, I too have found eternal love on Match.com. We met in early March of 1999 and are engaged to be married June fifteenth [2000]. Sending out the invitations in about another week. Wow, it is just soooooo right when it's right!"

Cecile, Portland, in Maine:

> "I met a great guy who moved in with me about six months ago. We plan on getting married in the fall."

Claire, in New Guinea:

"Soon after I last corresponded with you, I dropped out of the email romance circuit for a while but joined up again for a week during one of my trips home. I, too, feel very fortunate to have found my soul mate during that brief time. I'll be getting married in June when my job here is finished."

Susan, in Fremont, California:

"I have been dating someone quite seriously for the last year. We met in July and also met thru Match.com. I emailed him, which is quite a big change for me. I just kept going back to his profile, and something just said go for it. Tom is a private pilot, and we were born and raised not too far from each other back in the Midwest. I have even taken a trip with him and got to fly the plane, which might end up being my next profession."

Linda, in Portland, Oregon:

"I just met a nice guy through another Internet service, not Match.com. He treats me like a queen, so I treat him like a king. After four months, things look very, very, very good."

Liliana, in Kauai:

"I have met someone who lives less than a mile away from me on Kauai, but it took Match.com for me to find him. He is very nice and easy to be with, and I think things are going to work out nicely between us."

Sheri, in San Francisco:

"Lightning hasn't struck yet. Close once, but not quite enough. I haven't given up though."

Cassi, in Phoenix:

"I haven't come up with Mr. Right yet, but I'm still looking. I believe this to be a numbers game, and somewhere down the road the right one will come along. We are all in the same boat here."

Diane, in Chicago:

> "My romance is still intact although I am never quite sure as to when it will explode yet another time."

Sheila, in Houston:

> "I went a bit further with my quest online and met a very lovely sounding man online. We met in Richmond, and he turned out to be a nice person. Where it will go from here depends on a lot of things."

Of course, to close things out properly. I must add my own observations as well as those of my soul mate:

Me:

> "Ute and I chailed for a little over three months. I was going to fly over to Oahu, but it made more sense for her to come here. Moreover, she had never been to San Diego. When she got off the plane, I slipped her hand into mine; by the time we reached the baggage area, it was all over for both of us."

My soul mate, Ute:

> "Two weeks before we first met, Eric wrote, 'Don't put a person behind the words you read.... The chances that we match are slim. Like a novel, sometimes the inside of the book doesn't live up to the cover and thus doesn't get finished.' Yet the emails continued to fly back and forth across the ocean. It always *felt* right; it *was* right; it *is* right! And I knew it all along."

Ute and I began chailing in March. We finally met in July. I traveled to Hawaii for a week in October; she returned to San Diego for the Christmas holidays. I made a final trip to Hawaii in February to do the Great Aloha eight-mile Run with her.

The following June, Ute moved to San Diego where we (and Peanut, our four-legged buddy) now make our home. There is one sad note. Annie, my four-legged companion for seventeen years, has left me. She gave a sigh one day and that was it. Good-bye, my old pal. In the gaps, we stayed in touch with voice mail, email, night phone calls, postcards, electronic cards, and letters. It worked. It will for you.

More Help

Questions? Need some input? Looking for help with your profile? Not sure if your handle really reflects you? Have some thoughts or experiences you'd like to pass along to be (or not to be) used in a sequel to this book? Try my Web site, *www.CastYourNet.net* (yes ".*net*" rather than ".*com*").

The end...of your beginning.

Index

Notes

Notes

Notes

Notes

Notes